ISLAMIC ENDOWMENTS IN JERUSALEM UNDER BRITISH MANDATE

ISLAMIC ENDOWMENTS IN JERUSALEM UNDER BRITISH MANDATE

YITZHAK REITER

Department of Islamic and Middle Eastern Studies,
Hebrew University of Jerusalem

FRANK CASS
LONDON • PORTLAND, OR

First published in 1996 in Great Britain by
FRANK CASS & CO. LTD.
Newbury House, 900 Eastern Avenue
London, IG2 7HH

and in the United States of America by
FRANK CASS
c/o ISBS, 5804 N.E. Hassalo Street
Portland, Oregon, 97213-3644

Transferred to Digital Printing 2004

British Library Cataloguing in Publication Data

Reiter, Yitzhak
Islamic endowments in Jerusalem under British mandate
1. Waqf 2. Endowments – Jerusalem 3. Land tenure – Jerusalem
4. Acquisition of property (Islamic law) 5. Jerusalem –
History – 20th century
I. Title
333.3'09569442

ISBN 0-7146-4670-9 (cloth)
ISBN 0-7146-4342-4 (paper)

Library of Congress Cataloging-in-Publication Data

Reiter, Yitzhak
Islamic endowments in Jerusalem under British mandate / Yitzhak Reiter.
p. cm.
Includes bibliographical references and index.
ISBN 0-7146-4670-9 (cloth)
ISBN 0-7146-4342-4 (paper)
1. Waqf—Jerusalem—History. 2. Endowments—Palestine—History.
3. Palestine—History—1917–1948. I. Title.
KML271.35.R45 1996
297'.65—dc20 96–15450
CIP

Typeset by Regent Typesetting, London

Contents

List of figures and tables

Figures

Tables

Acknowledgements

I am indebted to those individuals and institutions who throughout the preparation of this work provided encouragement and technical and financial support. I was accorded financial support over the years by the Harry S. Truman Institute for Research and the Advancement of Peace and by the Hebrew University of Jerusalem. Professor Aharon Layish supervised the study; he and my colleagues at the Department of Islamic and Middle Eastern Studies at the Hebrew University were sources of constant encouragement. I acknowledge the goodwill of the late Shaykh Saʿd al-Dīn al ʿAlamī (Mufti and President of the Supreme Muslim Authority of the West Bank and East Jerusalem) in facilitating access to records in the various Islamic Archives of East Jerusalem. In the archives themselves I was generously assisted by Zayn al-ʿĀbidīn al-ʿAlamī (former director of the East Jerusalem Sharīʿa Court), by Shaykh Asʿad al-Imām (whose knowledge of the Waqf institution I was privileged to appreciate) and by Dr Ḥamad Yūsuf (director of the Section for Islamic Heritage Archive in Abū Dīs). I am grateful to Daniel Dishon for his delicate editorial work on the manuscript. Finally I owe special thanks to my wife Ilana and to my children (Ohad, Moran, Maʿayan and ʿInbar) for their tolerance and (lost) time.

Y.R.

Introduction

In 1935, at the height of the struggle over land ownership between the Palestinian national movement and the Zionists in Mandatory Palestine, Ḥājj Amīn al-Ḥusaynī, president of the Supreme Muslim Council (SMC), urged the Muslim Arab public to turn all their land into a Muslim endowment – a *waqf* (plural: *awqāf*). This would provide a permanent surety against land sales to Jews, since according to *sharīʿa* law, *waqf* properties may not be sold, and their administration is subject to the supervision of the *sharīʿa* court system. During the Mandatory period, the latter was subordinated to the SMC[1] and both were headed by al-Ḥusaynī.

The appeal by the supreme religious and political leader of Muslim Arabs in Palestine was subsequently endorsed by a national convention of *ʿulamāʾ* (Muslim clergy). But making widespread use of the *waqf* ran counter to its decline in other Islamic countries in the twentieth century. Several Muslim countries had already embarked on the abolition of the family *waqf* (*waqf dhurrī*, *waqf ahlī*), and the public *waqf*s (*waqf khayrī*) there were being subjected to sweeping reforms. These countries regarded the *waqf* as an archaic institution, meant to perpetuate the old social order and harmful to the modern economy; attempts were made to release real estate from the *waqf* status, which thwarted its economic development. In Turkey, the *waqf* had been abolished in 1926. In Egypt, Iraq and other countries, advocates and opponents of the *waqf* debated the issue heatedly.[2]

This may well explain the negligible response to Ḥājj Amīn's exhortation. Landowners were in no hurry to place restrictions on their property that would prevent its sale if and when economic developments made it imperative to dispose of it.

Clearly, there was a clash between two views of the *waqf*: some considered it unsuited to the new social and economic conditions, others held that it was worthy of preservation and even reinforcement in Palestine. The latter had in mind the political decision on the part of the British administration to set up the SMC and give it autonomous powers over *waqf* affairs. Consequently, the major issue discussed in this study is to what degree the *waqf*, as an institution of the old world order, proved capable of adapting itself to modern socio-economic conditions.

Reform of the *waqf* began in the Ottoman Empire in the mid-nineteenth century but fell short of being radical. In fact, the *waqf* retained its traditional character until the end of the Ottoman period. Customarily, Napoleon's invasion and the conquests of Muḥammad ʿAlī are considered to have ushered in the modern era in Palestine, but with regard to the *waqf* in Palestine, the truly important turning point was the start of the British Mandate. Despite much institutional continuity between the Ottoman and the Mandate period, it was the Mandatory administration which set new norms for running the *waqf*.

This is true in several senses. The first and most striking is the transition from Muslim to non-Muslim rule. With the exception of brief periods of Crusader rule between 1099 and 1187, Palestine had been governed by Muslims for 1,300 years. For the last 400 years it had been under the centralized rule of the Ottoman Sublime Porte. Ottoman Palestine had been divided into several administrative units that belonged to the *velāyets* of Beirut and Damascus; the *sanjaq* of Jerusalem was run directly by the Sublime Porte. Only for brief, transitory periods was most of Palestine under the rule of one man, as, for example, in the days of Ẓāhir al-ʿUmar al-Zaydānī (1750–75) and Aḥmad Pāshā al-Jazzār (1775–1804). The Muslim code of law – the *sharīʿa* – applied to Muslims, who thought of themselves as the *umma* (nation). Non-Muslims had the status of belonging to a recognized religious community (*ṭāʾifa*) under the *millet* system.

The British occupation of Palestine stood the situation on its head. Palestine was now ruled by a non-Muslim government, and the Muslims ceased to be the 'nation'. They, in turn, now had the status of a religious community – one of several. The *sharīʿa* was no longer the law of the land, and the jurisdiction of the *sharīʿa* courts was confined exclusively to matters of personal status and *waqf* law. The government, British and Christian, had committed itself to help set up a Jewish national home in Palestine. All the country's administrative agencies now came under the British Mandatory government in Jerusalem. The British had to find new ways of running the Muslim community or for it to run itself. They decided to invest the Muftī of Jerusalem with the supreme religious authority, designated him *al-Muftī al-Akbar* ('chief Muftī'; later, *Ra'īs al-'Ulamā'* ('Head of the '*Ulamā*'')), and made him head of the Muslim community in Palestine.

However, not only Palestine was severed from the Ottoman Empire. Most of its non-Turkish parts had come under foreign rule, and Turkey itself swiftly abolished the caliphate (1924) and severely restricted the application of the *sharī'a*. The Muslim world was fragmented and bereft of central leadership. The Muslims in Palestine had to adapt to the new situation and construct concepts that would make it possible for them to exist under non-Muslim rule, even though, at the time, they constituted the majority in the country. The Arab inhabitants of Palestine shared in the national awakening that swept through the region after the First World War, and the national cause became the pivot of their activities. They viewed their status under the British as temporary – bound to end with their liberation from alien rule. Religious sentiment was enlisted for the sake of the national goal, the assumption being that national liberation would, in turn, serve the Muslim objective – the restoration of Muslim rule.

Islamic law – the *sharī'a*, in which the *waqf* is firmly embedded – was meant to be applied by a Muslim ruler. One of the questions explored in the present study is how the *waqf* functioned under non-Muslim rule. A comparison of the *waqf* in Palestine with that of other countries that came under non-Muslim rule, and particularly under British rule, such as India and Egypt, is invalidated by the different political circumstances in the countries. Uri Kupferschmidt, who studied the SMC, has stressed its singular place in the history of Islamic bodies administering Muslim religious affairs under occupation.[3] The very establishment of the SMC and the broad autonomous powers vested in it by the British in religious matters, including *waqf* administration, attest to the difference between Palestine and other countries.

Another indicator of Palestine having entered a new chapter in its history is the intercultural encounter between Arab society and the New Yishuv, the pre-state Zionist Jewish community. It strengthened Western influence on Muslim Arab society and gave the latter greater exposure to the impact of modernization. But it also set the two national movements, the Palestinian-Arabs and the Jewish-Zionists, on a collision course and led them into a struggle for sovereignty and dominion over the same land, for access to the Holy Places, and ultimately for the very character of the country as a whole and of Jerusalem in particular. In waging the Palestinian national struggle, Ḥājj Amīn al-Ḥusaynī used, with considerable success, the sanctity to Muslims of Palestine, and especially of Jerusalem, so as to turn the Palestinian struggle into a pan-Islamic one. Devices used in this cause included the renovation of mosques on the Temple Mount, the burial of Muslim leaders there, the Western Wall dispute and the famous religious legal opinion (*al-fatwā al-khaṭīra*) forbidding Muslim landowners in Palestine to sell land to Jews. The *waqf* was also mobilized for the struggle, either by expanding the number of *waqf* employees – useful because they were subordinate to the SMC – or by direct use of *waqf* revenues for the purchase of land offered for sale by Muslims.

The economy of the country also underwent a transformation during the Mandatory period, moving from a traditional to a largely capitalist pattern. Rapid population growth required investment in building and development, and caused the growth of the domestic market, the expansion of the labour force and the development of infrastructures, services and new industries. Imports and exports grew in volume. Agriculture yielded its economic primacy to industry. Because the *waqf* properties were of economic value, all this affected the way they were administered.

Likewise, the British regime in Palestine had a considerable impact on the shaping of society. It introduced new norms of administration and a Western social outlook, including a concept of the function of the state different from that of the Ottomans. The state now assumed greater responsibility for providing public services. Unlike Ottoman practice, these services were initiated and financed by the state. This, in turn, affected the role of the public *waqf*.

It had always been a characteristic of the *waqf* to conceal its inner workings, as well as its revenues, from all but those directly associated with it. Being a subject of great political and financial sensitivity, details of *waqf* administration were known only to the chosen few – the *waqf* administrators (*mutawallī*s or officials of the central administration of *awqāf*) and their supervisors (the *qāḍī* and the SMC). Where endowments were not administered by the central *waqf* administration, the individual *mutawallī*s attempted to maintain discretion on *waqf* properties and accounts. Even the beneficiaries were only given minimal information, lest they find a pretext for claiming a greater share than the *mutawallī* was prepared to grant them, or seek grounds to dismiss him for mismanagement. Therefore, access to the *mutawallī*s' annual books of accounts – *daftar al-muḥāsaba* – is extremely rare. (We were able to obtain only a few.) The *sharīʿa* court records (*sijill*, pl. *sijillāt*) are therefore the main source of documentation for researchers on the internal administration of the *waqf*.

The primary source for the present study is the *sijill* of the *sharīʿa* court in Jerusalem during the Mandate – exceedingly important for historical research. It has already served as the basis for several studies in social history. Several articles have been devoted to bringing out the importance of the *sijill*, particularly the Jerusalem one, as a historical source.[4] With respect to *waqf* administration, the *sijill* is the most important primary research source we possess.

Waqf records are found in the *sijill* chiefly because *sharīʿa* law empowers the *qāḍī* to supervise *waqf* administration, and because the *qāḍī* played a specific administrative role in the Ottoman Empire. According to the *sharīʿa*, the *qāḍī* endorses the *mutawallī* as suitable, appoints him, authorizes him to deduct a fee for himself from the *waqf* revenues, sanctions conversions of *waqf* property, approves letting urban *waqf* properties for periods exceeding one year (or three years for rural holdings) and authorizes other transactions. Complaints by beneficiaries against *mutawallī*s – for denying beneficiaries their entitlements, for breach of faith, neglect or mismanagement – are adjudicated by the *qāḍī*. Since the nineteenth century, filing a *waqfiyya* (dedication deed; pl. *waqfiyyāt*) with the *sijill* constituted proof of the validity of a *waqf* and of the ownership of the property it held, for the purpose of property records. In the Ottoman period, the *sijill* of the *qāḍī* also contained all decrees by the *sulṭān* and of the Waqf Ministry on *waqf* matters, especially with regard to the appointment of *waqf* officials, their terms of employment, and the way their successors were to be selected.

The *sijill* provides much insight into *waqf* affairs because it contains bona fide legal documents of different types. However, its main shortcoming as a historical source is its failure to set out the broad context of the cases discussed. It has proven possible to fill in some of the missing details by means of interviews or by recourse to other sources (see below).

Although the *sijill* contains a great many documents of great diversity, only one major type has so far been selected for systematic research: the *waqfiyyāt*. A few studies do refer to other types of documents in the *sijill*, such as authorizations of transactions, sultanic decrees or records of appointments, but in most cases these are included by way of a sample.[5] The present study utilizes all *sijill* documents relating to the *waqf* that were recorded over a continuous period – the 30 years of British rule.

The *sijill* of Mandatory Jerusalem contains nearly 100 volumes (nos 416–512). Each volume contains, on average, about 400 pages of tightly spaced handwriting. Some documents take up a quarter page; others (legal decisions, *waqfiyyāt* and complex authorizations) cover several pages of folio. Together, they contain approximately 1,500 documents on various *waqf* matters, organized in two categories: rulings in lawsuits (*aḥkām, iʿlamāt*) and all other documents and authorizations (*ḥujaj*). The first category includes: entitlement disputes (*istiḥqāq*); auditing of *mutawallī*s' accounts and dismissal of *mutawallī*s (*muḥāsabat al-mutawallī wa-ʿazlihi*); trespassing on *waqf* properties (*ightiṣāb*), rent increases (*ziyādat al-ḥikr*), appointing the best-qualified person as *mutawallī* (*arshadiyya*), and temporary eviction of tenants of a *waqf* property for renovation purposes. The second group of documents (*ḥujaj*) includes: *waqfiyyāt*; modifications of *waqfiyya* terms; appointments of *mutawallī*s (or of a temporary replacement (*qāʾimaqām mutawallī*) in the absence of the appointee); appointments of supervisors (*nāẓir*); resignations of *mutawallī*s or supervisors; authorization of transactions such as exchange, sale, rental or purchase of property; authorization of long-term leases; authorization to renovate, convert or demolish *waqf* properties; authorization of exceptional outlays; authorization to take out a loan or repay a loan by the *mutawallī* to the *waqf*; authorization for the *mutawallī* to rent a *waqf* property for himself; authorization for the *mutawallī* to take a fee; authorization of tithe agreements, and powers of attorney.

The archives of the SMC, which contain tens of thousands of files of administrative correspondence, are housed in the Department of Islamic Heritage in Abū Dīs. Researchers find it difficult to work in the Abū Dīs archives, one reason being that the archivists no longer have the original SMC catalogue. This is so, they claim, because they found the documents lying around in haphazard piles. They re-sorted the documents using criteria of their own. Consequently, the files do not always contain the documents indicated in the catalogue. This rules out any attempt to conduct a quantitative study, since documents dealing with one subject are not kept together. Therefore, all that could be done was a sample study, which allowed me to acquire a direct impression of the way the SMC handled *maḍbūṭ* assets – those of *waqf*s not supervised by the *qāḍī* (see below) – as well as those that were *ghayr maḍbūṭ*.[6]

Other archive materials used in this study are the files of the Jerusalem District Court on land cases. Some 60 Mandate-era lawsuits concerning *waqf*s add important information on points on which the *sijill* has nothing to say. The study also makes use of the archives of the Chief Secretariat of the Mandatory Government in Palestine (CSO), kept in the Israel State Archives, with special emphasis on the files of the Islamic Affairs Section (K) and the Land Registry Section (F).

The administrative archive materials complement the legal documents of the *sijill*, since a legal document, even if pertaining to a case heard in court, does not always reflect the background of the dispute and the parties' true motives. At the most, it articulates the parties' arguments and gives the *qāḍī*'s ruling. To fill in the background, interviews were conducted with several individuals well acquainted with the Islamic establishment of the Mandatory period.

The present book is divided into four parts. Part 1 contains two chapters on the legal, administrative and institutional aspects of *waqf* management in Palestine at the end of the Ottoman period and during the British Mandate. Part 2 comprises a chapter on the *waqf* founders and properties and one on the objectives of the *waqf*. Part 3 (Chapters 5–7) describes the management of the *waqf* (the *mutawallī*s and the way they were appointed; their ongoing administration of properties, and the transactions they carried out). In Part 4, Chapter 8 discusses supervision of *waqf* administration by the *sharīʿa* court and the SMC.

NOTES

1. Y. Porath, *The Palestinian Arab National Movement 1929–1939: From Riots to Rebellion* (London: Frank Cass, 1977) pp. 97–98; *al-Jāmiʿa al-ʿArabiyya*, 24 January, 1935.
2. On the abolishment of the *waqf* institution in Turkey see B. Lewis, *The Emergence of Modern Turkey* (London: Oxford University Press, 1961) p. 407. On the debate in Egypt see G. Baer, *A History of Land Ownership in Modern Egypt 1800–1950* (London: Oxford University Press, 1960) pp. 147, 215–19; idem., '*Waqf* Reform in Egypt' in *Middle Eastern Affairs* (St Antony Papers no. 4, 1, 1958) pp. 61–76; A. Sekaly, 'Le problem des waqfs en Egypte', *Revue du Monde Musulmanne*, 3, 1–4 (1929) pp. 285ff.; M. ʿAlī Phāshā, 'Le waqf est-il une institution religieuse', *L'Egypte Contemporaine*, 18 (1927) pp. 385–402. For the position of the Minister for *Awqāf* in Egypt see *Ḥukm al-Sharīʿa fī al-Waqf al-Khayrī waʿl-Ahlī, Bayān min al-ʿUlamā'* (Cairo, 1346 h.); on Iraq see: M.A. al-ʿUmar, *al-Dalīl li-Iṣlāḥ al-Awqāf* (Baghdad, 1948), p. 40 ff.; M.S. al-ʿĀnī, *Aḥkām al-Awqāf* (3rd ed., Baghdad, 1965) pp. 145–6; M.M. al-Māḥī, *al-Ḥukūma al ʿIrāqiyya, Taqrīr ʿan Awqāf al-ʿIrāq wa-Wasā'il Iṣlāḥiha* (Baghdad, 1937) p. 113ff.
3. U.M. Kupferschmidt, *The Supreme Muslim Council; Islam under the British Mandate for Palestine* (Leiden: E.J. Brill, 1987) pp. 1–16.
4. F. Koprulu, 'L'Institution de Vakf et l'importance historique de documents de Vakf', *Vakiflar Dergisi*, 1 (1938) (section farncaise) pp. 3–9; 'A. Mannā', 'The *Sijill* as a Source for Study of Palestine during the Ottoman Period, with Special Reference to the French Invasion' in D. Kushner (ed.), *Palestine in the Late Ottoman Period* (Jerusalem and Leiden: Yad Itzhak Ben-Zvi and E.J. Brill, 1986) pp. 351–62; J. Mandeville, 'The Ottoman Court Records of Syria and Jordan', *Journal of the American Oriental Society*, 86 (1966) pp. 311–19; idem., 'The Jerusalem *Sharīʿa* Court Records: a Supplement and Complement to the Central Archives' in M. Maʿoz (ed.), *Studies on Palestine during the Ottoman Period* (Jerusalem: Magnes Press, 1975) pp. 517–24; 'A.

Rafeq, 'The Law Court of Damascus, with Special Reference to the Craft-corporations during the First Half of the Eighteenth Century' in *Les Arabes par leur archives* (Paris, 1976) pp. 141–59; A. Layish, 'The *Sijill* of the Jaffa and Nazareth *Sharīʿa* Courts as a Source for the Political and Social History of Ottoman Palestine' in M. Maʿoz (ed.), *Studies on Palestine during the Ottoman Period* (Jerusalem: Magnes Press, 1975) pp. 517–24.

5. See for example the following studies: L. Milliot, *Démembrement du habous: gza, guelsa, zīna', istighrāq* (Paris: E. Leroux, 1918); G. Baer, 'The Dismemberment of *Awqāf* in Early 19th Century Jerusalem', *Asian and African Studies*, 13, 3 (1979) pp. 220–41; A. Markus, 'Piety and Profit: the *Waqf* in the Society and Economy of 18th Century Aleppo' in G. Baer and G. Gilbar (eds), *Studies in the Muslim Waqf* (Oxford: Oxford University Press) (forthcoming).
6. 1,500 files from various administration aspects of the *waqf* were reviewed.

Jerusalem at the end of the Mandatory Period

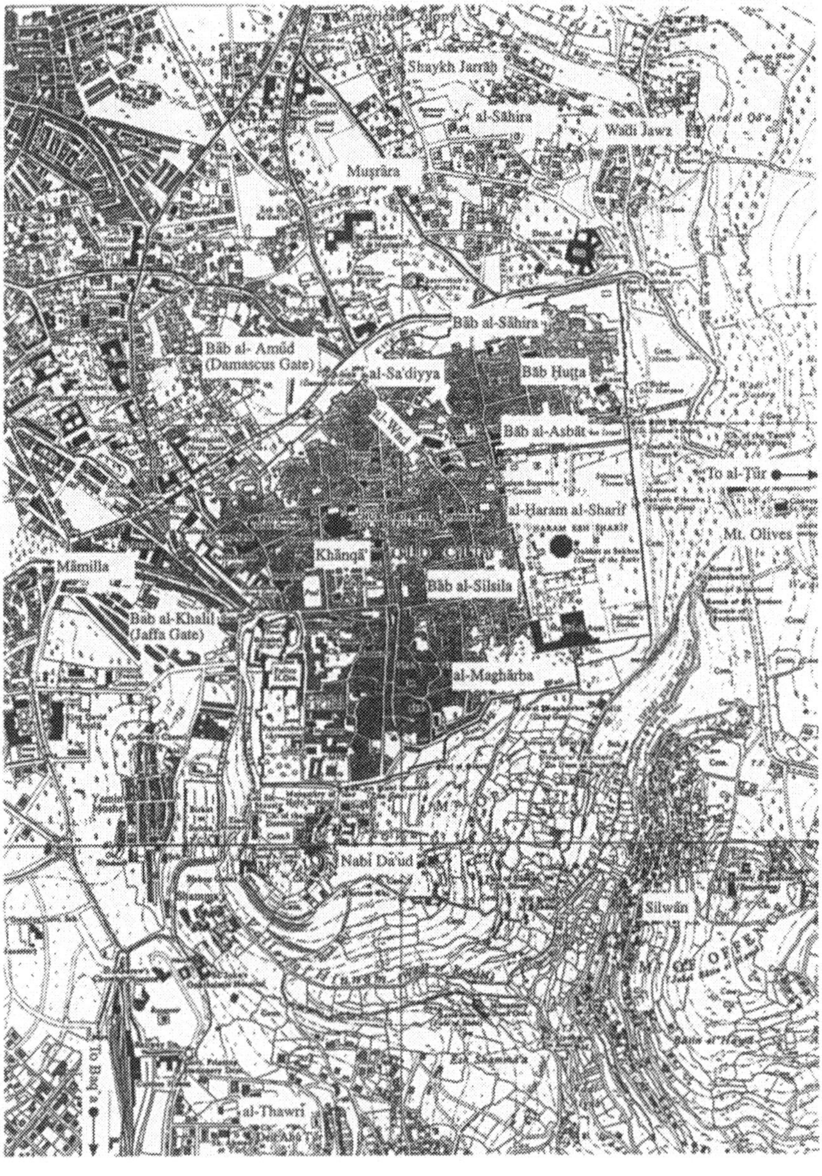

Part I

1

The struggle over *waqf* supervision – late Ottoman precedents

On 23 February 1913, Muḥammad Shafīq al-Mālik, director of the Jerusalem Waqf Department, received a cable with directives from the Waqf Ministry in Istanbul. It instructed him to incorporate the Nabī Mūsā Waqf into the district department of the Waqf Ministry. Until then, it had been administered by *mutawallī*s from two prestigious Jerusalem families – the Yūnis family and the Ḥusaynīs. The director hastened to do as bid but, to sweeten the pill, al-Mālik agreed to let members of the two families continue in their religious posts, but as salaried employees of the Waqf Ministry. The Ḥusaynīs and Yūnis countered by asserting that, under Ottoman law, the Nabī Mūsā Waqf belonged to the category of 'exceptions' (*mustathnā'*) – *waqf*s which the ministry had no right to interfere with (*istithnā' hādhihi al-awqāf min al-mudākhala fīhā*).[1] The court found for the plaintiff. (For full details of the suit, which also concerned two other *waqf*s, and for the arguments put forward by both sides, see below at the end of this chapter.)

The arguments put forward by each side reflect the confusion and obfuscation that overlay the problem of distinguishing between different types of *waqf* under Ottoman reformist legislation. But precisely these distinctions governed the administrative and supervisory powers that the Istanbul Waqf Ministry was authorized, under these very laws, to exercise. This confusion lasted well into the Mandatory period, leading to similar disputes between the SMC and the *mutawallī*s appointed by the *sharī'a* court, according to the latter's prerogatives.

The question that came up early in the Mandatory period concerned the powers of the SMC (the formal successor to the Ottoman Waqf Ministry) vis-à-vis *waqf*s that it did not administer directly. In any such dispute, the parties cited Ottoman precedents, because the British Mandatory government had chosen to uphold Ottoman law.[2]

To elucidate this issue, we must first briefly review the meaning of the term '*waqf*' as well as the history of its administration.

A *waqf* (pl. *awqāf*) is an endowment made according to Islamic law. A man or a woman may endow his/her property and thereby reserve its profit in perpetuity for charitable aims (public or private). The word comes from an Arabic root meaning 'stand'. It connotes that from the moment the *waqf* becomes valid, its assets, and the rights pertaining to them, can no longer be transferred: they come to a standstill. This bars the transfer of ownership or possession, long-term leases and mortgages, but allows income-generating short-term leases. The income from the assets must be used for the purposes set out by the founder in his endowment deed – the *waqfiyya*. The principle of the perpetuity of the endowment and its stated aim springs from the religious belief that charity earns a person a reward in the next world. An act of endowment must therefore be for perpetuity: as long as the founder's soul exists in the next world, he continues to be sustained by the acts of charity he performed when still alive.

The act of endowment was recorded by the *qāḍī* of the *sharīʿa* court, who then retained control of the fate of the assets and their administration. In certain matters (such as transactions in *waqf* assets), the administrator of the *waqf* and its supervisor (if there was one) were unable to take action without the *qāḍī*'s prior permission. The *qāḍī* also had the right to dismiss a *mutawallī* who exceeded his powers, even if the *mutawallī* was the founder himself.

The founder may decide who is to administer the *waqf* when it first becomes operative, and in the coming generations, in one of three ways: by naming someone personally, *ex officio*, or by setting criteria (such as 'the eldest of my [male] children', or 'the most capable of my offspring'). If he does not do that, the *qāḍī* is free to designate the administrator. In most endowments made for public needs in the Ottoman Empire, the founders appointed specific people for specific jobs.

With regard to *waqf*s, differences between the four orthodox legal schools were slight. The school dominant in the Ottoman Empire was the Ḥanafī, which was therefore also applied by the Palestine *sharīʿa* courts. Therefore, we hardly need revert to the question of the school as our study proceeds.

Sharīʿa law does not recognize a centralized *waqf* administration. Moreover, it explicitly prohibits the transfer of revenues from one *waqf* to another for the purpose of renovating it or defraying its expenses, unless the two *waqf*s happened to serve the same purpose.[3] However, despite these restrictions, medieval rulers often attempted to take over various *waqf*s and run them from the centre. On the whole, they failed.[4] But the *waqf*s which had their revenues earmarked for the holy cities of Mecca and Medina (*al-ḥaramayn al-sharīfayn*) were indeed centrally administered by the state, at least from the start of the Ottoman Empire.[5] Generally speaking, the Ottomans soon began to exploit some of the vast resources of the *waqf*s to finance, develop and establish various public enterprises. In so doing, they explicitly breached the founder's conditions, and this, in turn, was a grave infringement of *sharīʿa* law. The Ottoman sultans often entrusted the supervision of the *waqf*s to officials of proven loyalty. For example, the endowments of Sultans Mehmed II, Selīm I and Sulaymān the Magnificent were supervised by the Grand Vizier; those of Bayazid II and Ahmed I by the *Shaykh al-Islām* (Turkish: *sheyhülislām*).

The transfer of supervisory powers to the upper echelons of government diminished the prerogatives of the *sharīʿa* court. It was not formalized in legislation or laid down in administrative orders (at least not until the start of reform legislation in the first half of the nineteenth century); rather, it evolved by reason of the superior status of senior officials who, in the Ottoman hierarchy, were not subject to the instructions of local *qāḍī*s.[6] This is important for two reasons: first, it paved the way for the transfer of *waqf* management to the state without directly challenging *sharīʿa* court jurisdiction or provoking the *ʿulamāʾ*; when a Waqf Ministry was eventually formed, there was already a tradition for some endowments to be supervised without reference to the *sharī'a* courts. Second, the state-appointed supervisor (*nāẓir*) exercised a loose type of control which the *mutawallī*s preferred over the close supervision on the part of the *qāḍī*.

Already in the eighteenth century, *Sulṭān* 'Abd al-Ḥamīd I (1774–1789) had set up a special administration to manage his own imperial endowments. The new office, named Ḥamīdiyya after its founder, was subordinate to the *Awqāf al-Ḥaramayn* administration but had features characteristic of an autonomous body. When the results proved favourable, several other *waqf*s belonging to the ruling elite were attached to the *al-Awqāf al-Ḥamīdiyya* administration. Such endowments were called *mulḥaqa* (annexed) and the bureau was renamed 'The Administration of the Ḥamīdiyya Endowments and their Annexes'.[7] This historical detail was to become important for an understanding of the concept of *mulḥaq* in later days.

Sulṭān Maḥmūd II (1807–1839) laid the foundations of what would become the Ministry of Imperial Endowments – *Naẓārat al-Awqāf al-Humāyūniyya*. The ministry was headed by a former director of the mint and was entrusted with management and supervision of imperial *waqf*s and of the endowments of the two holy cities. In 1863, regulations were laid down for the management of *waqf*s through the ministry's regional administrators.[8] Although amended from time to time, they remained at the base of *waqf* administration until the end of Ottoman rule.[9] Among other things, they made provisions for routine investigation of the legal status of *waqf* land, especially state land (*mīrī*), and for the investigation of family *waqf*s whose beneficiaries had all died or part of whose revenue was earmarked for the two holy cities. Such endowments as were found to be *mulḥaq* (subject to ministry supervision) had to be placed under definite ministry control (they became *maḍbūṭ*).[10] Also, under the new regulations, the approval of transactions involving *waqf* property was no longer the *qāḍī*'s exclusive prerogative; henceforth, they required endorsement by authorities of the state.

The Waqf Ministry was given the following powers vis-à-vis *awqāf mulḥaqa*:

1. the right to retain one-quarter or one-third of the revenue of each endowment (a practice current for a long time);[11]
2. the right to approve or turn down any renovation costing more than 500 piasters;[12]
3. the right to audit *waqf* accounts regularly, including a comprehensive annual audit. *Awqāf mulḥaqa* and *maḍbūṭa* must keep accurate records of their income and expenditure;
4. the right to require that an additional permit from the ministry be obtained for *waqf* transactions;
5. to prevent *waqf*s employing unnecessary staff;[13]
6. to require endorsement of the appointment of a *mutawallī* by the *qāḍī*, following recommendations of the Ottoman district council (*majlis idāra*) and the director of the Waqf Department.[14]

These broad powers with regard to *awqāf mulḥaqa* were inconsistent with the tradition prevalent in Palestine that *awqāf mulḥaqa* were family endowments and therefore not to be directly administered by the central *waqf* administration.

Haim Gerber, examining the archives of the *majlis idāra* of Jerusalem, found evidence that the district council had issued public tenders for renting out both *mulḥaq* and *maḍbūṭ waqf*s. It was not clear how the district councils had acquired powers with respect to *mulḥaq waqf*s.[15] He concluded that the Ottomans had taken over the *mulḥaq waqf*s under the same (1863) regulations.[16]

To resolve this problem, we should construe the term '*mulḥaq*' in a way that differs from the standard Palestinian usage. *Awqāf mulḥaqa* were actually full-fledged imperial endowments, as we explain below. It hardly stands to reason that such stringent restrictions, with such serious curtailment of the powers of the *qāḍī*s, should have been applied to non-imperial endowments. The only text known to us that makes a precise legal distinction between different types of *waqf*s is the book on *waqf* laws by Omer Hilmi, President of the Supreme Court of Appeals in Istanbul, published in 1899. One may assume that the definitions by Hilmi, chairman of a committee that edited the law code (*majalla*), reflected the distinction existing at the time the ministry was set up in the first half of the nineteenth century. Hilmi distinguishes between three types of *waqfs*:

a. *Awqāf maḍbūṭa* (administered, governed), that is, *waqfs* administered by the Waqf Ministry. These are subdivided into two categories:

1. Endowments created by *Sulṭāns* and their families, for which the endowment deed lays down that, whatever the circumstances, the *Sulṭāns* themselves have the right to administer the *waqf* directly. The *Sulṭān* then empowered the Minister of Imperial Waqfs to manage the *waqf* on his behalf.
2. Family endowments in which all the offspring whom the founder's *waqfiyya* designated as administrators were deceased.

b. *Awqāf mulḥaqa* ('annexed'), that is, endowments administered by a special *mutawallī* under the supervision of the Waqf Ministry. This situation came about because in most such cases the founders named high-ranking officials as *nāẓirs* (administrators, or overseers): the Grand Vizier, *Shaykh al-Islām, Dār al-Sa'āda*, the two *Qadi 'Askars* (military judges), the *Fatwā Amīnī* (head of Legal Opinions Department), and the *qāḍīs* of Istanbul and three cities. They remained the official administrators, but later came under supervision of the Waqf Ministry. *For this transfer of supervisory powers to become legal, the nazirs must themselves transfer their prerogatives to the Waqf Minister* [my emphasis].

c. *Awqāf mustathna'a* (exceptional), that is, endowments administered by a special *mutawallī* not subject to any Ministerial supervision or intervention. Examples are endowments created by Ottoman conquerors in newly won territories or by notables.[17]

These definitions show that, from a juridical point of view, the only criteria which distinguished between *mulḥaq*, *maḍbūṭ* or mustathna' *waqfs* were the terms of the endowment deed. The ministry took over from the *sulṭān* as the *mutawallī* of imperial endowments, as well as from senior officials named as *nāẓirs* by the founders. In both cases, the *waqf* minister needed authorization in order to discharge his duties legally. The ministry has no right to supervise or intervene in the management of any endowment that was not imperial or 'statist' in nature: that is, not subsumed under either of the two above categories of *maḍbūṭ*. The latter endowments fell into the category of 'exceptions' – *mustathna'*. But then, why does Hilmi cite only the endowments of conquerors and notables as exceptional? The answer most likely to be correct is that the three categories of *waqf*s figuring in the civil code were not meant to include all endowments in the empire. They were evidently culled from the specific legislation under which the ministry was established or from the ministry's internal regulations, and they refer to imperial endowments only. As its name (*Naẓarat al-Awqāf al-Hümāyūniyya*) indicates, the ministry did not purport to deal with anything but imperial (*hümāyūniyya*) endowments. The endowments of 'conquerors and notables', about which we have only vague information, were evidently state endowments that defied categorization. They remained undefined because the *waqfiyya* entrusted the administrative functions not to senior officials but to members of the founder's own families. *Mulḥaqa* endowments were simply state endowments – created by sultans and officials – that had been annexed to the ministry for supervision. As we have seen,[18] the term was invoked to designate state endowments that had been incorporated into the Ḥamīdiyya administration.

Further evidence of this is the wording of an order dated 1870 (which deals with bequeathing *ijāratayn* rights; on *ijāratayn* see Chapter 7). It does not mention the word '*mulḥaq*'. *Mulḥaq* endowments, it would seem, had already become *maḍbūṭ* in all respects: the order distinguishes between two types of endowments throughout the empire: *maḍbūṭ* and non-*maḍbūṭ*. *Maḍbūṭ waqf*s were merely under the supervision of the ministry; their day-to-day administration was in the hands of a founder-appointed *mutawallī*. Non-*maḍbūṭ waqf*s were administered by *mutawallī*s and subject only to loose supervision on the part of the ministry.[19] Some degree of ministry supervision was thus applied to both categories. Exceptional endowments were a sub-group in the non-*maḍbūṭ* category (. . . *al-awqāf al-mustathna'a allatī hiya* *min al-awqāf al-ghayr maḍbūṭa . . .*).[20] Consequently, family endowments are *awqāf mustathna'a*, as defined by Hilmi, but are *awqāf ghayr maḍbūṭa* under nineteenth-century Ottoman law.

The conventional view among Israeli scholars – that family endowments belong to the *mulḥaq* type – is thus erroneous. *Awqāf mulḥaqa* were imperial endowments in all respects, and their administration was annexed to that of the *maḍbūṭ waqf*. The fact that only Israeli scholars express this opinion helps us in tracing the source of the error to the Mandatory period, and especially to the way the British understood Ottoman legislation. This hypothesis is supported by the way that John B. Barron, director of revenue after the British conquest of Palestine, defines *mulḥaq*-type endowments in a 'guide' to the *waqf* itself and to its administration in Palestine in particular:

> The revenue of these *waqf*s are left or ceded by private persons, partly for the benefit of religion and partly for the benefit of some person named or succession of persons, such benefits varying with and according to the will of the donors. They are also known in Palestine as 'Private Waqfs'.[21]

Barron expresses his doubts as to whether the nineteenth-century regulations for establishing district *waqf* administrators had ever been enforced in Palestine and suspects that the accounts of the *mulḥaq waqf*s, with reference to family endowments, had been audited in practice by the Waqf Department.[22] He is not the only observer who was mistaken on this subject. In his book on Ottoman land law, Tute also claims that most *awqāf mulḥaqa* were family endowments.[23] As late as 1935, Goadby and Doukhan still state in their book on land regulations:

> So long as the special purposes for which the dedication was made continue, the mutwally (administrator) of the family Waqf administers the family Waqf. Such a *waqf* is Ghair Mazbutta, or as it is more often termed, Mulhaqa (attached), because the Idara (administration) does not belong to the Awqaf administration, but is only under its supervision.[24]

We can therefore trace the mistaken interpretation of the term '*mulḥaq*' by modern scholars to its initial misunderstanding on the part of British officials during the Mandate.

One who evidently knew the correct definition of a *mulḥaq waqf* was the administrator of the Jerusalem Waqf in the late Ottoman and early Mandatory period, ʿĀrif Ḥikmat al-Nashashībī. During his tenure, the shaykh of the Nabī Dā'ūd *zāwiyya* (*ṣūfī* lodge), first administered by the Ottoman Waqf Ministry and later by the SMC, petitioned the *Ma'mūr al-Awqāf*, asking that the Waqf Department finance the hiring of a *Qur'ān* reader in the *zāwiyya*. Nashashībī passed on his request to the SMC, together with a translation into Arabic of the *firmān* (sultanic decree) appointing the shaykh as head of the *zāwiyya*. The *firmān* stated, *inter alia*, that the *zāwiyya waqf* formed part of endowments owned by the state and the Waqf Ministry (*min awqāfinā al-mulkiyya al-tābiʿa li-naẓārat al-awqāf*). Nashashībī pointed out that this endowment was one of the *mulḥaq* endowments administered by state-appointed *mutawallī*s (*hādhā al-waqf min al-awqāf al-mulḥaqa allatī tudār bimaʿrifat mutawallīn makhṣūṣatan muwajjaha liʿahdatihim al-tawliyya bi-barāwāt sulṭāniyya*).[25] Furthermore, the fact that the revenues of the two villages belonging to it – Bayt Sīra and Dayr ʿAmrū – were pledged to the *zāwiyya* gives us to understand that the Nabī Dā'ūd endowment was imperial in nature and defined as *mulḥaq*. The Shaykh Abū al-Wafā' *zāwiyya* endowment in Jerusalem was also considered *mulḥaq*, and its revenues were forwarded to a 'Ministry of *Mulḥaq* Endowments' (*ḥazīnat awqāf hümāyūnnī mulḥaqa*) which supervised it.

A precise definition of the *mulḥaq* endowment is important because it helps us to make clear whether endowments administered by private *mutawallī*s, most of which were family endowments, were under state supervision during the Ottoman period or not. Since, as argued above, family endowments do not come under the category of *mulḥaq* endowments, one might say that they were not subject to state supervision (that is to say, in addition, to that exercised by the *sharīʿa* court). At least this was true until 1904, when the Local Waqf Committees Law was enacted. This empowered the local committees to audit the *mutawallī*s' accounts and to replace them if their management was unsound. It was the only law among the many Ottoman reform laws to prescribe the annual auditing of *mutawallī* accounts by the Waqf Ministry.

The 1904 law contradicted the 1917 *sharī'a* court Procedures Law, which gave the *qāḍīs* (rather than the local committees) authority to replace *mutawallīs*. This created some confusion under the Mandate (when both laws were considered to be valid). In fact, each *sharī'a* court acted as it saw fit. A dispute soon broke out between the president of the SMC, Ḥājj Amīn al-Ḥusaynī, who ordered the *sharī'a* court to apply the Local Waqf Committees Law, and the Sharī'a Court of Appeals, which gave precedence to the Procedures Law. The court argued that, having been passed after the Local Committees Law, the Procedures Law overrode (*yansakh*) the earlier statute.[26] Ḥājj Amīn had to back down and surrender his authority to appoint and dismiss *mutawallīs* (this is discussed at greater length in Chapter 8), even though the British ordinance of 1922, setting up the SMC, had empowered it to supervise the *mutawallīs*. Paragraph 15 of the ordinance states:

> The mutewallis shall administer mulhaka Wakfs [sic] in accordance with existing laws and they shall submit their accounts annually to the local committees for examination.

It is noteworthy that a similar dispute had existed in another formerly Ottoman area, namely in Iraq. Reform laws enacted there in 1929 exempted family *waqfs* from supervision by the Waqf Ministry. However, in the practice of Iraqi lawyers and administrators, family *waqfs* were, in any case, not considered *awqāf mulḥaqa*. The status of the latter, under the narrower interpretation applied in Iraq, was therefore not affected by the 1929 legislation.

The Jerusalem *sijill* of the period 1900–14 contains no reference whatsoever to the concept of *mulḥaq*. Under the category of '*waqf maḍbūṭ*' it mentions, in 1903 and again in 1912, the al-Ḥaram al-Sharīf endowments as being administered by the Waqf Ministry. The Khāṣṣikī Sulṭān Waqf received no mention at all in the *sijill* during these years, but there is no doubt that it, too, was administered by the ministry through the Waqf Department.

However, other large public endowments – for example, the Khānqā'a al-Ṣalāḥiyya Waqf and the Nabī Mūsā Waqf – were not managed by the state; neither were the *waqf*s of *ṣūfī* houses of worship.

Alongside the term '*maḍbūṭ*', another distinction was being made according to the purpose of the *waqf*: endowments for public purposes, called '*waqf khayrī*', and family endowments, called '*waqf dhurrī*'. Under *sharī'a* law, no such distinction existed, because the *sharī'a* regarded the establishment of a family endowment as a charitable act. But the difference evolved naturally because the two types of *waqf*s were handled under different administrative procedures: family endowments were managed by a *mutawallī* from the founder's family, while the creators of most public *waqf*s wanted them to be administered by a public figure on behalf of the government. The use of the terms '*khayrī*' and '*dhurrī*' related to the administration rather than to the character of the *waqf*. A single property could be partly of one, partly of the other kind. In one case, for example, half of a house was designated *maḍbūṭ* and the other half *dhurrī*.[27]

In 1913–14, the Waqf Ministry attempted to take over management of the Nabī Mūsā Waqf and the other endowments of the tombs of prophets (the term 'prophet' being used here in the *qur'ānic* sense). A *waqf* official in Istanbul instructed the Jerusalem Waqf Department to take charge of three *waqf*s: Nabī Mūsā, Nabī Yūnis and Nabī Lūṭ. The instructions were issued after the ministry's department for the registration of old endowments had found that there were no *waqfiyya* for these endowments; neither were there records of stipulations for appointing a *mutawallī*, nor a known standard practice (*ta'āmul*) for doing so.[28] The original appointment of the claimants' forebears not having been renewed, they lacked a formally appointed administrator, so the Istanbul official claimed. Since they were *khayrī* rather than *dhurrī*, and since the law required the transfer to Waqf ministry management of any *waqf khayrī* (exempt if administered by an appointee endorsed by the sultan), they must come under the ministry.[29] Muḥammad Ṣāliḥ al-Ḥusaynī, together with six others from the al-Ḥusaynī and Yūnis families, brought action in the Sharī'a Court of Jerusalem, asking it to enjoin the district

Waqf Department not to deprive them of the administration of the *waqf*. Muḥammad al-Mālik, director of the Jerusalem Waqf Department, argued before the court that the Nabī Mūsā and two other *waqf*s were not family endowments but public ones. Therefore, under the law, their administrators were to be appointed by the *sulṭān*, but this had not been done. Nabī Mūsā, he stated, therefore belonged to the category of '*waqf maḍbūṭ*' and should be administered by the state. The members of the Yūnis and al-Ḥusaynī families produced a *firmān* from 1728 appointing three of their forebears to jointly manage the endowment and laying down that the positions of *mutawallī* and shaykh should then pass from father to son. They further claimed that, under the recently-enacted law, the Nabī Mūsā endowment was considered 'exceptional' – mustathna', outside the scope of ministry intervention.[30] On the basis of the above *firmān*, the *qāḍī* ruled that the petitioners were to continue to administer the endowment. He appointed 12 administrators, each a descendant of one of the appointees named in the original *firmān* and each approved by the families. The ruling was confirmed by the *sharī'a* office of judicial review in Istanbul.[31] In this case, the *sijill* documents contradict Gerber's conclusion that large endowments, including Nabī Mūsā, were *maḍbūṭ*.[32]

The case illustrated that *waqf*s not managed by the ministry were categorized as *mustathna'*, rather than *mulḥaq*. The Young Turks attempted to effect a gradual takeover of all public endowments by tracing those that lacked properly documented administrators. For example, when the administrator of the al-'Umarī Mosque Waqf in Bethlehem died in 1911, its management was transferred to the Waqf Department on the grounds that the position of *mutawallī* had fallen vacant.[33] Kupferschmidt states that by the First World War, the Ottoman authorities had taken over 70 endowments in Palestine under such pretexts.[34] Thus, without formal legislative action, they replaced the distinction between *maḍbūṭ* and *ghayr maḍbūṭ* with a distinction between *khayrī* and *dhurrī*. Their actions were prompted by a modern view of the state as obliged to provide certain public services for its citizens.

NOTES

1. *Jerusalem Sharī'a Court Records* (henceforth: *Sijill*) 409/33/730 (vol. 409, p. 33, no. 730).
2. Paragraph 46 of The Palestine Order-in-Council 1922 validated all Ottoman laws in Palestine until November 1914.
3. O. Hilmi, *A Treatise on the Laws of Evkaf* (trans. C.R. Tyser and D.G. Demetriades, Nicosia, 1899) art. 340.
4. M. Abū Zahra, *Muḥāḍarāt fī al-Waqf* (2nd ed., Cairo: Dār al Fikr al-'Arabī, 1971) pp. 12–13.
5. B. Lewis, 'al-Ḥaramayn'. *The Encyclopaedia of Islam* (2nd ed., Leiden: E.J. Brill), 3, pp. 175–6; M. Hoexter, '*Waqf* al-Ḥaramayn and the Turkish Government in Algiers', in G. Baer and G. Gilbar (eds), *Studies in the Muslim Waqf* (Oxford: Oxford University Press) (forthcoming); idem, 'The *Waqf* and the State' in *Studies in the Muslim Waqf* (London: Oxford University Press) (forthcoming).
6. Aḥmad Pāshā al-Jazzār nominated the *qāḍī* of Acre as supervisor of his imperial *waqf* of 1786, while granting a yearly pension to *Dār al-Sa'āda*. See Y. Reiter, 'The *Waqf* Institution in Acre' (unpublished M.A. Thesis in Hebrew, Hebrew University of Jerusalem, 1986) pp. 49–50.
7. R.J. Barnes, *An Introduction to Religious Foundations in the Ottoman Empire* (Leiden: E.J. Brill, 1987), note 14.
8. *Dustūr* (Arabic translation by Nawfal Nawfal, Beirut 1301 h.) 2, p. 134 ff.
9. On the regulations see: H. Gerber, Ottoman Rule in Jerusalem 1890–1914 (Berlin: Klaus Schwarz Verlag, 1985) pp. 182–3; R.J. Barnes, *An Introduction to Religious Foundations in the Ottoman Empire* (Leiden: E.J. Brill, 1987) p. 141–6; J.B. Barron, *Mohammedan Waqfs in Palestine* (Jerusalem, 1922) pp. 23–6.
10. J.B. Barron, Mohammedan Waqfs in Palestine (Jerusalem, 1922) p. 16.
11. Paragraphs 11, 13, 19 of the regulations. The sum was called *māl maqtū'*.
12. Any renovation over that sum to 2,000 G. needed the authorization of the council and the *mudīr*.
13. Paragraph 32 of the regulations.
14. Paragraph 26 of the regulations.
15. H. Gerber, *Ottoman Rule in Jerusalem 1890–1914* (Berlin: Klaus Schwarz Verlag, 1985) p. 190.
16. Ibid., p. 183.
17. O. Hilmi, *A Treatise on the Laws of Evkaf* (trans. C.R. Tyser and D.G. Demetriades, Nicosia, 1899) arts. 33–5.
18. R.J. Barnes, *An Introduction to Religious Foundations in the Ottoman Empire* (Leiden: E.J. Brill, 1987), note 14.
19. *Al-Awqāf al-mawjūda fī bilād al-dawla al-'aliyya qismān, aḥaduhumā al-awqāf al-maḍbūṭa wal-thānī al-awqāf ghayr al-maḍbūṭa. fal-awqāf al-maḍbūṭa hiyya al-awqāf allatī takūn tawliyyatuhā wa-idāratuhā aw tawliyy-atuhā bi'ahda mashrūṭ 'alayhā lakin idāratuhā faqaṭ maḍbūṭa wa-maṣāliḥuhā kāfatan tudār min ṭaraf khazīnat al-awqāf al-humāyūniyya ra'san wal-awqāf ghayr al-maḍbūṭa hiyya al-awqāf al-mudāra min ṭaraf mutawallīhā ma'a inḍimām naẓārat khazīnat al-awqāf al-humāyūniyya wa-ma'alūmatihā. Dustūr* (1st series, Arabic translation by Nawfal Nawfal,

Beirut 1301 h.)) 2, 145–55. Paragraph 1 of the Law of *Jumādā Thānī* 1287 h.

20. Paragraph 18 of the Law of *Jumādā Thānī* 1287 h.
21. J.B. Barron, *Mohammedan Waqfs in Palestine* (Jerusalem, 1922) p. 26.
22. Ibid.
23. R.C. Tute, *The Ottoman Land Code* (Jerusalem, 1927) p. 12.
24. F.M. Goadby and M.J. Doukhan, *The Land Law of Palestine* (Tel Aviv, 1935) p. 74.
25. Archives of *The Center for Islamic Heritage (Qism al-turāth al Islāmī)* (hereinafter *CIH*), files 1/2/45, 13/22/1.
26. Eisenman's interpretation is misleading. See R.H. Eisenman, *Islamic Law in Palestine and Israel* (Leiden: E.J. Brill, 1978) p. 78.
27. *Sijill* 397a/189/536.
28. *Sijill* 409/33/730.
29. *Laysa waqfan dhurriyan bal huwa min al-awqāf al-birriyya al-khayriyya wa-mithl hādhā al-waqf idh lam yunsab ʿalayha aḥadan mutawallīn dhā barā'a sulṭāniyya fa-amr idāratihā ʿāi'd wa-rājiʿ ilā khazīnat al-awqāf al-jalīla*
30. '. . . *Wa-mutābaʿat al-ḥukm wal-irāda al-sanniyya al-ṣādira akhīran bi-istithnā' hādhihi al-awqāf min al-mudākhala fīhā wa-baqā' waḍʿiyatuhā al-qadīma ʿalā mā kānat ʿalayhi . . .*'
31. The *Sharīʿa* review offices in Istanbul were *Majlis al-Tadqiqāt al-Sharʿiyya* and the *Fatwākhāne*.
32. H. Gerber, *Ottoman Rule in Jerusalem 1890–1914* (Berlin: Klaus Schwarz Verlag, 1985) p. 185.
33. *Israel State Archives* (henceforth: *ISA*), *Land Court*, 753b, file 42/31.
34. U. M. Kupferschmidt, *The Supreme Muslim Council: Islam under the British Mandate for Palestine* (Leiden: E.J. Brill, 1987) p. 115.

2

The Mandatory government and the *waqf*

PATTERNS OF *WAQF* ADMINISTRATION

Broadly speaking, the basic legal concept of British rule in Palestine was to go on applying Ottoman law such as it was in the final years of the Ottoman Empire (and particularly the *majalla* code). But the disappearance of the Istanbul Waqf Ministry and of the highest religious office-holders of the old order left them with no choice but to devise new patterns of administration for the *waqf*s. The concomitant structural changes emerged in three stages:

1. from the British conquest to the establishment of the SMC (1917–21);
2. the period of Ḥājj Amīn al-Ḥusaynī's presidency of the SMC (1922–37);
3. the tenure of the three-man *Awqāf* Committee (1938–48).

Up to the establishment of the SMC

The British conquest merged the (independent) *sanjaq* of Jerusalem with the *sanjaq*s of Acre and Nablus, which had previously belonged to the *wilāya* of Beirut.[1] The *sanjaq* of Jerusalem had long administered the subdistricts (*qaḍā'*) of Jaffa, Hebron and Gaza.

At the end of the Ottoman period, the *mudīr awqāf* (district administrator of *waqf*s) had his seat in Jerusalem; the *maḍbūṭ* endowments were administered by an official of lower rank who had the title of *ma'mūr awqāf*.[2] Immediately after taking over, the

British appointed local committees to operate alongside the *ma'mūr*. They expected these committees to exercise real power, but the new organizational structure collapsed swiftly. The *ma'mūr*s often regarded their positions as family sinecures, and therefore foiled any effort on the part of the committees to intervene in their affairs.

At the top of the structure stood a British-appointed central committee for *waqf* affairs. It had its offices in Jerusalem and was chaired by the Mufti of Jerusalem; its membership consisted of delegates from each local committee. After the British completed the conquest of northern Palestine in September 1918, they decided at first to administer the *waqf*s of the Acre and Nablus *sanjaq*s separately from those of other areas, but in October 1919 these, too, were placed under the authority of the central committee. Its functions, as set forth by the chief administrator, included confirmation (requiring the consent of the chief administrator himself) for transferring *waqf* revenue from one area to another for the benefit of the Palestine Muslim community as a whole.[3] Furthermore, it was to draft budget proposals, supervise the appointment of *waqf* officials and oversee *waqf* management.[4] One of the *waqf* administrators was made a government official and placed in charge of implementing the committee's decisions. He was to act as an intermediary between the central committee and the military administration. The former Ottoman appointments committee (known as *Lajnat Tawjīh al-Jihāt*) that had assisted the *mudīr* continued to function but was made subordinate to the central committee.

These bodies came to constitute the British central *waqf* administration in Palestine; through it, the British discharged the duties formerly performed by the central Ottoman administration: the military governor approved the *waqf* budget, his representative took part in central committee meetings, and an officer for *waqf* affairs was appointed alongside the military governor of every administrative district.[5] Barron estimates annual *waqf* revenues in Palestine during the Ottoman period at £E (Egyptian pounds) 22,000 and expenditures at £E17,000. The balance of £E5,000 was forwarded to the Waqf Ministry in Istanbul (except for years when al-Aqṣā Mosque or other *waqf* buildings needed large-scale maintenance work).[6] Unlike the Ottomans, the British did not appropriate surpluses, since none remained after the conquest. The war had brought the state of *waqf* properties and the collection of revenues to an exceptional low. By 1920, *waqf* revenues had grown again and had reached about £E35,000.[7]

When the civil administration was established in July 1920, it was resolved to seek a permanent organizational pattern for the Muslim community. This was done both in response to complaints from Muslims and for political motives: to conciliate the largest group in the Arab population. Originally, the high commissioner accepted a proposal by the director of the Lands Department who, concerned about the damage the *waqf* system was causing the economy, suggested prohibiting the creation of new endowments. He proposed to set up a committee composed of a *qāḍī*, a member of the *waqf* administration, an official of the Lands Department, and a Muslim notable to approve exchange and other transactions involving *waqf* properties. (A similar committee was then operating in Cyprus.)[8]

This, however, did not remain official policy for long. On 9 November 1920, the high commissioner convened several muftis, other *'ulamā'*, and Muslim notables (nine in number), together with seven senior government officials, to discuss ways to organize Muslim religious affairs and manage the *waqf*s. This forum, subsequently called the Committee for Muslim Religious Affairs, made the following recommendations:

1. The government should continue supervising the management of the *waqf*s.
2. Sharī'a court judges (*qāḍī*s) should be appointed by a Muslim body.
3. A committee should be set up to propose ways to implement these recommendations.

In a confidential memorandum dated 13 January 1921, J.B. Barron, the director of income and taxes and the Mandatory administration's expert on *waqf* affairs, proposed the next step. It is worth rendering his proposal (hitherto unpublished) in detail, as a piece of valuable and original thinking on the matter, even though it ran counter to the policy eventually adopted. Barron proposed that the Ottoman regulations of 1863 for district *waqf* directors should remain valid but that several terms used there be changed: 'Waqf Ministry' to be replaced by 'the Government of Palestine', '*mudīr awqāf*' by '*ma'mūr awqāf*', and '*majlis*' by 'Central Waqf Committee'.[9] According to Barron's memorandum, the new *waqf* administration should be headed by a Committee of Four, which would be the supreme Muslim religious authority in Palestine. Its functions were to be:

1. to prepare the *waqf* budget and submit it to the high commissioner for approval; any changes that might be required from time to time would also have to be approved by the high commissioner; when dealing with financial matters, the committee would call in a government representative;
2. to appoint or dismiss *ma'mūr*s and the committee secretary, to approve appointments of *mutawallī*s for *mulḥaq* (non-*maḍbūṭ*) endowments, and to appoint or dismiss *waqf*-appointed employees of religious and educational institutions;
3. to approve, subject to the high commissioner's consent, loans by *waqf*s and mortgages on or sales of *waqf* property (insofar as *sharī'a* law permitted such transactions);
4. to approve renovation or rental of assets in sums exceeding £E300.

Under the Committee of Four would come the Central Waqf Committee, made up of the *ma'mūr*s of Jerusalem, Nablus and Acre, and four *sanjaq* representatives: two from Jerusalem with its subdistricts of Judea, Beersheva, Gaza and Jaffa; one from Nablus, and one representing Haifa and the Galilee. Its chairman would be appointed by the government. The liaison between the Committee of Four and the Central Committee would be the secretary of the Committee of Four, a member of the Central Committee. His salary would be paid by the *waqf*. (Barron had his doubts on this point and proposed that the secretary-designate, 'Ārif Ḥikmat al-Nashashībī, remain on the government payroll, even though he believed the Muslims would not agree to this.) Central Committee members would have their expenses reimbursed, but would receive no salary. The Central Committee would carry out the instructions of the four-member committee, supervise the work of the local committees, oversee officials of individual *waqf*s, appoint *waqf* officials (with the exception of certain appointments reserved for the Committee of Four) and discipline them if necessary. It would submit draft budgets, audit and verify income and expenditure, and pass its findings to the Committee of Four.

Under the Central Committee, in turn, would operate local *waqf* committees composed of the *ma'mūr* and two unsalaried notables, to be appointed by the government in consultation with the Committee of Four. These would carry out the instructions of the Central Committee and supervise *waqf* management on the regional level. Barron also proposed that the *mutawallī*s of non-*maḍbūṭ waqf*s (which he called '*mulḥaq*') carry out the instructions of the *waqf* administration and submit their accounts to the Central Committee for an annual audit. The *ma'mūr*s would submit a quarterly report on *waqf* income and expenditures to the secretary of the Central Committee. Another proposal by Barron which, again, he believed the Muslims would not accept, was to set aside one-twelfth of the yearly tithes of the *waqf* and deposit this sum in an emergency investment fund for a term of six years.[10]

Barron's assessment concerning what the Muslims would and would not accept (presumably made after contacts with Muslims such as Ḥussām al-Dīn Jārallah and 'Ārif Ḥikmat al-Nashashībī, both then on the government payroll) were far too optimistic. His proposal gave the government sweeping powers of intervention in *waqf* affairs; this was certainly not true of the rival proposal for a Committee for Muslim Religious Affairs. As stated above, Barron's recommendations were not adopted.

In 1921, the Committee for Muslim Religious Affairs proposed to form a central Muslim body composed of the supervisor of *sharī'a* courts, the above-mentioned Ḥussām al-Dīn Jārallah and four other members. These would be selected by a committee made up of two representatives from each district or sub-district, elected by persons entitled to vote in mufti elections under the Ottoman law of AH1328/1910. The same committee would also choose a supreme committee replacing the Ottoman Waqf Ministry for the purpose of *waqf* management and supervision.[11] The proposal laid down that a government representative with the status of advisor would attend the meetings of the Muslim body. The government would be authorized to audit *waqf* accounts whenever it saw fit. The high commissioner would be empowered to approve or veto the *waqf* budget 'for financial considerations only'.[12] When the Muslim public rejected the proposal as implying substantial government involvement in *waqf* and *sharīʿa* court affairs, a new committee was formed to propose the structure and authority of a supreme *sharīʿa* Muslim council and an alternative method for managing *waqf* and *sharīʿa* affairs.[13] Its guidelines became the basis of official policy for the following 15 years.

The SMC (up to 1937)

The order establishing the Supreme Muslim Council was signed by the high commissioner on 20 December 1921 and gazetted on 1 January 1922. It granted the council full autonomy in *waqf* matters, allowing it, practically speaking, to take over, in most *waqf* affairs, the former functions of the Ottoman government. Its powers were:[14]

1. to manage and supervise Muslim endowments, to draft and approve their annual budgets and to bring them to the notice of the government (but not to have them approved by it);
2. to propose candidates for the office of *qāḍī* in *sharīʿa* courts; their actual appointment, however, required government approval; where the government withheld its approval, it was obliged to justify its refusal within 15 days;
3. to appoint muftis from among three candidates whom a special selection committee would propose in accordance with rules to be laid down by the SMC; the Mufti of Beersheba would be elected by the heads of the Bedouin tribes;
4. to appoint the director-general of the *waqf* administration, *ma'mūrs*, other *waqf* officials, all *waqf*-appointed employees of various institutions and *sharīʿa* court officials;

5. to supervise the general and local *waqf* committees and their employees;
6. to dismiss, if necessary, *waqf* and *sharīʿa* court officials and any employee paid out of a *waqf* budget, and to apprise the government of the reason for the dismissal;
7. to demand the return of any property taken over by the Ottomans or the British that could be shown, after investigation, to have been *waqf*-owned. The SMC, for its part, would undertake to honour the original stipulations of donors regarding its use;
8. to modify, amend or supplement any provision concerning the *waqf*s or to publish new regulations; this was to be done by means of a special procedure, requiring a two-thirds majority in the selection committee, as well as government consent; the government was to be informed of any such decision;
9. to approve, by unanimous vote, transactions involving *waqf* properties independently of a *sharīʿa* court decision.

The SMC was to publish an annual report on its activities and budget. The Muslim community would monitor SMC operations by means of the SMC selection committee. The order provided for the formation of a General Waqf Committee, chaired by the Mufti of Jerusalem and including the director-general of the *waqf*, the *ma'mūr*s and a member of each local (district-level) *waqf* committee. The general committee would prepare the annual budget and present it to the SMC. Local *waqf* committees would be set up in districts and sub-districts at the discretion of the SMC. For this purpose, the SMC would be composed of the mufti of the district in question (or, in the absence of a mufti, the eldest of the *ʿulamā'*), the *ma'mūr* and two local notables. The functions of the local committee would be those given to the district council by the Ottoman law of 1904.[15] This implied that the district commissioner would no longer retain jurisdiction in *waqf* affairs.

Subject to approval of the SMC, the committee would appoint, dismiss or discipline *waqf* officials. The order also placed *mulḥaq* endowments under the authority of the *waqf* administration and required them to submit annual accounts to the local committees.

The government would continue to collect tithes through a single central office and to assist the Muslim community in financial matters.

One of the most significant provisions in the order was Paragraph Four, which empowered the SMC to propose regulations for *sharīʿa* courts. The procedure for doing so was to be laid down later. The government, for its part, would not initiate legislation in *waqf* matters. In placing the SMC above the *sharīʿa* courts, the order gave the SMC powers going beyond those formerly exercised by the Ottoman Waqf Ministry and awarded it some of the authority originally held by the *Shaykh al-Islām*. As it turned out, the SMC never made use of this prerogative.[16]

The very appointment of Ḥājj Amīn al-Ḥusaynī, the chief mufti, as president of the SMC ran counter to the policy of decentralization that the Ottomans had introduced in the nineteenth century by granting the district council and the local committees powers of their own. By contrast, Ḥājj Amīn was both *ra'īs al-ʿulamā'* and *al-muftī al-akbar*, and served simultaneously as president of the SMC and chairman of the General Waqf Committee. As the director-general of endowments and the *waqf ma'mūr*s belonged to the latter, this effectively turned the general committee into an appendage of the SMC, rather than its acting as an additional agency capable of checking and balancing the activities of the SMC.[17] Moreover, some members of local committees were officials of the SMC or were chosen and appointed by it. The Jerusalem local committee, for example, was chaired by Ḥājj Amīn himself. Although he did not himself participate in the committee meetings, one of its members was his stand-in, representative and apparently something of a flunkey.[18] There was another member of the al-Ḥusaynī family on the committee, and the *ma'mūr al-awqāf* in Jerusalem was a Ḥusaynī, too, as well as a confidant of Ḥājj Amīn.[19] The SMC eventually appointed six local committees: in Jerusalem, Jaffa, Hebron, Gaza, Nablus and Acre.

The SMC archives show that the local *waqf* committees neither exercised supervisory function nor monitored the activities of the SMC regarding *waqf*s; rather, they became part of the SMC apparatus, and played a rather insignificant part at that. They received their letters of appointment from none other than the *ma'mūr al-awqāf*, who was himself a committee member. For example, Shaykh Muḥammad-Ṣāliḥ al-Ḥusaynī received his letter of appointment from one of the officials of the *ma'mūr*, who signed it on behalf of the *ma'mūr*. The letter instructed the local committee 'to participate, together with the *ma'mūrs*, in supervising the activities of the Waqf Department'. The letter added that the appointment had been made in accordance with the Appointments Law of 1913 (not – as would have been the correct formula – in accordance with a clause in the order establishing the SMC, which was based on the 1904 Local Waqf Committee Law).[20]

The local committee was to offer recommendations on the renovation of *waqf* property, carry out on-the-spot inspection of properties before renovation or transactions, endorse transactions, function as a bid-soliciting committee, let property, approve grants for renovation of mosques and other religious places in the district and the surrounding villages, approve welfare grants from the budget of the Takiyya of the Khāṣṣikī Sulṭān Waqf and approve a budget for the Nabī Mūsā festivities.[21] It was also to approve audits (*muḥāsaba*) of the account books of *mutawallīs* and to oversee the supervisor of such family endowments as had been temporarily placed under the administration of the Waqf Department. This approval was, however, a mere formality – the picture emerging from the SMC archive materials therefore confirms Kupferschmidt's assumption that the local committees were not important actors in the *waqf* system.[22]

The waqf *administration after 1937*

In October 1937, after the assassination of Lewis Andrews, the Acting District Commissioner of the North, Ḥājj Amīn al-Ḥusaynī fled the country. He was then dismissed from his positions as president of the SMC and chairman of the Central Waqf Committee. Under the Defence Regulations (The Muslim Waqf) of 1937, the powers of the SMC regarding *waqfs* were transferred to a three-man government committee.[23] Its members were Justice Green (chairman), I.L. Kirkbraide (Assistant Chief Secretary) and

Shaykh Ḥussām al-Dīn Jārallah.[24] From this time forward, the SMC and the General Waqf Committee ceased to deal with *waqf* matters except on the instructions of the new committee; the powers formerly vested in them by law for supervision and management of *waqf*s now lapsed.[25]

In March 1938, Amīn al-Tamīmī, a relative of Ḥājj Amīn, was dismissed from the SMC and replaced by Shaykh Kamāl Isma'īl.[26] The other three SMC members remained in office.[27] In June 1938, an addendum to the Defence Regulations was gazetted, divesting the SMC of its power to administer *waqf*s, but authorizing it to discharge all other functions and obligations set forth in the original law setting it up.[28] By 1946, changes in the membership of the three-man committee had led to its being made up of Muslims only.

In 1947, Shimoni wrote:

> It was first believed that this committee would replace the Muslim Council, but during 1938 it became clear that the council members residing in Palestine were prepared to co-operate with the committee. Then some of their powers were restored, and the three-man committee now acts only in lieu of the president of the council and as a supervisory committee. True, the Council's powers and latitude have been greatly cut down, and all it is today is a government committee of sorts.[29]

Kupferschmidt believes that after 1937, the SMC became what it should have been from the very start: an administrative agency managing Muslim religious affairs.[30] On the administrative level, no change took place in the functions of the SMC and the *waqf* administration. The positions of SMC president and *Ra'īs al-'Ulamā'* were not filled again. The three-man *waqf* committee came to supervise the activities of the SMC closely (see Chapter 8).

To sum up, the SMC continued to function after 1937 in much the same format as before the issuing of the 1937 Defence Regulations. But the British government now intervened to a much greater extent in *waqf* management and in the affairs of institutions financed by the central *waqf* administration. Yet this involvement did not affect the overall performance of the SMC and the *waqf* institution. In the main, it was meant to prevent the political use of *waqf* resources against the Mandatory government.

THE BRITISH AND THE SMC

The establishment of the SMC had been the outcome of exhaustive negotiations between the British authorities and representatives of the Muslim community. The formation of the British civil administration had aggravated Arab grievances against the Palestine Mandate and against the British policy of furthering the establishment of a Jewish National Home. The British desire to conciliate the Arabs led to a policy of non-intervention in Muslim religious affairs. The order establishing the SMC gave it *de facto* autonomy ('unwarranted autonomy', in Kupferschmidt's words).[31] In practical terms, this placed the *waqf*s under the unqualified control of the SMC. The Mandatory government waived the right to supervise them. It thought of intervention in *waqf* matters as interference in the affairs of the Muslim community, and Ḥājj Amīn took advantage of the quasi-religious character of the *waqf* to warn the British that any such intervention would offend Muslim sensitivities.[32] Herbert Samuel, the first high commissioner, said that the Mandate regime did not wish to usurp the prerogatives of the *Shaykh al-Islām*.[33] He defined British policy on *waqf* matters as 'based on the Turkish precedent except for the fact that we have been far more generous'.[34] The *sharīʿa* courts did not insist on exercising their traditional right of supervision. It would have been possible for them to do so, for even though they were ostensibly part of the government judicial system, the government reserved no more than marginal powers for itself. When a financial crisis hit the SMC in 1930, the British refrained from using it as a lever to tighten their control.[35]

In line with their conciliatory policy, the British waived the requirement periodically to re-elect the president of the SMC, acquiescing to the Muslim claim that he had been elected for life.

To underline their generosity, they transferred back to the SMC numerous properties that the Ottomans had expropriated, thus reversing some of the Ottoman reforms and adding considerably to the SMC's financial strength.[36] Several examples are given below.

Mundaras *endowments*

The Ottoman reforms had included the transfer of revenue from certain *waqf*s to finance general education. This policy had the effect of secularizing the *waqf*, since by then public services such as education had been defined as a responsibility of the state rather than one to be provided, as in the past, by individuals through making endowments. In an order dated 1883, the Ottomans earmarked income from family endowments whose beneficiaries had all died (*awqāf mundarasa*)[37] for educational purposes (to be administered by local education committees). Under the Mandate, the government first refused to recognize properties registered in the name of the local education committees as *waqf* assets. In 1923, the chief secretary wrote to the president of the SMC that the government acknowledged the earmarking for education of income from such properties and had therefore decided to register them as belonging to the government. The income would be held in trust for education, and its management would be entrusted to the local education committees under the supervision of the Education Department.[38]

But the British soon waived this source of revenue and transferred the management of these endowments to the central *waqf* administration of the SMC. In 1923, 788 *awqāf mundarasa* of economic value were returned to the SMC; of these, 332 were in Jerusalem alone, 86 in Gaza, 122 in Safed, 144 in Jenin, 41 in Hebron, 17 in Nablus, 3 in Tulkarm, 38 in Ramallah and Bethlehem and 1 in Tiberias.[39] Their aggregate annual income was officially estimated at £E8,000 but was actually much larger, and their combined value was of great economic significance.[40] Other *awqāf mundarasa* were disputed; their status was not resolved until the 1930s.[41]

In 1932, the SMC set up a public education committee (*lajnat maʿārif ahliyya*) composed of the local *waqf* committee and three notables. Its purpose was to manage the *awqāf mundarasa*, set the budgets of Muslim schools, inspect their activities and review appointments to and dismissals from their staff. Its budget was kept as a trust by the *waqf* exchequer.[42]

Transfers from the British authorities to the SMC

Already in July 1920, during deliberations in the Committee for Muslim Religious Affairs, the Central Waqf Committee had presented the government with a list of 68 *waqf* properties whose revenues had been confiscated by the Ottoman authorities as part of their reforms, and had demanded their reinstatement. For example, the Khāṣṣikī *Sulṭān* Waqf, whose revenues were pledged to soup kitchens (*ʿimāra*), had been abolished under a 1913 statute that did away with all soup kitchens.[43] It seems that the British were strongly affected by local grievances against the Ottomans and wished to appear as an enlightened regime greatly constrasting with them. Consequently, they tended to accept the local interpretation of *waqf* reforms as acts of 'expropriation'. Even as early as that, British officials supported the 'return' of *waqf* properties and revenues to the Muslims as preferable to their being taken over by Mandatory (Christian) authorities.[44] The Ottomans had transferred an annual sum of £E1,150 to the Waqf Department in exchange for the income from the Khāṣṣikī Sulṭān Waqf, and another £E850 for property renovations. The British first raised the sum to £E4,200, then, after the SMC was established, to £E10,400.[45] They also returned public endowments that the Ottomans had taken over, including the *Sulṭān* Qaitbai Waqf and five *madrasas* in the Old City of Jerusalem.[46]

Tithes

The British continued to apply the Ottoman policy of centralized state collection of tithes and the transfer of the endowments' share in them to their administrators. However, they discontinued the late Ottoman custom whereby the average revenue collection over the preceding five years was made the base for computing the current tithes. After the economic crisis of 1929, the government decided to reduce tithes sharply, first by 30 per cent and then by 50 per cent. Since the tithes were the main source of SMC income, the cuts affected it greatly. Moreover, there was then another reason for the deterioration of the SMC's financial situation – the vicissitudes of the Palace Hotel project (see Chapter 7 under; Changing the *waqf*'s original nature). The SMC argued that its income should not fall victim to the government's policy of reducing taxes. At a certain stage, the British accepted this argument, and starting in July 1931, paid it £P (Palestinian pounds) 1,750 per month as an advance, irrespective of agricultural production and without inspecting the SMC accounts.[47] Some time later, the government agreed with the SMC on a sum based on the average of the tithes over the five years preceding the assessment year. In accordance with this computation, the SMC received £P30,000 for 1930–31 and £P23,000 a year from 1932 onwards.

The sides also agreed to appoint a committee chaired by a judge to examine old SMC claims to additional tithes to which its entitlement had not so far been recognized. Taking the committee's work seriously, the director of the Lands Department sent all land registrars a list of villages whose tithes the SMC had claimed, asking them to check the legal status of the lands in question. He asked them to make immediate use of experts on Turkish ownership documents and to personally inspect his work.[48] The SMC then broadened its claims, demanding the tithes of villages that the government had listed because there was no proof that their incomes had been dedicated to the *waqf*. At the request of the SMC, the British asked the Turkish government as early as 1925 to provide documents relating to the *waqf*. The documents arrived and were submitted to the SMC for perusal about four years later, but again the SMC was not satisfied. In 1929, the president of the SMC dispatched his confidant, Amīn Bey al-Tamīmī, himself a member of the SMC, to Istanbul in order to photograph Ottoman land registry documents. But al-Tamīmī was not given a list of individuals or agencies whose documents were required. He spent two years in the Turkish capital, and his letters to Ḥājj Amīn describe the difficulties of working with

Turkish archives: high fees for duplicating registration documents, registrations in Latin characters, and so on. The director of the al-Salt *waqfs* in the East Bank wished to avail himself of al-Tamīmī's services. In a secret correspondence with Ḥājj Amīn, he asked him to instruct al-Tamimi to photograph documents pertaining to the Abū ʿUbayda al-Jarrāḥ Waqf, comprising 70,000 dunams of irrigated farmland on the East Bank, which the British wished to take over.[49] In the mean time, it transpired that most of the dedication deeds and documents required for proving *waqf* entitlements had been stored in the old office of the Ottoman Waqf Department in Jerusalem. Al-Tamīmī's mission became unnecessary, and he was summoned back to Palestine and appointed to supervise the work of two *waqf* officials (the director of the al-Aqṣā library, Shaykh Yaʿqūb al-Bukhārī, and Muḥammad Hijāzī) who were given the task of sorting the old documents.[50] A committee headed by Justice Webb examined the claims of the SMC on the strength of the documents it had submitted and found some justified. In 1932, after the committee had presented its recommendations, the government quickly paid the SMC an advance. The sum paid by the British enabled the SMC to purchase land as part of the campaign against selling land to Jews.[51]

The Webb Committee's recommendations set the stage for another tithe disposition agreement between the government and the SMC in 1934. Under it, payment to the SMC for tithes was raised from £P23,000 to £P30,000 per year, retroactively from 1931, in addition to a one-time payment of £P43,690 for tithes that had accrued until 1931. The money was earmarked for renovations at al-Aqṣā Mosque and the Ḥaram (Cave of the Patriarchs) in Hebron, the repayment of debts, and the purchase of land for use by fellahin. In exchange, the SMC waived any additional claims.[52] This was a very generous settlement, because it increased the SMC's share from 12.5 per cent of government tithe revenue to about 20 per cent.[53]

Yet another agreement was drafted in 1944. Tithe payments were now raised to £P80,000 per year, retroactively from 1942.[54] This increase was described as a government grant (*minḥa*). The SMC vacillated for three years, finally approved the accord on

7 July 1947, but asked to amend the term 'annual grant' to read 'annual payment', reflecting its view that, rather than being a British gesture, the remittance was due to the SMC by right.[55]

The SMC also negotiated for the payment of tithes to such non-*maḍbūṭ waqf*s as were entitled to them. Agreement was reached for a yearly payment of £P1,512.92 per year to the SMC for four *waqf*s: Nabī Mūsā, Nabī Dā'ūd, Shaykh Aḥmad al-Dajānī and Abū Midyan. British consent for the SMC to serve as a conduit for the transfer of tithes to these *waqf*s gradually enabled the SMC to take control of their management. By early 1948, when the SMC was already administering some of these endowments, it asked the government to increase its remittance in view of the difficult economic situation.[56]

SMC revenue in 1946 was approximately £P140,000, as itemized in Table 2.1.

TABLE 2.1 SMC REVENUE IN 1946

Source of revenue	*£P*
Rental and leasing of *maḍbūṭ waqf* properties	27,505
Tithes and registration fees	77,906
Donations	2,288
Sidnā 'Alī (tithes)	4,111
*Mundaras waqf*s	8,502
Repayment of loans	2,798
Miscellaneous	16,549
Total	139,659

Out of this total, £P88,595 were government transfers (tithes and registration fees, and the revenue from Sidnā 'Alī and *mundaras waqf*s). The SMC's overall balance for that year came to £P19,546.[57]

The SMC used the ample funds it received from the government to employ a staff of about 600, in addition to about 550 marriage registrars, 90 teachers and 188 in charge of renovations on *al-Ḥaram al-Sharīf*.[58] It also succeeded in expanding its property portfolio by purchasing and developing additional land and developing other properties it already held. The *al-Ḥaram al-Sharīf* renovation budget also made use of resources other than transfers: for example, donations from Muslims in Palestine as well as elsewhere in the Muslim world. This project, budgeted at £P170,000, was managed as a special fund, separately from the regular SMC budget.[59] The *sharīʿa* courts cost the government some £P10,000 per year. The orphans' fund, also managed separately from the regular SMC budget, amounted to £P145,000 lent at interest, in the course of the land struggle, to farmers who had run into difficulties.[60] The orphans' fund and the al-Haram al-Sharif renovation fund were not subject to any supervision whatsoever, whether governmental or public.

THE STATUS OF THE *SHARĪʿA* COURTS

The enhanced status and powers of the SMC in *waqf* affairs came at the expense of the *sharīʿa* courts, which found their authority curtailed and their status diminished. Although the Ottomans had not managed to apply the Local Waqf Committees Law of 1904 concerning supervision of family *waqf*s, the British, in paragraph 15 of the order establishing the SMC, gave the SMC supervisory powers over *mulḥaq* (non-*maḍbūṭ*) *waqf*s. The administrators of these endowments were to 'honor the instructions of the Waqf administration' – a general statement whose purport is not clear. More specifically, they were required to submit yearly financial statements to the local *waqf* committees, which, in turn, were subordinate to the SMC.

None the less, the SMC, while entrusted with exclusive administrative and supervisory powers over *maḍbūṭ*-type endowments, was dependent on the *sharīʿa* courts in all matters for which, under *sharīʿa* law, the Ottoman Waqf Ministry required approval by a *qāḍī*. This was specifically so with respect to transactions of the *ijāratayn*, *ḥikr* and *istibdāl* type. Paragraph 8(2) of the order establishing the SMC stipulated unanimous consent of SMC members for such transactions before they came up for approval in the *sharīʿa* court, but such approval was still required for *maḍbūṭ* and non-*maḍbūṭ* *waqf*s alike.[61] In the Ottoman period, the consent of the Waqf Ministry had been needed for approval, but in the reverse order: first came the approval of the *qāḍī*, who had to verify whether the transactions met *sharīʿa* conditions; only then was the ministry approached. This points to the diminution of the status of the *sharīʿa* court under the Mandate. True, its approval, once given, could no longer be abrogated by a secular civil body, as had been the case in the Ottoman period; but now an agency of a clearly secular nature was empowered to determine which applications would be brought before the *qāḍī* and which not.[62] Theoretically, the *sharīʿa* court could decline to approve transactions the SMC wished to carry out, if it considered them contrary to *sharīʿa* law. In practice, however, such a refusal was exceedingly unlikely, since the *qāḍī*s were largely dependent on the SMC: the latter could dismiss them (though it had to explain to the high commissioner the reason for doing so); if the SMC wished to avoid involving the British, it could punish a *qāḍī* by transferring him to a position in another town.

Although the SMC founding order had not said so explicitly, the SMC needed the approval of the *sharīʿa* court in all *waqf* matters for which the former Ottoman ministry had required such approval. Alongside transaction permits, the consent of the *qāḍī* was needed for basic modification of property, changing the method of revenue collection (tithes), rental for a period exceeding the norm (*ijāra wāḥida*) and the like. In practice, the SMC did indeed seek *sharīʿa* court approval for transactions of this kind (although we do not know if this was true of all transactions).[63]

Initially, the *sharīʿa* courts were also authorized to adjudicate endowment affairs of members of other religious communities. Non-Muslims could make endowments only by applying to the *sharīʿa* court, basing their applications on the *sharīʿa* law. But in 1922, an Order in Council restricted the powers of *sharīʿa* courts to Muslim endowments. For non-Muslim endowments already in existence, they retained their former power with regard to questions of the founding and validity of the endowment. Other matters were brought before the tribunals of the donor's religious community if the religious law of his community addressed itself to endowments; if not, they came before the civil court.[64]

The *sharīʿa* courts lacked the power to enforce their rulings; instead, they depended on the civil courts to do so.[65] In order to plead in the *sharīʿa* courts, a lawyer had to apply to the government's Department of Justice, not to a Muslim body.

The jurisdiction of the *sharī'a* court over land ownership disputes had been curtailed by the Ottomans back in 1914, but they continued to adjudicate land cases that touched on the status of a *waqf*.[66] As regards non-*ṣaḥīḥ waqf*s, the Land Law of 1858 had already stripped the *sharī'a* courts of their prerogatives.[67] Soon after the British conquest, the new administration issued an order barring civil courts of the first instance, as well as *sharī'a* courts, from adjudicating land ownership cases. In 1921, special land courts were set up, and jurisdiction in such matters was finally removed from the competence of the *sharī'a* courts. The 1925 Civil and Religious Courts Ordinance (Jurisdiction) went a step further, stipulating that any matter relating to ownership or possession of land was to be adjudicated in a civil court, even if one of the parties claimed that the case involved *waqf* property. The SMC disliked the idea of *waqf* disputes between itself and the government coming before civil courts, but the Ottoman precedent was too strong to overcome. Nevertheless, the SMC attempted to change the situation, and the Islamic Congress of February 1926 passed a resolution urging the government to restore jurisdiction over *waqf* land to the *sharī'a* courts.[68] Its appeal was ignored by the Mandatory government.

THE IMPACT OF BRITISH LEGISLATION ON THE *WAQF*

Until 1937, official British policy was to refrain from intervention in religious affairs, whether Muslim or not. This included *waqf* matters. However, the British government felt obliged to deal with all religious communities on an equal footing. This meant, from the very start, curtailing the privileges the Muslims had enjoyed in the Ottoman Empire. The British applied their liberal Western *Weltanschauung* in their administration, but were not less guided by political and public considerations. The underlying principle of their policy was to preserve the status quo in religious affairs; only such changes were to be made as were indisputably necessitated by the change of regime. Accordingly, reforms were introduced through indirect legislation, unlikely to conflict with the *sharī'a*. None the less, economic and administrative problems of the kind bound to preoccupy any government led the British to take legislative action that affected the *waqf*.

The Charitable Trusts Ordinance

In Islam, the *waqf* is an important instrument of charity. Moreover, since Islam bars individuals from making wills as they choose, founding a *waqf* was the only possible way of circumventing the *sharīʿa* laws of succession. Later civil legislation offered modern alternatives to the laws of inheritance and different ways to practise charity, and was thus capable of undermining and weakening the *waqf* as an institution. The British viewed *waqf*s as quasi-religious bodies and tended to leave their administration in Muslim hands in order to avoid antagonizing the Muslim population. However, they were ill at ease with *waqf*s being subordinated to religious courts. The Ottomans, in the twilight of their rule, had passed legislation allowing the formation of charitable associations under civil rather than *sharīʿa* law.[69] The British gradually drove in the wedge further, the first step being an ordinance permitting the creation of endowments in civil courts under secular law. This followed the English concept of a trust. The Endowments for Charitable Trusts Ordinance of 1924[70] allowed any individual to dedicate a property for purposes of charity, education or religion, and assigned jurisdiction in such matters to the district courts. Next came the Charitable Trusts (Public Trustee) Ordinance of 1925, which made it possible to convert a *waqf* established in a *sharīʿa* court into a secular charitable endowment.[71] This interference with the *waqf* was effected indirectly by civil legislation; by creating a secular alternative to the *waqf*, it could theoretically have done the *waqf* considerable harm. Its practical effects have not yet been researched. In offering an alternative to, rather than banning, the *waqf*, this law implied British appreciation that the *waqf* was of intrinsic value (unlike their policy towards the SMC, which was guided by political considerations). In India, the British administration had abolished family *waqf*s as contrary to the norms of British law.[72] The French and Italians had similarly attempted to impose their own legal norms on the Muslim inhabitants of their African colonies.

The Succession Ordinance

Another law likely to affect the *sharīʿa* adversely and, as a result, to vitiate the link between them and the *waqf*, was the Succession Ordinance of 1923. This adopted the 1913 Ottoman law of inheritance. Being based on the principles of German inheritance law, the 1913 Ottoman law had created new ways of circumventing *sharīʿa* laws. The law set forth various rules for bequeathing *miri* property, the main ones being by family branches, with grandchildren receiving a part of their grandfather's legacy together with their parents, and equal shares for sons and daughters. Under this method, which was called *al-intiqālī*, the legator's wife would receive a share of one-quarter, instead of only one-eighth as laid down by *sharīʿa* law; the share of the legator's mother was increased as well. Up to 1992, the *sharīʿa* court in East Jerusalem ruled according to both methods: *sharīʿa* law applied to *mulk* property, *intiqāliyya* law to *mīrī* property. The Succession Ordinance was therefore an important departure that made it possible, in most cases, for Muslims to draw up an unrestricted civil-law will of the British type.[73]

Land registration

During the Ottoman period, jurisdiction over the transfer of land and the determination of ownership belonged exclusively to the *sharīʿa* court. Any legislation requiring the registration of land or confirmation of *waqf* ownership by government offices was a threat to the jurisdiction of the *sharīʿa* courts. Land registration began in the Ottoman period, under the Land Law of 1858. Cadastral registration (Turkish: *ṭāpū*; Arabic: *ṭābū*) based on demarcations made by surveyors was introduced in the last years of Ottoman rule, but the authorities did not succeed in entrenching this practice in Palestine. In order to establish a new *waqf* or recognize the entitlements of existing *waqf*s, it was necessary to register them in the cadastral ledgers and obtain a *kūshān* (authorized ownership document). Under British rule, it became impossible to register an endowment in a *sharīʿa* court without the prior consent of the Land Registry Department. The Land

Transfer Ordinance of 1920 stipulated that any transfer of land required the prior written consent of the Registry Office.[74] In the context of *waqf*s, this was intended to create records permitting inspection of land. The registry would thus be able to distinguish between types of land ownership and, for instance, to prevent the endowment of *mīrī* land, which was forbidden under the Ottoman Land Law of 1858, which regarded *mīrī* land as state-owned. Whenever the *qāḍī* was asked to register a *waqf*, he had first to forward the request to the Land Registry Department and obtain its consent. Only when the registrar stated that there was no legal impediment to turning the property into a *waqf* could the *qāḍī* validate the endowment by a legal ruling. Once this had been done, the *waqf* administrator had to re-register the land in the *ṭābū* as an endowment. To illustrate: the wife and children of ʿAlī al-Turk, who had founded a family *waqf* in the Mandatory period, succeeded in annulling it after his death, because he had died before registering the property as a *waqf* in the *ṭābū*.

Expropriation of waqf *land for public purposes*

The underlying principle of the *waqf* was the permanence of the dedication, both with regard to its use and with regard to the property itself, which was meant to be a living memorial to the founder. It was therefore forbidden to sell or transfer *waqf* properties, except in special circumstances and under the strict supervision of the *qāḍī*. However, the Ottomans had enacted several laws that permitted expropriation of land for public purposes.[75] Although Ottoman legislation thus applied the concept of 'eminent domain', including expropriation, the negotiations and procedure necessary to set the level of compensation made such action exceedingly difficult. The Ottoman law was incorporated into British legislation, with some necessary modifications, on 20 May 1919. Law No. 28 of 1 August 1926[76] then set forth regulations governing land expropriation, pursuant to a series of earlier Acts which had made it possible to expropriate historic and ancient sites or lands needed for military purposes.[77] The new statute, based on a law enacted in Britain in 1845, differed from the Ottoman law in two respects: (1) in enabling the expropriating authority to take immediate possession of the property, provided the high commissioner's approval was obtained, and (2) in its award of jurisdiction, in the absence of agreement on compensation, to the local court of competence in land affairs. The law sanctioned expropriation of land of any type, including *waqf*, laying down that compensation equal to the value of the *waqf* must be remitted to the *waqf* administration.[78] Empowering a civil authority to expropriate *waqf* property without reference to the *sharīʿa* court flew in the face of the entire *sharīʿa* concept of the principle of the *waqf*.

Rent control (tenant protection)

Sharīʿa law limits the maximum rental period of an urban *waqf* to one year, and of farmland to three years, except when the founder states otherwise in the endowment deed. Rents must be 'appropriate' – in keeping with the property's value on the free market. Civil legislation making the rental of *waqf*s unlimited in time, or controlling the level of the rent, is contrary to *sharīʿa* law. None the less, the serious housing shortage of the 1930s led to the imposition, by the British authorities, of rent control and the prolongation of leases for as long as tenants paid the rent set by the government. The relevant legislation followed the model of English law. An order issued in 1933 allowed municipalities to issue by-laws in this matter. It was replaced with full-fledged legislation in 1934,[79] and subsequently by another law that remained in effect until the end of the Mandate: the Rent Restriction Ordinance, applying to residential housing from 1940 and to business premises from 1941.[80] Its purpose was to protect tenants from eviction after the expiry of their original lease and to control rent levels.[81] It did not distinguish between *waqf* and other properties, thus rendering it contrary to *sharīʿa* law.

To sum up, British policy had a decisive impact on *waqf* management until 1922, and again, to a large extent, after 1937 (through the SMC). Between 1922 and 1937, however, during Ḥājj Amīn al-Ḥusaynī's presidency of the SMC, the British had no way to influence or supervise the way the SMC managed the endowments. With respect to the transfer of property and budgets to the SMC, the British proved generous indeed. By the same token, British legislation greatly reduced the powers of the *sharīʿa* courts to supervise non-*maḍbūṭ waqfs*, to rule on transactions involving *waqf* properties and to adjudicate ownership disputes involving *waqfs*. On the one hand, the British implemented some of the Ottoman reform legislation, including statutes that the Ottomans had not had time to apply in Palestine. On the other hand, in their desire to accommodate the SMC, they undid some of the Ottoman reforms. Some British legislation affected the *waqfs*, though only indirectly; it was meant to apply British social norms, but the Muslim public was disinclined to make use of the options thus provided to them.

NOTES

1. The *sanjaq* of Nablus included the *qaḍā*'s of Nablus, Tul- Karm and Jenin; the *sanjaq* of Acre included the *qaḍā*'s of Haifa, Acre, Nazareth, Tiberias and Safed.
2. *Ma'mūrs* were in post in Jaffa, Hebron, Gaza, Acre and Nablus. See J.B. Barron, *Mohammedan Waqfs in Palestine* (Jerusalem, 1922) p. 46.
3. Ibid., pp. 46–7.
4. Ibid., p. 48.
5. Ibid., p. 47; U.M. Kupferschmidt, *The Supreme Muslim Council: Islam under the British Mandate for Palestine* (Leiden: E.J. Brill, 1987) pp. 20–3.
6. Ibid.
7. *The Palestine Weekly*, 22 October 1920.
8. The proposal of 7 October 1920 was approved by the High Commissioner on 17 October 1920. *ISA, Chief Secretary Office* (henceforth: *CSO*) F, 3775, file 19.
9. J.B. Barron, *Mohammedan Waqfs in Palestine* (Jerusalem, 1922) p. 46; U.M. Kupferschmidt, *The Supreme Muslim Council: Islam under the British Mandate for Palestine* (Leiden: E.J. Brill, 1987) p. 21; *Official Gazette*, 15 May 1921.
10. *ISA, CSO*, 3775, file 8, art. 14 of Barron's letter to the Legal Secretary.
11. The proposal of The Committee for Muslim Religious Affairs was approved by thr High Commissioner on 12 March, 1921 and published in the *Official Gazette*, no. 43 of 15 May 1921.
12. U.M. Kupferschmidt, *The Supreme Muslim Council: Islam under the British Mandate for Palestine* (Leiden: E.J. Brill, 1987) pp. 22–3, 80–1, 86–7.
13. Ibid., p. 22.
14. A. Layish, 'The Muslim *Waqf* in Israel', *Asian and African Studies*, 2 (1966) p. 52. Y. Shimʿoni, *The Arabs of Palestine* (Hebrew, Tel-Aviv: ʿAm ʿOved, 1947), p. 76; B.S. Shitrit, *The Supreme Sharīʿa Muslim Council* (Hebrew,

n.p., 1949), 8.

15. For example of listing names of nominees in the local *Waqf* committees, see *Salname Vilayet Beyrut*, 1311–1312 (Istanbul, n.d.) p. 136, 139.
16. Cf. J.B. Barron, *Mohammedan Waqfs in Palestine* (Jerusalem, 1922) p. 52.
17. U.M. Kupferschmidt, *The Supreme Muslim Council: Islam under the British Mandate for Palestine* (Leiden: E.J. Brill, 1987) p. 147.
18. In 1930, Sa'd al-Dīn al-Khaṭīb held that office, in 1942 the committee members were Shaykh Ḍiyyā' al-Dīn al-Khaṭīb (chair), Shaykh 'Abd al-Bārī Barakāt and Dā'ūd al-Fityānī.
19. U.M. Kupferschmidt, *The Supreme Muslim Council: Islam under the British Mandate for Palestine* (Leiden: E.J. Brill, 1987) p. 147, note 3.
21. *CIH*, 13/32/5,12/60.
21. *CIH*, 13/34/5,19/60.
22. U.M. Kupferschmidt, *The Supreme Muslim Council: Islam under the British Mandate for Palestine* (Leiden: E.J. Brill, 1987) p. 147.
23. *Official Gazette*, no. 730, suppl. II, 973.
24. *Official Gazette*, no. 731 (18 October 1937) suppl. 2, 935. See also B.S. Shitrit, *The Supreme Sharī'a Muslim Council* (Hebrew, n.p., 1949) p. 11.
25. Ibid.
26. *Official Gazette*, no. 769 of 21 March 1938.
27. Replacements were nominated by the government in case of retirement or old age of serving members. U.M. Kupferschmidt, *The Supreme Muslim Council: Islam under the British Mandate for Palestine* (Leiden: E.J. Brill, 1987) p. 256; B.S. Shitrit, *The Supreme Sharī'a Muslim Council* (Hebrew, n.p., 1949) p. 10.
28. The Defence Regulations (Supreme Muslim Council) (no. 2), 1938; *Official Gazette*, no. 788, suppl. 2, p. 662; B.S. Shitrit, *The Supreme Sharī'a Muslim Council* (Hebrew, n.p., 1949) p. 10.
29. Y. Shim'oni, *The Arabs of Palestine* (Hebrew, Tel-Aviv: 'Am 'Oved, 1947), p. 80.
30. U.M. Kupferschmidt, *The Supreme Muslim Council: Islam under the British Mandate for Palestine* (Leiden: E.J. Brill, 1987) p. 255.
31. Ibid., p. 28.
32. Ibid., p. 117.
33. Y. Porath, *The Emergence of the Palestinian-Arab National Movement 1918–1929* (London: Frank Cass, 1974), p. 196.
34. *ISA, CSO*, 192, minutes of 5 May 1922 quoted by U.M. Kupferschmidt, *The Supreme Muslim Council: Islam under the British Mandate for Palestine* (Leiden: E.J. Brill, 1987) p. 118.
35. U.M. Kupferschmidt, *The Supreme Muslim Council: Islam under the British Mandate forPalestine* (Leiden: E.J. Brill, 1987) p. 46.
36. Ibid., p. 118.
37. *Mundaras* means that its purpose is abolished or the entitlements of beneficiaries have lapsed. Y. Shim'oni, *The Arabs of Palestine* (Hebrew, Tel-Aviv: 'Am 'Oved, 1947), p. 86.
38. *ISA, CSO*, F, 3775, file 21.
39. *ISA. Land Court*, B/763, file 19/35.
40. J.B. Barron, *Mohammedan Waqfs in Palestine* (Jerusalem, 1922) p. 57; U.M. Kupferschmidt, *The Supreme Muslim Council: Islam under the British*

Mandate for Palestine (Leiden: E.J. Brill, 1987) p. 120, note 94.

41. U.M. Kupferschmidt, *The Supreme Muslim Council: Islam under the British Mandate for Palestine* (Leiden: E.J. Brill, 1987) pp. 121–2.
42. The nominees were officers in SMC affiliated institutions. *CIH*, 13/32/5, 14/60, 13/33/5,16/60.
43. H.A. Khayat, '*Waqfs* in Palestine and Israel – from the Ottoman Reforms to the Present' (Ann Arbor, MI, University Microfilms, 1962), 83–85; *CIH*, 1338/2,1/4/45.
44. U.M. Kupferschmidt, *The Supreme Muslim Council: Islam under the British Mandate for Palestine* (Leiden: E.J. Brill, 1987) p. 118.
45. J.B. Barron, *Mohammedan Waqfs in Palestine* (Jerusalem, 1922) p. 58.
46. Ibid.
47. U.M. Kupferschmidt, *The Supreme Muslim Council: Islam under the British Mandate for Palestine* (Leiden: E.J. Brill, 1987) p. 46.
48. *ISA, CSO*, F, 3775, files 11 and 12. Judge Webb headed the Committee. Other members were J.C. Cress from the treasury and Mitrī Ḥanā from the land department.
49. For the corespondence between Ḥajj Amīn and al-Tamīmī see *CIH*, 13/29/3,1/55.
50. U.M. Kupferschmidt, *The Supreme Muslim Council: Islam under the British Mandate for Palestine* (Leiden: E.J. Brill, 1987) p. 46.
51. Ibid., p. 49.
52. For the agreement see M.A. al-Imām al-Ḥusaynī, *al-Manhal al-Ṣāfī fī al-Waqf wa-Aḥkāmihi* (Jerusalem, n.d. (1982)) pp. 127–42.
53. U.M. Kupferschmidt, *The Supreme Muslim Council: Islam under the British Mandate for Palestine* (Leiden: E.J. Brill, 1987) pp. 182–4.
54. Ibid., pp. 184–5; for the agreement see M.A. al-Imām al-Ḥusaynī, *al-Manhal al-Ṣāfī fī al-Waqf wa-Aḥkāmihi* (Jerusalem, n.d. (1982)) pp. 276–7.
55. *CIH*, 13/47/5,24/55, letter from the SMC to the Chief Secretary.
56. *CIH*, 13/47/5,24/55.
57. *ISA, SMC*, P/988, file 38.
58. U.M. Kupferschmidt, *The Supreme Muslim Council: Islam under the British Mandate for Palestine* (Leiden: E.J. Brill, 1987) pp. 60–2.
59. Ibid., pp. 170–2.
60. Ibid.
61. Layish believes that the SMC was not subject to *Sharī'a* Court approval, A. Layish, 'The Muslim *Waqf* in Israel', *Asian and African Studies*, 2 (1966) p. 43.
62. Cf. Ibid., p. 42.
63. See Chapter 7.
64. A. Layish, 'The Muslim *Waqf* in Israel', *Asian and African Studies*, 2 (1966) p. 41–3.
65. Paragraph 56 of the Palestine Order-in-Council. Great Britain, Colonial Office, *Report by His Majesty's Government to the Council of the League of Nations on the Administration of Palestine and Trans-Jordan for the Year 1935* (London, 1936).
66. A. Layish, 'The Muslim *Waqf* in Israel', *Asian and African Studies*, 2 (1966) p. 45.
67. Ibid., p. 46.

68. U.M. Kupferschmidt, *The Supreme Muslim Council: Islam under the British Mandate for Palestine* (Leiden: E.J. Brill, 1987) pp. 125.
69. Law of 1914.
70. *Palestine Laws*, Chapter 14. A. Layish, 'The Muslim *Waqf* in Israel', *Asian and African Studies*, 2 (1966) p. 43.
71. *Palestine Laws*, Chapter 15. A. Layish, 'The Muslim *Waqf* in Israel', *Asian and African Studies*, 2 (1966) p. 43; on the trusts ordinance see F.M. Goadby and M.J. Doukhan, *The Land Law of Palestine* (Hebrew, Tel Aviv, 1935) pp. 89–95.
72. D. Pearl, *A Textbook on Muslim Law* (London, 1979) pp. 165ff.; G.C. Kozlowski, *Muslim Endowments and Society in British India* (Cambridge: Cambridge University Press, 1985) p. 56; A. Fayzee, *Outline of Muḥammadan Law* (3rd ed., London: Oxford University Press, 1964) pp. 290ff.
73. F.M. Goadby and M.J. Doukhan, *The Land Law of Palestine* (Hebrew, Tel Aviv, 1935) p. 111.
74. *Palestine Laws*, Chapter 81, Paragraph 4. A. Ben Shemesh, *The Land Laws of Palestine* (Hebrew, Tel Aviv, 1953) p. 256.
75. The expropriation law of 21 Jumādā al-Awwal 1296h/1879, amended in 17 April 1330 mali/1914. Expropriation by municipalities was enacted on 7 Rabīʿ al-Awwal 1332h/1914. F.M. Goadby and M.J. Doukhan, *The Land Law of Palestine* (Hebrew, Tel Aviv, 1935) p. 315.
76. *Palestine Laws*, Chapter 77.
77. F.M. Goadby and M.J. Doukhan, *The Land Law of Palestine* (Hebrew, Tel Aviv, 1935) p. 316.
78. Ibid. pp. 315–31, 348.
79. Ibid., 194; M. Doukhan, *Land Laws in the State of Israel* (Hebrew, 2nd ed., Jerusalem, 1953) p. 216.
80. *Palestine Laws*, 6, p. 3234ff.
81. M. Doukhan, *Land Laws in the State of Israel* (Hebrew, 2nd ed., Jerusalem, 1953) p. 216.

Part 2

3

Founders and properties

FORMATION OF *WAQFS* IN JERUSALEM

The number of *waqf* dedications in a certain area and over a given period by founders from among a population of a certain size may indicate the importance of the *waqf* in the society being observed. Of special interest for such a study is how the modern era has affected the *waqf*. Because, as a traditional institution, it sustained the old social order in more ways than one, one might assume that the number of new *waqf*s decreased during recent decades. Modern circumstances rendered some functions of the *waqf* unnecessary. For example: the so-called 'sultanic' (imperial) endowments had been intended to fill the void left by the Ottoman state regarding some types of public services such as education, health, welfare and others. When the Mandatory government took responsibility for such services and financed them from the state budget, these *waqf*s became redundant.

To shed light on the status and the trends of development of the *waqf* in Mandatory Palestine, one may compare the number of new endowments in Ottoman Jerusalem with other periods and places. To analyse and evaluate the role of the *waqf* in any given period, we should assess its function at that time: why do individuals turn their possessions into *waqf*s? Their motives can be understood to a certain extent by looking at two interrelated factors. The first is the goal that the *waqf* founder set himself and the identity of the beneficiaries of his *waqf*. (For our present purpose, the designated *waqf* administrator is considered one of them.) With respect to family *waqf*s, *waqf* entitlements have been studied by Layish, who thought of them as a way to circumvent the *sharīʿa* laws of succession. Powers, for his part, views the family *waqf* as one component of a wider Islamic inheritance system.

The second factor is the personal, social and economic background of the founders. Crecelius, for example, describing *waqf*s in seventeenth- and eighteenth-century Egypt, deduced from the large number of military elite members among the founders that their main motive had been to 'launder' unlawfully-obtained property and entitle their offspring to inherit it.[1] No attempt has yet been made to explore the connection between the personal background of founders and their motives for creating a *waqf*.

This chapter analyses data on the gender, age and personal status of founders in an attempt to find a correlation between these indicators and the motives for creating endowments. Unlike research on the Middle Ages, it is possible to obtain personal details on founders during the Mandate, because many of them are still alive and have consented to being interviewed.

The most detailed corpus of data on the formation of *waqf*s is the survey by Barkan and Ayverdy on Istanbul *waqf*s.[2] According to the data in this survey, 2,515 endowments were made in Istanbul by 1546 – on average 25–30 per year. Another source of information is Kāmil al-Ghazi's book on Aleppo.[3] There, in the second half of the eighteenth century, Muslims created 577 endowments, approximately ten per year. In the nineteenth century, the number of *waqf* formations decreased to 6.2 per year.[4] These figures tell us from the outset that the number of endowments was much greater in the capital than in a provincial town – even a large one – and that the number of endowments in the same city changed from period to period.

Crecelius's data, culled from the records of three *sharīʿa* courts in Cairo, illustrate the fluctuations in the number of endowments between one period and another. In five sub-periods between 1640 and 1802, the annual average ranged from 18.1 to 55.[5] Crecelius attributes at least some of these fluctuations to political changes affecting the status of the central Ottoman government in Egypt. He believes, as stated above, that the military elite used the *waqf* to launder illicitly obtained property and to evade taxes.[6]

Before the Ottoman conquest in 1517, the *taḥrīr* records show only 70 *waqf*s extant in Jerusalem.[7] Shortly before the British occupation in 1917, about 2,000 *waqf*s were registered in the Jerusalem *sijill*. Thus the yearly average number of *waqf*s formed in Jerusalem during the entire Ottoman period was between four and five. These data, however, are problematic for several reasons:

1. The area of jurisdiction of the Jerusalem *sharīʿa* court changed during the period, especially in the nineteenth century. At certain times, Gaza and Hebron *waqf*s were registered in Jerusalem.
2. At times, Jerusalem *waqf*s were registered in *sharīʿa* courts in Damascus and Cairo, and vice versa.[8]
3. Some of the endowments were made by Christians and Jews (especially in the second half of the nineteenth century; cf. Chapter 2).[9]
4. Under *sharīʿa* law, a *waqf* need not be registered in a *sijill* to be valid.[10] And indeed, some endowment deeds – presumably a small number – were not registered.

Obviously, the most important *waqf*s in Jerusalem were formed for public purposes. In the middle of the sixteenth century, the Ottoman *taḥrīr* records listed 88 endowments in Jerusalem, 60 (68 per cent) of them for public purposes. Most of these had been made by Ayubid, Mamluk and Ottoman dignitaries. The records show that the vast majority were formed in order to finance religious institutions, in particular Sufi establishments, and most of the dedicated properties were major villages and farms outside Jerusalem.[11] The number of family endowments increased in the Ottoman period, as did the share of urban properties so endowed.

The only findings on *waqf* formation in various localities that can be paired with population estimates are those pertaining to Jerusalem. According to Baer, 46 *waqf*s were created in Jerusalem between 1805 and 1820.[12] The annual average of three is lower than that found in cities such as Aleppo, Cairo and Istanbul. However, the Muslim population of Jerusalem in the early nineteenth century was no larger than 5,000, at a time when that of the other cities reached hundreds of thousands.[13] The per capita share of endowments was thus several times higher in Jerusalem than in the Ottoman capital or other large urban centres.

TABLE 3.1 CREATING ENDOWMENTS IN MANDATORY JERUSALEM

No.	*Date*	*Founder's name*	*Waqf type*	*Sijill*
1	17.10.18	Fāṭima As ʿad ʿAbd al-Qādir al-ʿAlamī	Family	416/119/184
2	7.12.20	ʿIsā Muḥammad ʿAlī Abū Sabitān	Family	421/74/184
3	21.9.21	As ʿad ʿAlī ʿUthmān Ṭaha al-Dajānī	Family	422/260/334
4	2.12.21	Ibrāhīm Muḥammad Yaḥyā Qulaybū	Family	423/87/3
5	24.1.22	Ibrāhīm Muḥammad Yaḥyā Qulaybū	Family	423/133/38
6	20.3.23	Yāsīn Muḥammad ʿAql	Family	427/86/17
7	10.5.23	Aḥmad Saʿīd Ṣāliḥ Munā al-Saʿdī	Family	427/91/22
8	29.5.23	Khalīl ʿAbdallāh ʿAṭallāh al-Hidmī	Family	427/132/136
9	1.6.23	ʿAlī ʿAbd al-Raḥmān al-ʿUmarī and his wife	Family	427/141/142
10	4.6.23	Muḥammad Yūsuf ʿAbd al-Rāziq al-ʿAlamī	Family	427/147/148
11	3.7.23	Yāsīn Saʿīd Muḥammad al-Dasūqī	Family	427/174/173
12	8.10.23	Ibrāhīm Ḥamad Ḥamad Muḥammad Ghibn	Family	427/245/245
13	4.11.25	ʿAbd al-Razzaq Barakāt Abū al-Filāt	Family	436/45/52
14	29.3.26	ʿUmar ʿAbd al-Qādir Muṣṭafā Būja	Family	433/123/77
15	16.5.26	ʿUmar ʿAbd al-Qādir Muṣṭafā Būja	Family	433/131/82
16	19.5.26	Subḥī ʿAbdallāh Bakr Aḥmad al-Dajānī	Family	437/33/37
17	19.5.26	ʿAbd al-ʿAzīz Shākir al-Dajānī	Family	437/37/41
18	19.5.26	Ḥasan Ṣidqī al-Dajānī	Family	437/38/42
19	29.6.26	Mūsā Ḥusayn ʿAbdallāh al-Muhtaḍā	Family	437/144/167
20	4.7.26	ʿUmar ʿAbd al-Qādir Muṣṭafā Būja	Family	433/123/77
21	4.7.26	Muḥammad Yūsuf ʿAbd al-Rāziq al-ʿAlamī	Family	437/78/90
22	9.5.27	Khalīl ʿAbdallāh Ibrāhīm al-Hidmī	Family	439/122/107
23	10.8.27	Sāliḥ ʿAlī Basīsū al-Takrūrī	Public	441/31/41
24	21.6.30	Saʿad al-Dīn ʿAbd al-Qādir al-Khalīlī	Family	446/60/11
25	27.6.30	Ḥasan Muḥammad Aḥmad al-Ṭilimsānī	Public	451/111/171
26	23.3.31	Jamīla Bakr Muḥammad Shishbirl	Family	454/1/81
27	12.5.31	Idrīs Mūsā Ḥasan al-Qaṣrī al-Maghribī	Family	454/19/109
28	26.10.31	Muḥammad Khalīl Muḥammad al-Māliḥī	Family	455/6/296
29	1.11.31	Nimr Ḥasan Muḥammad al-Nābulsī	Family	455/13/303
30	15.12.31	ʿAbd al-Raḥmān Nijm al-Dīn al-ʿAlamī	Family	453/98/12
31	2.4.32	Muḥammad ʿAbd al-Raḥmān Abū al-Faḍl al-ʿAlamī	Family	446/107/56
32	25.5.32	ʿAlī Fawzī Muḥammad al-Imām al-Qaṣrī	Family	455/132/135
33	25.5.33	Wahība Dā'ūd Yūsuf Ḥabrumān	Family	461/26/40
34	14.2.34	Muḥammad Maḥmūd Ibrāhīm al-Arnā'ūt	Family	462/36/4
35	16.12.34	Ḥusayn Maḥmūd Aḥmad Abū Khātir	Family	467/53/448
36	6.2.35	Yāsīn Saʿīd Muḥammad al-Dasūqī	Family	467/98/46
37	6.2.35	Yāsīn Saʿīd Muḥammad al-Dasūqī	Family	467/98/47
38	18.4.35	Prince of Ḥaydarābād	Public	467/142/109

39	16.11.35	Maḥmūd ʿAbd al-Razzaq al-Dajānī	Family	467/76/19
40	13.2.36	ʿAbd al-Raḥmān ʿUthmān al-Rimāwī	Public	471/77/42
41	10.8.36	Muḥammad ʿAbd al-Muʿṭī Aḥmad al-Quṭub	Family	471/133/123
42	30.3.37	Muḥammad Sulaymān Muḥammad al-Sāʿiḥ	Family	474/80/125
43	10.5.37	ʿAbd al-Raḥmān Ḥāmid Muḥammad al-Tājī	Public	474/100/155
44	17.7.37	Masʿūd Bilāl al-Ṣūṣ al-Maghribī	Family	474/133/212
45	5.10.37	Ḥājj Muḥammad Amīn al-Ḥusaynī	Mixed	475/25/42
46	25.8.38	Idrīs Mūsā al-Qaṣrī al-Maghribī	Family	475/8/13
47	18.4.38	Amīna and Maḥbūba ʿAbd al-Razzaq Qulaybū	Family	470/145/11
48	10.8.38	ʿĀrif Aḥmad ʿAbd al-Qādir al-Zamāmīrī	Family	477/36/190
49	16.12.39	Yāsīn Saʿīd Muḥammad al-Dasūqī	Mixed	479/104/265
50	13.4.40	Riḍā Ḥasan Darwīsh al-Ṣalāḥī	Family	478/175/68
51	2.3.41	ʿUmar Ḥusayn ʿĀbidīn	Family	482/7/46
52	2.10.41	Khalīl Ṣādiq Chelebī al-Nammarī	Family	484/23/235
53	9.10.41	Amīna Ḥasan Yūsuf al-Dasūqī	Family	484/32/340
54	4.4.42	Amīna Badr Muṣṭafā Khalīl al-Khālidī	Public	476/89/8
54	7.4.42	Amīna Badr Muṣṭafā Khalīl al-Khālidī	Public	476/110/18
56	8.10.42	Asʿad Muḥammad Asʿad Shānīn	Family	486/54/415
57	12.11.42	ʿAlī Yūsuf Saʿīd Kamāl	Family	86/96/481
58	20.6.43	Fāṭima ʿAbd al-Majīd Firʿawn	Family	490/10/16
59	6.9.43	ʿAbd al-Majīd Dāʾūd Sulaymān Barakāt	Family	490/26/35
60	8.11.45	Anīs and Rāghib ʿAbd al-Raḥīm Darwīsh	Family	504/90/551
61	8.1.45	ʿUmar ʿAbd al-Munʿim al-Jūlānī	Family	505/5/642

A century later, between 1900 and 1917, 141 new *waqf*s were registered in the Jerusalem *sijill*, but only 45 of them were founded by Muslims.[14] This shows that the annual average of new Muslim *waqf*s in Jerusalem during these years – three – had not changed, but the number of non-Muslim endowments had grown significantly. Meanwhile, the population of Jerusalem had grown, and there had been considerable economic development in all of Palestine. A diminution in the importance of the *waqf* can therefore be noted among Jerusalem Muslims by the early twentieth century.

Seventy-two new endowments were established in Jerusalem during the Mandatory period, including 11 by Jews. (The latter were made before the Trusts Ordinance of 1925 went into effect.) The Muslim endowments are set out in Table 3.1. On average, two Muslim endowments were therefore made per year. This is consistent with the basic hypothesis that the nearer one gets to the modern era, the less the *waqf* is used for social and economic goals. The decrease is even more significant when one recalls the vigorous economic development as well as the growth of the Muslim population in Jerusalem and its surroundings in the twentieth century. (Altogether, the population there grew eightfold from the early nineteenth century to the end of the Mandatory period.)

Comparison of the number of *waqf*s established in Jerusalem in the Ottoman and the Mandatory periods suggests that in Ottoman times, the *waqf* was central to urban life. The per capita number of endowments in Jerusalem exceeded that of Istanbul. The reason probably lies in the sanctity of Jerusalem in Islam and its special status. In the Ottoman era, Jerusalem was a neglected city with a small population confined, for most of the period, within the Old City walls. Consequently, by the late nineteenth century, about 80 per cent of the Old City land and the buildings on it had become *waqf*s. By the end of the Ottoman period, as modernization made its inroads, the pace of *waqf* formation slowed down perceptibly. For the same reason, the use of the *waqf* for social purposes decreased under the Mandate; indeed, it did so more rapidly than the creation of *waqf*s for other objectives.

THE FOUNDERS: SOCIAL, ECONOMIC AND PUBLIC CHARACTERISTICS

During the Ottoman period, *waqf* formation was very much a matter for the upper classes – the *Sulṭān* and his court, the military elite, the *ʿulamāʾ* and the high-ranking administrative cadre.[15] In a society based on a small elite and a large majority of lowly 'subjects' (*raʿāya*), this was only natural. Studies on the *waqf* during the Ottoman period support this inference. In Edirne, 57 per cent of *waqf*s formed in the fifteenth and sixteenth centuries were established by members of the elite (especially from among the military).[16] In Cyprus, most *waqf*s formed shortly after the Ottoman conquest were created by Ottomans of high military rank, who also administered them.[17] In Cairo, from the second half of the seventeenth century until the end of the eighteenth century, the share of *waqf*s set up by members of the military elite ranged from 9 to 29 per cent.[18]

Mobility in the upper classes increased with the approach of the modern era. The Mamluks and the military cadres gave way to administrators, clerics and big traders. The same is true of *waqf* founders.[19] In the towns, urban notables (*aʿyān*) became clearly dominant, both as founders and administrators. In eighteenth- and nineteenth-century Aleppo, many *waqf* founders belonged to five such families. They included local merchants, administrators and a small number of clerics.[20] In Jerusalem, about one-third of endowments in the early nineteenth century were created by notables, although these and their families accounted for no more than 15–20 per cent of the Muslim population of the city at the time.[21]

There is, of course, a strong correlation between the extent of property dedicated, the nature and purpose of the endowments and the types of people who established them.[22] Exceptionally large *waqf*s, chiefly those including farmland, were made by members of the ruling elites. According to the commonly accepted theory, arable land in the empire – the main source of state revenue – was state property. Consequently, such land was endowed by sultans or by members of the ruling class with the consent of the *Sulṭān*. Both were imperial *waqf*s and belonged to the state. Most sultanic endowments were land under cultivation, endowed to finance and maintain various public institutions. By contrast, many modest *waqf*s, generally consisting of one dwelling unit, were set up by members of the lower middle or lower classes. Unlike Edirne in the fifteenth and sixteenth centuries, most new *waqf*s in seventeenth-century Bursa were formed by members of the lower class.[23] In the eighteenth and nineteenth centuries, 65 per cent of endowments in Aleppo were made by members of the lower middle and lower classes.[24] Most research naturally focuses on the large, state-type endowments, even though by the end of the Ottoman period, such *waqf*s had become a minority. Smaller endowments, mostly family *waqf*s, have not yet been made the topic of systematic research.

Notables as founders

According to early nineteenth-century findings gathered by Baer, 7 of the 23 endowments established in Jerusalem between 1805 and 1814 were made by Ottoman officials and 6 by families of local notables.[25] Disregarding the *waqf*s of Ottoman officials, we find that 44 per cent of the above endowments were made by members of the most important families in the city. A century later, this proportion had hardly changed (see Table 3.2). From 1900 until the British conquest, 55 per cent of the 42 new endowments were created by lower- or middle-ranking families. But many endowments (about 42 per cent) were established by members of important families, such as the Khālidīs (3), the Nashashībīs (4), the Dajānīs (2), the al-ʿAlamīs (4), the al-Imāms (3), the Ḥusaynīs (1), the Abū al-Saʿūds (1), and the Dizdārs (1).[26] By contrast, the proportion of notables among *waqf* founders decreased sharply during the Mandate years, when some 80 per cent of founders (39 out of 49) were unrelated to families of notables. In other words, the share of the latter had come down to their proportion in the overall Muslim population of the city (20 per cent). The ten founders from among the notables belonged to four ranking families: the Ḥusaynīs, the ʿAlamīs, the Dajānīs, and the Khālidīs. Other influential families in Jerusalem, such as the Nashashībīs, the Dizdārs, and the Abū al-Saʿūds, are not found among the *waqf* founders. Several prestigious families, such as the Dizdārs, who had held positions in the Ottoman forces of the local garrison, and the Abū al-Saʿūds, who had belonged to the Ottoman religious establishment, now found their status diminished because their descendants had ceased to hold offices that had traditionally 'belonged' to the family.[27]

The percentage of notables among the founders is slightly higher if we exclude the four founders who were not Jerusalem residents[28] and the three who lived in nearby villages.[29] The data include one *waqf* established by a Ramallah notable[30] and another founded by means of a donation from an Indian dignitary, Prince of Ḥaydarābād. Through British diplomatic channels, he contributed £P7,543 for the Islamic University which the Islamic Congress of 1931 had resolved to establish. Ḥājj Amīn al-Ḥusaynī had appealed for donations for it. The sum was deposited in a bank and not used until 1938.[31]

Most of the founders now belonged to medium-sized families of a social status lower than the notables; they include the Būja, ʿAṭallah, Shishbirl, Māliḥī, Ḥabrumān, Arnaʾūṭ, Zamāmīrī, Dasūqī, Shāhīn, Kamāl, and Firʿawn families. Some others, such as the al-Quṭub and al-Nammarī families, belonged to the middle ranks in size and social status; some of their members held positions in the religious establishment.

Five endowments established by Jerusalem residents of North African origin deserve special attention.[32] The dedication of Maghribī *waqf*s in Jerusalem is an ancient tradition, and this was undoubtedly its continuation. The largest and the most famous Maghribī endowment is the Abū Midyan Waqf, which included the Western Wall plaza. Another *waqf* was established for the Maghribī *zawiyya*. Massignon lists 98 Maghribī *waqf*s in Jerusalem.[33] Most residents of North African origin in Jerusalem benefited from the large Abū Midyan Waqf and lived in buildings owned by it. This may explain the popularity of the *waqf* as such among members of the community. There seems to be a correlation between the formation of *waqf*s and the cultural norms of specific social groups. It is also noteworthy that four of the founders belonged to families originally from Hebron.[34]

The diversity of founding families in Mandatory Jerusalem reflects twentieth-century social changes in the city. These are characterized on the one hand by a rise in the fortunes of lower-ranking families, especially in terms of their economic activity and, on the other hand, by the influx of families from Hebron, whose stature in Jerusalem rose over time.[35]

The large, prestigious families, such as the Ḥusaynīs, Khālidīs, ʿAlamīs, Dajānīs, Nashashībīs, Quṭaynas and the ʿAsalīs, already had family *waqf*s dating back to the Ottoman period and generating handsome revenues. One characteristic of the overall socio-economic change in Jerusalem in the Mandatory period was the creation of *waqf*s by members of medium- and lower-ranking families who had gathered some property. The dedication of such properties as *waqf*s may have been part of the process of increasing social mobility.

TABLE 3.2 SOCIAL STATUS OF FOUNDERS

No.	*Date*	*Founder's name*	*Notable*	*Origin*	*Capacity and Public Status*
1	17.10.18	Fāṭima As ʿad ʿAbd al-Qādir al-ʿAlamī	X		(Woman)
2	7.12.20	ʿĪsā Muḥammad ʿAlī Abū Sabitān		al-Thawrī	Contractor
3	21.9.21	As ʿad ʿAlī ʿUthmān Ṭaha al-Dajānī	X		Perfume Trader
4	2.12.21	Ibrāhīm Muḥammad Yaḥyā Qulaybū		Hebron	Unknown
5	20.3.23	Yāsīn Muḥammad ʿAql		Lifta village	Unknown
6	10.5.23	Aḥmad Saʿīd Ṣāliḥ Munā al-Saʿdī			Store owner
7	29.5.23	Khalīl ʿAbdalla ʿAṭalla al-Hidmī			Grocer
8	1.6.23	ʿAlī ʿAbd al-Raḥmān al-ʿUmarī and his wife			Unknown
9	4.6.23	Muḥammad Yūsuf ʿAbd al-Rāziq al-ʿAlamī	X		Owner of estates and Member of Municipality
10	3.7.23	Yāsīn Saʿīd Muḥammad al-Dasūqī			Contractor
11	8.10.23	Ibrāhīm Ḥamad Ḥamad Muḥammad Ghibn			Unknown
12	4.11.25	ʿAbd al-Razzaq Barakāt Abū al-Filāt		Maghribī	Trader
13	29.3.26	ʿUmar ʿAbd al-Qādir Muṣṭafā Būja		Hebron	Unknown
14	19.5.26	Subḥī ʿAbdalla Bakr Aḥmad al-Dajānī	X		Unknown
15	29.6.26	Mūsā Ḥusayn ʿAbdalla al-Muhtaḍā			Education officer
16	10.8.27	Sāliḥ ʿAlī Basīsū al-Takrūrī		Maghribī	Unknown
17	21.6.30	Saʿad al-Dīn ʿAbd al-Qādir al-Khalīlī			Owner of estates
18	27.6.30	Ḥasan Muḥammad Aḥmad al-Ṭilimsānī		Maghribī	Unknown
19	23.3.31	Jamīla Bakr Muḥammad Shishbirl			(Woman)
20	12.5.31	Idrīs Mūsā Ḥasan al-Qaṣrī al-Maghribī		Maghribī	Shopkeeper
21	26.10.31	Muḥammad Khalīl Muḥammad al-Māliḥī			Unknown
22	1.11.31	Nimr Ḥasan Muḥammad al-Nābulsī		Nablus	Factory owner
23	15.12.31	ʿAbd al-Raḥmān Nijm al-Dīn al-ʿAlamī	X		Shaykh of Nabī Samuel

24	2.4.32	Muḥammad ʿAbd al-Raḥmān Abū al-Faḍl al-ʿAlamī	X		Unknown
25	25.5.32	ʿAlī Fawzī Muḥammad al-Imām al-Qaṣrī		Turkish	Unknown
26	25.5.33	Wahība Dāʾūd Yūsuf Ḥabrumān		Hebron	(Woman)
27	14.2.34	Muḥammad Maḥmūd Ibrāhīm al-Arnāʾūt			Unknown
28	16.12.34	Ḥusayn Maḥmūd Aḥmad Abū Khātir		Silwān	Contractor
29	18.4.35	Prince of Ḥaydarābād		India	Prince
30	16.11.35	Maḥmūd ʿAbd al-Razzaq al-Dajānī	X		Unknown
31	13.2.36	ʿAbd al-Raḥmān ʿUthmān al-Rimāwī		Jericho	Imam and pracher
32	10.8.36	Muḥammad ʿAbd al-Muʿṭī Aḥmad al-Quṭub			Qayyim in al-Aqṣā Mosque
33	30.3.37	Muḥammad Sulaymān Muḥammad al-Sāʿiḥ			Principal of Rawḍat al-Maʿārif
34	10.5.37	ʿAbd al-Raḥmān Ḥāmid Muḥammad al-Tājī		Ramla	Owner of estates
35	17.7.37	Masʿūd Bilāl al-Ṣūṣ al-Maghribī		Maghribī	Unknown
36	5.10.37	Ḥājj Muḥammad Amīn al-Ḥusaynī	X		President of SMC
37	18.4.38	Amīna and Maḥbūba ʿAbd al-Razzāq Qulaybū			(Women)
38	10.8.38	ʿĀrif Aḥmad ʿAbd al-Qādir al-Zamāmīrī			Contractor
39	13.4.40	Riḍā Ḥasan Darwīsh al-Ṣalāḥī	X		Principal of Orphans' School
30	2.3.41	ʿUmar Ḥusayn ʿĀbidīn		Hebron	Trader
41	2.10.41	Khalīl Ṣādiq Chelebī al-Nammarī			Owner of estates
42	9.10.41	Amīna Ḥasan Yūsuf al-Dasūqī			(Woman)
43	4.4.42	Amīna Badr Muṣṭafā Khalīl al-Khālidī	X		(Woman)
44	8.10.42	Asʿad Muḥammad Asʿad Shāhīn			Store owner and *Mukhtār*
45	12.11.42	ʿAlī Yūsuf Saʿīd Kamāl			Contractor
46	20.6.43	Fāṭima ʿAbd al-Majīd Firʿawn			(Woman) Wife of no. 24 above
47	6.9.43	ʿAbd al-Majīd Dāʾūd Sulaymān Barakāt			Trader
48	8.11.45	Anīs and Rāghib ʿAbd al-Raḥīm Darwīsh		Nablus	Grocer and shoe manufacturer
49	8.1.45	ʿUmar ʿAbd al-Munʿim al-Jūlānī		Nablus	Porter/owner of taxi company

Women as founders

It is an interesting social phenomenon, ostensibly at odds with the traditional view of the inferior status of women in Muslim society, that women owned property, dealt in real estate and also established and even administered endowments. The *sijill* provides factual information on this point which we do not find in other sources.[36]

In the fifteenth and sixteenth centuries, approximately 20 per cent of the endowments in Edirne and 37 per cent in Istanbul were established by women.[37] In Aleppo in the seventeenth and eighteenth centuries, 41 per cent (!) of all the founders (including non-Muslims) were women.[38] In Cairo, during the same period, the percentage of women among *waqf* founders ranged from 26–45 per cent.[39] In Jerusalem, in the early nineteenth century, one-quarter of the founders were women.[40] In Jaffa, according to Baer, women constituted some 23 per cent of the founders in the early nineteenth century and 43 per cent in the Mandatory period![41]

These data display a picture radically different from the conventional characterization of women in Islam. However, it is important to emphasize that women usually established smaller endowments. In Istanbul, for example, the above-mentioned 37 per cent of women founders pledged only 17 per cent of *waqf* properties. Their share in administering endowments was even lower.[42]

One would expect the share of women in economic life to have been greater during the Mandatory period than under the Ottomans: Palestinian society was then in transition from traditionalism to modernity. The Jerusalem *sijill* refutes this expectation. Its records show that women accounted for 28.5 per cent of Muslim *waqf* founders in 1900–17,[43] but only 13 per cent in the Mandate years.[44]

Women who created endowments in Mandatory Jerusalem came from prestigious and unimportant families alike. The property they pledged had come to them through inheritance shortly before the *waqf* was established. Seven of the eight women founders were single (whether spinsters, divorced or widowed);

only two had children. One of them, Wahība Ḥabrumān, who had been married when she made the dedication, designated her husband, Yūnis, as the sole beneficiary after her for as long as he lived; only after his death would her four children become beneficiaries. The second, Jamīla Shishbirl, named her children as beneficiaries. From among the childless women, two allocated the *waqf* revenues to nephews, two to persons not related to them (apparently orphans), and one made the endowment for the establishment of a hospital.

As noted above, several women had obtained the pledged property by inheritance only shortly before. Their age and their childlessness made them think it best to determine the future of the property themselves, rather than have it distributed according to the *sharīʿa*. Fāṭima al-ʿAlamī, for example, dedicated the entire estate that had come to her from her sister, Amīna – a one-sixth share of five dwellings.[45] Amīna al-Khālidī, who created one of the largest endowments of this period in Jerusalem and earmarked it for the establishment of a Muslim hospital, had inherited her property from her parents and had received half of the estates of her deceased brother and sister.[46] But for her endowment, the properties would have gone to two nephews whom she wished to disinherit because she regarded them as disreputable spendthrifts.[47]

Why was the proportion of women founders in Jerusalem high under the Ottomans but low under the Mandate, and why was it especially high in Mandatory Jaffa? The personal circumstances of the Muslim women founders in Jerusalem – most of them elderly widows – suggest that they regarded the *waqf* as a useful way to arrange the transfer of property within the family while retaining control over it during their lifetimes. This is also known to have been the motive of an elderly woman in Mandatory Syria whose children had died and whose sole heirs were two young grandchildren. She founded a *waqf* in order to ensure their succession and entrusted its administration to a *sharīʿa* court official.[48]

Economic status and occupation of founders

One indicator of *waqf* founders' economic circumstances is the extent of the properties that they pledged. Of all the endowments established in Mandatory Jerusalem, only six included more than one property.[49] None was exceptionally large if compared to *waqfs* set up by the Ottoman elite.

The occupation of 28 founders is known; that of 6 women and 14 male founders is not. From among the 28, 14 were merchants or property owners and administrators; 6 were building or renovation contractors; 4 were religious functionaries, and 4 were engaged in education (see Table 3.2).[50]

This composition reflects the socio-economic change characteristic of the Mandatory period, when economic developments were causing the rise of a new and affluent middle and upper middle class. An outstanding example of this transformation was ʿUmar al-Jūlānī,[51] a member of a Hebron family, who began his working life as a porter. A self-made man, he eventually became wealthy. Today, he owns a well-known taxi company. The military and administrative and religious elite, who were so salient among Ottoman *waqf* founders, had been replaced by merchants, contractors and the like, who belonged to small families not descended from notables.

Office-holders among the waqf *founders*

Only 8 of the 49 founders held public office: 2 were members of the municipal council, 2 of the SMC (one was its president), 2 were principals of SMC-affiliated schools, 1 a neighborhood *mukhtār*, and 1 an Indian prince. Only two of these founders – the *mukhtār* of the Bāb Ḥuṭṭa neighborhood and one of the municipal councillors – established family endowments. The other endowments were formed for public purposes. As already mentioned, Prince of Ḥaydarābād's *waqf* was for the establishment of an Islamic university in Jerusalem.[52]

Ḥājj Amīn al-Ḥusaynī himself created a *waqf* under circumstances worth noting. A former Turkish Army officer, Zakariyya Bey al-Dāghastānī, a permanent resident of Egypt, left his money to two orphanages: one in Jerusalem and the other in Turkey. (It was in the latter that he himself had been educated.) The donation was initially registered in the Jerusalem *sijill* as a will. Several years later, Ḥājj Amīn seems to have persuaded Dāghastānī to abrogate the will and to place the money at his disposal; he would use it for setting up an economic venture intended to provide the Jerusalem orphanage with steady revenues. The venture was to be registered as a *waqf*. To go through with the plan, Ḥājj Amīn carried out an *istibdāl* (exchange) transaction, using land in Shaykh Jarrāḥ that belonged to the *waqf* of the Dome of the Rock (see Chapter 7 under 'Sale for economic development'; for details on *istibdāl*, see Chapter 7 under '*Istibdāl*'); this land now became his personal property. On it, as well as on the site of a row of shops in Jaffa administered by the SMC as a *mundaras waqf*, Ḥājj Amīn erected commercial buildings that he quickly registered as a *waqf* with himself as founder, only several days before he fled the country in October 1937. According to the *waqfiyya*, £P500 of its income would be forwarded annually to Cairo, for Dāghastānī Bey; the balance was to be invested in a revenue-creating venture with the orphanage as the beneficiary. Practically speaking, Ḥājj Amīn thereby turned the donation into an economic enterprise of the SMC. The deed also appointed Amīn Bey al-Tamīmī, an SMC member and a confidant of Ḥājj Amīn, to administer the *waqf* in the latter's absence.[53]

'Abd al-Raḥmān al-Tājī, an SMC member from Ramallah, dedicated a building there that he had built on *maḍbūṭ waqf* land. He designated it as a *madrasa* (religious college) in his name. Ṣāliḥ al-Takrūrī, a childless municipal councillor of Maghribī origin, named orphans as beneficiaries of his endowment.

Waqf *founders by age, personal and family status*

One of the important factors in analysing the founders' motives at the time of the dedication is to take their personal circumstances into account. At least six founders are known to have been very old when they created their endowments,[54] and two of them were on their deathbeds.[55] Twelve of the founders were called '*Ḥājj*', suggesting that they, too, were rather old. As for family status, our analysis of endowment deeds, augmented by additional information from personal interviews, shows at least 20 founders who were childless or who had no male offspring.[56]

The advanced age of most of the *waqf* founders at the time they established the *waqf*s is an important finding that has not, so far, been taken into account by researchers. Elderly people are more concerned than others with the fate of their property after death, and it stands to reason that they would wish to keep the family property intact. Childless founders were even more troubled by this issue. Under Islamic inheritance law, their property would have gone to relatives outside the nuclear family; by contrast, their interest was to perpetuate their name, works and property – best done through setting up a *waqf*. Their fate in the afterworld was another likely consideration. Members of the Jerusalem Islamic religious establishment explained in interviews that believers at the final stage of their lives wish to observe commandments promising a reward in the world to come. Setting up a *waqf* is considered such a commandment.

To sum up: although the *waqf* as an institution came under strong criticism in Muslim countries, the formation of *waqf*s in Jerusalem did not cease in the period reviewed here. True, public *waqf*s lost much of their pre-eminence in the changed circumstances of modern state power, accounting for the paucity of endowments of this type during the Mandatory period. None the less, their functions had not become altogether obsolete. Moreover, the *waqf* maintained its relevance for Muslim society for political reasons connected with the establishment of the SMC, the broad powers it was granted in *waqf* affairs and in religious matters in general, and the political function given it by Ḥājj Amīn al-Ḥusaynī. The most striking change during the Mandatory period was in the social background of the *waqf* founders. Modernization made it possible to accumulate wealth rapidly, and newly-rich middle- or lower-class founders regarded the *waqf* to some extent as a vehicle of social mobility. It was likely to bring them closer to the notables administering long-established and prosperous family *waqf*s. Being, generally speaking, conservatives, Muslims were not often tempted to avail themselves of the civil-law option to draw up their will as they chose. They preferred to circumvent the *sharīʿa* inheritance laws by means of the *waqf*, which had become a recognized and legitimate component of the *sharīʿa*. For the 30 years of British rule, the Jerusalem *sijill* records only nine wills and one gift.[57] For a large proportion of the founders – those who were childless – the *waqf* was the accepted way of settling the future of their property. Without it, their property would have gone to the state or to distant relatives whom the founders may not have favoured. Furthermore, as we have seen, acts of piety were characteristic of the age group most of them belonged to.

WAQF PROPERTIES

Most *waqf* revenue in Jerusalem in the early Ottoman period derived from agricultural property.[58] By contrast, most of the 45 endowments made by Muslims in the first 17 years of the twentieth century, until the British occupation of Jerusalem, were urban ones: 26 entire residences, and parts of 44 others; 13 shops and parts of 102 others; 2 urban plots and parts of 21 others; 2 bakeries and parts of another 2; parts of 2 olive presses; a part of a bathhouse; a mosque; a well, and 3 vegetable gardens inside the city and parts of 14 others. The only agricultural properties dedicated in this period were some 35 of 42 olive plantations in villages outside Jerusalem. These were dedicated as a family *waqf* by a wealthy Jerusalem notable, ʿUthmān Sulaymān al-Nashashībī, whose endowment was one of the largest of the period.[59] The transition from mostly agricultural to mostly urban property became noticeable in the late Ottoman period. It was caused by changes in the social status of the founders and in the purposes of the endowments – of which the vast majority were already of the family type.

In Mandatory Jerusalem, too, most new *waqf* properties were urban. This is consistent with the fact that most of them were family *waqfs*. The property of an urban family was, above all, its dwelling, sometimes augmented by additional property that it used for its livelihood: apartments for rental, shops, workshops or vacant building lots.

TABLE 3.3 PROPERTIES DEDICATED IN MANDATORY JERUSALEM

Endowment no.	*Property no.*	*Properties*	*Shares*	*Location*	*Notes*
1	1	House	4/21	Jaffa	Inherited from her sister
	2	House	4/21	Jaffa	"
	3	House	4/21	al-Sharaf	"
	4	House	4/21	al-Sharaf	"
	5	House	4/21	al-Sharaf	"
2	6	House	Complete	al-Thawrī	
	7	House	Complete	Damascus Gate	
	8	House (20 rooms)	Complete	"	
	9	House (17 rooms and 4 stores)	Complete	"	
3	10	House	1/7	Nabī Dā'ūd	
4	11	House and big store attached	About 21/24	Wād al-Tawāḥīn	
5	12	House	Complete	N. of al-Thawrī	On 750 sq. feet
6	13	House	Complete	Liftā	
7	14	House	Complete	Damascus Gate	
8	15	Two houses	Complete	Bāb al-Asbāṭ	
9	16	Big house (42 rooms) 2 stores, garden	Complete	Shaykh Jarrāḥ	Tulūl al-Maṣābin
10	17	House (13 rooms)	Complete	Bāb al-Asbāṭ	
	18	House (14 rooms)	Complete	Bāb al-Asbāṭ	
11	19	House (8 rooms)	Complete	al-Sa'diyya	
12	20	House (2 apartments)	Complete	Liftā	
13	21	House	Complete	Baq'a	On *mirī* land
14	22	House	2,400/. 9,216	Bāb Ḥuṭṭa	
	23	House	48/384	Bāb Ḥuṭṭa	
	24	House	11/88	Bāb Ḥuṭṭa	
	25	House	588/2816	Near Ma'mūniyya	
15	26	House	Complete	al-Sa'diyya	
16	27	100 piasters	Complete	Nabī Dā'ūd	For constructing a house
17	28	100 piasters	Complete	Nabī Dā'ūd	"
18	29	100 piasters	Complete	Nabī Dā'ūd	"
19	30	House	Complete	Jerusalem	

20	31	House	Complete	al-Sa'diyya	Addition to existing endowment
21	32	House (6 rooms)	Complete	Bāb al-Asbāṭ	"
22	33	House (5 rooms)	Complete	Bāb al-Asbāṭ	"
23	34	House	Complete	Baq'a	Plot and trees
24	35	Land (3,200 feet), house and store	Complete	Muṣrāra	
25	36	House	8/24	Maghribī Quarter	
26	36	House	8,300/ 13,824	Damascus Gate	On *waqf* land
27	38	House (2 storeys)	Complete	Damascus Gate	
	39	Store	About 18/24	Bāb al-Silsila	
28	40	House	Complete	Bāb Ḥuṭṭa	
29	41	House	Complete	Mālḥa	
	42	House	Complete	Damascus Gate	*Mīrī* land
30	43	House (4 rooms)	364/6,912	Bāb al-Sāhira	
31	44	House	Complete	Damascus Gate	
	45	House (8 rooms)	789/1,600	'Aqbat al-Thawr	Also trees on *mīrī* land
	46	House (2 rooms)	18/24	'Aqbat al-Thawr	
	47	House (5 rooms)	68/72	Jaffa Gate and garden	
	48	Store	399/ 414,720	al-Wād	
	49	Store	32,520/ 103,680	al-Wād	On land leased by *ijāratayn*
	50	Store	32,520/ 103,680	al-Wād	" "
	51	Store	32,520 103,680	al-Wād	"
	52	Store	32,520/ 103,680	al-Wād	From al-Aqṣā *waqf* on *waqf* land
	53	Store	32,520/ 103,680	al-Wād	"
	54	House and store	Complete	Damascus Gate	"
	55	House	Complete	al-Wād	
	56	House (13 rooms) and 5 stores	Complete	al-Wād	
32	57	House (20 rooms) and store	Complete	Tulūl al-Maṣābin	

	58	House (8 rooms	Complete	Tulūl al-Maṣābin	
33	59	House and 4 stores	240/864	Bāb Ḥuṭṭa	
34	60	House (6 rooms)	25,200/ 120,960	Bāb Ḥuṭṭa	
35	61	House (8 rooms)	Complete	Abū Thawr	
	62	House (12 rooms)	About 1/6	al-Sa'diyya	
	63	House (5 rooms) and store	Complete	Damascus Gate	
	64	House (3 rooms) and 2 stores	14/24	al-Naṣārā	
36	65	Citrus with a house	6/24	Jaffa	
37	66	House and store	90/128	Damascus Gate	
38	67	Agricultural land: 1,000 dunams	Complete	Zaytā village	Value: 7,542 piasters
39	68	Plot (760 sq.m.)	Complete	Qaṭamūn	Acquired by *istibdāl*
	69	Plot (819 sq.m.)	Complete	Qaṭamūn	"
40	70	House	Complete	Jericho	On *waqf mundaras*
41	71	House	Complete	Shaykh Jarrāḥ	On *mīrī* land
42	72	Plot with store	Complete	Damascus Gate	Plot 1,926 sq.m.
43	73	Building (2 halls and 12 rooms)	Complete	Ramla	On *waqf* land
44	74	Apartment (2 rooms)	Complete	Maghribī area	In *waqf* house
45	75	Four stores and 7 apartments	Complete	Shaykh Jarrāḥ	On land acquired by *istibdāl*
	76	12 stores	12/24	Jaffa	*Waqf mundaras*
46	77	House and store attached	Complete	al-Sa'diyya	
47	78	House (7 rooms)	77/2,304	Wād al-Tawāḥīn	
48	79	House (210 rooms) and store	Complete	Bāb al-Sāhira	Including the plot
49	80	House	21/96	Damascus Gate	
50	81	House	Complete	Haifa	
	82	House	Complete	Haifa	
	83	House	Complete	Haifa	
51	84	Mosque and house (4 apartments)	Complete	Wa'r al-Khaṭīb	On plot 1,350 sq.m.

52	85	House and 3 stores	1/3	Damascus Gate	Joint to his grandfather's *waqf*
53	86	House and 4 stores	2/5	Damascus Gate	Purchased from her father
54	87	Land (9,852 sq.m.)	1/9	al-Qubba	Mortgaged
	88	Building (24 rooms and 8 stores)	Complete	Jaffa Gate	Mortgaged
	89	School and 3 big buildings	1/2	Jaffa Gate	Inherited from her brother and sister
	90	House (4 rooms) and plot (315 sq.m.)	1/2	Jaffa Gate	"
	91	Land (3,257 sq.m.)	1/2	Jaffa Gate	"
	92	Big house, coffeehouse on 2,187 sq.m.	1/2	Jaffa Gate	
	93	Land (1,681 sq.m.)	1/2	Jaffa Gate	
	94	10 stores and room on 1,135 sq.m.	Complete	Jaffa Gate	On plot 1,135 sq.m.
	95	House (6 stores, 24 rooms) on planted 917 sq.m.	1/2	Jaffa Gate	
	96	Land (494 sq.m.)	1/2	Jaffa Gate	
55	97	Store	1/4–1/2	Old City	Inherited from her mother
	98	Store	1/4–1/2	Old City	
	99	Store	1/4–1/2	Old City	
	100	Store	1/4–1/2	Old City	
	101	Store	1/4–1/2	Old City	
	102	Store	1/4–1/2	Old City	
	103	Garden and 3 stores	1/4–1/2	Old City	Used as printing shop
	104	Bakery used as factory	1/4–1/2	Damascus Gate	Tile factory
	105	House	Complete	al-Sharaf	
	106	House	Complete		Inherited from her brother
	107	Moveables and furniture	Complete	From her house	To equip the endowed hospital
	108	House	Unknown	al-Wād	Inherited from her father

	109	House	Unknown	al-Wād	Inherited from her father
	110	House	1/2	al-Wād	
	111	Store	1/2	Sūq al-Bazār	
	112	Store	9/24	Sūq al-Bazār	
	113	Store	5/24	Sūq al-Bazār	
56	114	House	Complete	Bāb Ḥuṭṭa	
57	115	Plot (290 feet) and room	Complete	Bāb al-Sāhira	
	116	Land (63 sq.m.)	Complete	Jurrat al-Danaf	
58	117	House	Complete	Jerusalem	On plot 810 sq.m.
59	118	Apartment and 2 stores on 1,157 feet	Complete	al-Thawrī	On 1,157 sq. feet *muqāṭa'a*
	119	House (6 rooms) with plot	Complete	al-Thawrī	
60	120	House (14 rooms)	14,390/ 622,008	al-Wād	
61	121	Building (32 rooms and 10 stores)	Complete	Ma'mūnallāh	

One hundred and twenty-one assets were turned into *waqf*s in Jerusalem during the 30 years of the Mandate.[60] Only one of them was large: the donation by Prince Ḥaydarābad already mentioned above. Ḥājj Amīn al-Ḥusaynī used this money to purchase 1,000 dunams of agricultural land in Kafr Zaytā (in the Tulkarm sub-district) as part of the struggle over land purchases in Palestine, and to dedicate that land as a *waqf* for the foundation of the Islamic university in Jerusalem (rather than using the funds directly for the university, as the founder had intended). His purpose was to keep the land out of Jewish hands. Pledging the revenue from the land for the university was mere lip service, since the meager revenue in question was hardly sufficient for the founder's original declared purpose. The land purchase by the SMC was to set a pattern for the Muslim community to thwart land acquisiton by Jews.[61]

Another five Mandate-era endowments were medium-to-large.[62] Muḥammad Abū al-Faḍl al-'Alamī dedicated four dwellings, five shops, and various parts of three houses and six stores.[63] Ḥājj Amīn al-Ḥusaynī invested a donation of £P8,000 from al-Dāghastāni in the construction in Jerusalem and Jaffa of houses and shops, which he registered as a *waqf* in his own name.[64] Amīna al-Khālidī dedicated many properties for establishing a hospital for the Muslim poor.[65] As'ad Shāhīn dedicated a large building (32 rooms and 10 shops) in the Mamilla neighborhood.[66] The total scope of properties dedicated in Mandatory Jerusalem was 100 buildings, most of them residential (but including a school and a mosque), 100 shops and business premises, a tile factory and a printing house. Also dedicated were approximately 11 dunams of urban land (in addition to the 1,000 dunams of farmland in Kafr Zaytā), one orchard, one vegetable garden, the chattels of one woman founder,[67] and three sums of money that were set aside for the construction of a house.[68]

Most of the dedicated properties were located in areas of economic growth in the Old City bazaars, the Damascus Gate and Herod's Gate vicinity outside the city wall, and the Jaffa Gate and Mamilla areas. Properties in prestigious new Arab neighborhoods such as Baq'a and Qaṭamūn were also dedicated. Some of the endowed properties were located in villages outside Jerusalem: al-Ṭūr, Abū Thawr and Liftā. (These were later included in the city boundaries.) Several endowed properties were outside Jerusalem: in Jaffa, Ramallah, Haifa and Jericho.[69]

In sum, the properties made into *waqf*s in Jerusalem during the Mandate were largely urban. Although the total fell short of the preceding period in size and number, the prevailing trends of economic development made the properties quite valuable.

This list, however, gives us only a partial picture of the extent of *waqf* properties in Jerusalem. To round it out, we should examine all the 2,000 endowment deeds registered in the Jerusalem *sijill* during the Ottoman period. These encompassed much of the land and many of the buildings of Ottoman Jerusalem – according to some opinions, as much as 80 per cent.[70] Some of the dedicated properties were outside the city proper, and some disappeared from the lists of *waqf*s for various reasons: neglect, natural wear and tear, or transactions involving them. It must be recalled that Ottoman Jerusalem, its sanctity nothwithstanding, remained a rather small town in terms of area (intramural) and population (which did not exceed 20,000 until the end of the Ottoman period). The first population movement from within the city walls to the surrounding ground (in the late nineteenth century) is reflected in the *sijill* in the release of *waqf* lands on the Jerusalem periphery and the acquisition of property in new parts of the city, particularly north of Damascus and Herod's Gate (Bāb al-Sāhira), today's main business district in eastern Jerusalem. It is estimated that roughly one-third of all business premises in this part of the city are *waqf* properties.[71]

The SMC files contain no single document summarizing the *maḍbūṭ waqf* properties in Jerusalem. According to a report on *waqf* revenue in Jerusalem for the year AH1358/1939/40, the SMC administered 211 *awqāf maḍbūṭa* that were rented out. They included 77 shops, 10 apartments, 2 cafés, a bakery, a caravanserai, a public bath, 6 plots of vacant land, the Palace Hotel, the *sharīʿa* court building and the land surrounding Solomon's Pool (Birkat al-*Sulṭān*) and Mamilla Pool. In that year, the aggregate revenue was £P4,604. In addition, there were 121 shops that apparently belonged to endowments handed over provisionally to the Waqf Department after the office of *mutawallī* had become vacant.[72]

All the foregoing properties had economic value. However, there were also dozens of religious buildings among the Jerusalem *waqf*s. These were either mosques (including those on the *al-Ḥaram al-Sharīf*) or else cemeteries, shrines, religious colleges, several schools, a *zāwiyya* and other Sufi places of worship, and orphanages.

By the late Ottoman period, the centuries-old tradition of making city land into *waqf*s had turned much of the city's built-up area into endowed property. Moreover, as the *sijill* shows, most *waqf*s were let under generations-long leases, and the entitlements passed on from one generation to the next.[73] Both facts combined to make the Jerusalem real-estate market rather static.

NOTES

1. G. Baer, 'Jerusalem's Families of Notables and the *Waqf* in the Early Nineteenth Century' in D. Kushner (ed.), *Palestine in the Late Ottoman Period* (Jerusalem and Leiden: Yad Itzhak Ben-Zvi and E.J. Brill, 1986) pp. 109–22.

2. O.L. Barkan and E.H. Ayverdi, *Istanbul Vakiflari Tahrir Defteri 953 (1546)* (Istanbul, 1970).
3. Kāmil al-Ghāzī, *Nahr al-Dhahab fī Ta'rīkh Ḥalab* (Aleppo, 1342h), 2, p. 535ff.
4. R. Roded, 'The *Waqf* in Ottoman Aleppo' in G. Baer and G. Gilbar (eds), *Studies in the Muslim Waqf* (Oxford: Oxford University Press) (forthcoming); M. Kurd *'Alī, Kitab Khiṭṭat al-Shām* (Damascus, 1927) p. 116.
5. D. Crecelius, 'Incidences of *Waqf* Cases in Three Cairo Courts', *Journal of the Social History of the Orient*, 29 (1986) p. 182.
6. Ibid., p. 187.
7. M. Ipširlī and M. al-Tamīmī, *Awqāf wa-Amlāk al-Muslimīn fī Filasṭīn* (Istanbul: Munaẓamat al-Mu'tamar al-Islāmī, 1982) p. 20ff; M. Ipširlī, 'The *Waqf* of Palestine in the Sixteenth Century according to the Tahrir Registers' in *The Third International Conference on Bilād al-Shām: Palestine, 19–24 April 1980*, 2 (1984) pp. 96–107.
8. *Waqf* Sinān Pāshā is an example: most of its properties are in Palestine, but it was registered in Damascus.
9. A. Shpitzen, 'Legal Personality and Jewish Endowments in the Late Nineteenth Century Jerusalem' (Hebrew), *Qatedra*, 19 (April 1981) pp. 73–82; R. Shaham, 'Christian and Jewish *Waqfs* in Palestine during the Ottoman Period', *Bulletin of the School of Oriental and African Studies*, 54 (1991) pp. 460–72.
10. S.D. Goitein and A. Ben Shemesh, *Muslim Law in the State of Israel* (Hebrew, Jerusalem, 1957) p. 160.
11. D.S. Powers, 'Revenues of Public *Waqfs* in Sixteenth Century Jerusalem', *Archivum Ottomanicum*, 9 (1984) pp. 163–202; M. Ipširlī and M. al-Tamīmī, *Awqaf wa-Amlāk al-Muslimīn fī Filasṭīn* (Istanbul: Munaẓamat al-Mu'tamar al-Islāmī, 1982) p. 20ff.
12. G. Baer, 'The Dismemberment of *Awqāf* in Early 19th Century Jerusalem' *Asian and African Studies*, 13, 3 (1979) p. 225; G. Baer, 'Jerusalem's Families of Notables and the *Waqf* in the Early 19th Century' in D. Kushner (ed.), *Palestine in the Late Ottoman Period* (Jerusalem and Leiden: Yad Yitzhak Ben Zvi and E.J. Brill, 1986) p. 110.
13. G. Baer, 'Jerusalem's Families of Notables and the *Waqf* in the Early 19th Century' in D. Kushner (ed.), *Palestine in the Late Ottoman Period* (Jerusalem and Leiden: Yad Yitzhak Ben Zvi and E.J. Brill, 1986) p. 117.
14. A. Shpitzen, 'Legal Personality and Jewish Endowments in the Late Nineteenth Century Jerusalem', (Hebrew) *Qatedra*, 19 (April 1981) pp. 73–82; R. Shaham, 'Christian and Jewish *Waqfs* in Palestine during the Ottoman Period', *Bulletin of the School of Oriental and African Studies*, 54 (1991) pp. 460–72.
15. On *'Ulamā'* as *waqf* founders and beneficiaries see 'A. al-Sayyid Marsot, 'The Political and Economic Function of the *'Ulamā'* in the 18th Century', *Journal of the Economic and Social History of the Orient*, 16, 2–3 (1973) pp. 130–54.
16. H. Gerber, 'The *Waqf* Institution in Early Ottoman Edirne', *Asian and African Studies*, 17 (1983) p. 31.
17. R.C. Jennings, 'The Development of *Evkaf* in a new Ottoman province: Cyprus, 1571–1640' in G. Baer and G. Gilbar (eds), *Studies in the Muslim*

Waqf (Oxford: Oxford University Press) (forthcoming).

18. D. Crecelius, 'Incidences of *Waqf* Cases in Three Cairo Courts', *Journal of the Social History of the Orient*, 29 (1986) pp. 181–92.
19. R.C. Jennings, 'The Development of *Evkaf* in a new Ottoman province: Cyprus, 1571–1640' in G. Baer and G. Gilbar (eds), *Studies in the Muslim Waqf* (Oxford: Oxford University Press) (forthcoming).
20. R. Roded, 'The *Waqf* and the Social Elite of Aleppo in the Eighteenth and Nineteenth Centuries', *Turcica*, 20 (1988) pp. 71–91.
21. G. Baer, 'Jerusalem's Families of Notables and the *Waqf* in the Early 19th Century' in D. Kushner (ed.), *Palestine in the Late Ottoman Period* (Jerusalem and Leiden: Yad Yitzhak Ben Zvi and E.J. Brill, 1986) p. 117.
22. H. Gerber, 'The *Waqf* Institution in Early Ottoman Edirne', *Asian and African Studies*, 17 (1983) p. 31ff.
23. H. Gerber, *Economy and Society in an Ottoman City: Bursa 1600–1700* (Jerusalem: Magnes Press, 1988) p. 150.
24. R. Roded, 'The *Waqf* and the Social Elite of Aleppo in the Eighteenth and Nineteenth Centuries', *Turcica*, 20 (1988) pp. 71–91.
25. G. Baer, 'Jerusalem's Families of Notables and the *Waqf* in the Early 19th Century' in D. Kushner (ed.), *Palestine in the Late Ottoman Period* (Jerusalem and Leiden: Yad Yitzhak Ben Zvi and E.J. Brill, 1986) p. 110.
26. *Sijills* 397–416.
27. On these families early in the 19th century see ʿAdel Mannāʾ, 'The *Sanjaq* of Jerusalem between Two Invasions (1798–1831), Administration and Society' (unpublished Ph.D. dissertation, The Hebrew University of Jerusalem, 1986) pp. 131, 160–1.
28. Nos. 22,29,31,34 in Table 3.1.
29. Nos. 2,5,28 in Table 3.1.
30. No. 34 in Table 3.1.
31. No. 29 in Table 3.1; U.M. Kupferschmidt, *The Supreme Muslim Council: Islam under the British Mandate for Palestine* (Leiden: E.J. Brill, 1987) p. 217.
32. Nos. 12,16,18,20,35 in Table 3.1.
33. L. Massignon, 'Documents sur certains *Waqfs* de lieux saints de l'Islam' *Revue des etudes Islamique* (1951), 43–76.
34. Nos. 4,13,26,40 in Table 3.1.
35. On the migration of Hebronites to Jerusalem see I. Zilberman, 'Change and Continuity amongst Muslim Migrants in a Suburb of Jerusalem' (unpublished Ph.D. dissertation, Cambridge University, 1988).
36. See as an example R.C. Jennings, 'Women in Early 17th Century Ottoman Judicial Records – the *Sharīʿa* Court of Kayseri', *Journal of the Economic and Social History of the Orient*, 18 (1975) pp. 176–89. A. Markus, 'Men Women and Property: Dealers in Real Estate in the 18th Century Aleppo', *Journal of the Economic and Social History of the Orient*, 26, 1–2 (1983), 137–63.
37. H. Gerber, 'The *Waqf* Institution in Early Ottoman Edirne', *Asian and African Studies*, 17 (1983) p. 37.
38. R. Roded, 'The *Waqf* in Ottoman Aleppo' in G. Baer and G. Gilbar (eds), *Studies in the Muslim Waqf* (Oxford: Oxford University Press) (forthcoming).

39. D. Crecelius, 'Incidences of *Waqf* Cases in Three Cairo Courts', *Journal of the Social History of the Orient*, 29 (1986) p. 179.
40. G. Baer, 'Women and the *Waqf*: An Analysis of the Istanbul *Taḥrīr* of 1546', *Asian and African Studies*, 17 (1983) p. 10.
41. Ibid.
42. Ibid, p. 11.
43. *Sijills* 397–416.
44. Nos. 1,31,26,33,44,47 in Table 3.1.
45. *Sijill* 416/119/184.
46. *Sijill* 476/89/82.
47. In Amīna al-Dasūqī's *Waqfiyya* it is stated that she acquired part of the endowed property from her father. *Sijill* 484/32/340.
48. R.C. Deguilhem Schoem, 'History of *Waqf* and Case Studies from Syria in the Late Ottoman Period and French Mandate' (Ann Arbor, MI, University Microfilms, 1986), 190.
49. See below.
50. Most of the biographical information on the founder's profession is based on interviews with Shaykh As'ad al-Imām.
51. No. 61 in Table 3.1 and no. 49 in Table 3.2.
52. *Sijill* 467/142/109.
53. *Sijill* 475/25/42.
54. Nos. 1,3,6,29,43,47 in Table 3.1.
55. Nos. 1, 6 in Table 3.1.
56. Nos. 3,6,12,25,40,47 in Table 3.1.
57. *Sijill* 467/120/72; 466/39/235; 453/82/337; 475/89/39; 476/28/13; 476/141/5; 478/349/76; 483/192/152; 483/266/295; for the gift see *Sijill* 416/98/154.
58. D.S. Powers, 'Revenues of Public *Waqfs* in Sixteenth Century Jerusalem', *Archivum Ottomanicum*, 9 (1984) p. 163.
59. *Sijills* 397–416. For the *Waqfiyya* see *Sijill* 414/201/510.
60. The description of the properties in the *Waqfiyya* makes it impossible to estimate their value.
61. For more on this donation and its fate see Chapter 7.
62. Nos. 9,31,54,55,61 in Table 3.3.
63. No. 31 in Table 3.3.
64. No. 45 in Table 3.3.
65. Nos. 54, 55 in Table 3.3.
66. No. 61 in Table 3.3.
67. No. 107 in Table 3.3.
68. Nos. 16–18 in Table 3.3.
69. Nos. 1,2,65,70,73,76,81–83 in Table 3.3.
70. Interview with Shaykh As'ad al-Imām, 30 April, 1990.
71. Ibid.
72. *CIH*, 13/39/2,2/58/10.
73. See Chapter 7.

4

Beneficiaries and the devolution of shares

Islam imposed compulsory rules for the inheritance of property. In Sunnī law, wills are subject to two limitations: no more than one-third of the estate may be willed, and nothing may be willed to a legal heir. The system, however, is very flexible.[1] Muslim jurists developed the concept of gifts *inter vivos*, under which property may be transferred at any time before death, with no restrictions whatsoever.

Thus, beside the compulsory inheritance rule, a partial will or a testamentary *waqf*, there exist a multitude of methods for *inter vivos* gifts, allowing proprietors to apportion their estates freely. The existence of the post mortem alongside the *inter vivos* concept offered Muslims a wide range of strategies for dividing their estates. This was further broadened by the full control of founders over the distribution of entitlements, making the family *waqf* an alternative to the other two methods.

That there is a contradiction between the two legal norms of property devolution – family *waqf* and inheritance – cannot be disputed. It is mentioned in Islamic legal literature since the second century AH (eighth century AD). Aharon Layish has stressed the 'extensive use of the [family] *waqf* mechanism to circumvent the law of succession so as to deprive qur'anic heirs'. It was used, according to Layish, to grant greater *waqf* entitlements to members of the nuclear family, at the expense of members of the extended family.[2] David Powers considered the family *waqf* a gift *inter vivos*. He wrote: 'As part of the larger Islamic inheritance system, endowment law accorded Muslim proprietors a legal means to circumvent the effects of the inheritance rules by allocating usufruct rights to specified people in specified amounts and to regulate the transmission of those rights from one generation of beneficiaries to the next.'[3] The function of the *waqf*, Powers held, was to keep property together and to regulate the transmission of usufructory rights from one generation to the next in a way that established a broader and more inclusive lineal descent group.[4]

To challenge the rules and norms of the inheritance law by establishing a *waqf*, a founder must have strong and specific motives. This may explain the fact that regardless of the importance of the *waqf* as such and regardless of the large properties involved, few people founded *waqf*s. The Jerusalem *sijill* shows that from the beginning of the sixteenth century to the present, the number of family *waqf* founders – an average of two to three per year – has been small compared to the great majority who stayed within the bounds of the inheritance law.[5] In Jerusalem between 1917 and 1948, for example, hundreds of legacies were left in accordance with the law, but only 61 endowments were made (39 family and 22 public *waqf*s); 14 wills were made, and 1 revoked. Because registration in the *sijill* served as the legal source for the exercise of ownership rights, we assume that all endowment deeds (*waqfiyyāt*), gifts, wills and legal decisions on inheritance were so registered.

Alongside the norms of property devolution considered so far, there exists another: customary practice. We know of many cases in which heirs did not divide patrimonial real estate at all, with the eldest son alone or the male children holding on to the property to the exclusion of sisters and other legal heirs. Sometimes, male heirs contravened inheritance law by exerting pressure on their sisters to waive their rights in their father's estates. This was particularly likely to happen when a sister needed the consent of her elder brother to get married.[6]

The question poses itself why family *waqf* founders preferred the legal method of the *waqf* rather than simply applying customary practice to challenge the inheritance law. We shall discuss this presently.[7]

By awarding gifts or establishing family *waqf*s, a proprietor could diminish the size of the estate that would eventually go to his legal heirs. Our corpus of material from Jerusalem, however, contains only one example of a proprietor employing a complex strategy of property distribution by making use of *waqf*s, inheritance, wills or gifts.

For a family *waqf* endowed according to the Ḥanafī school of law (dominant in the Ottoman Empire), founders also retain personal control by appointing themselves lifetime *mutawallī*s and by retaining the right to revise the *waqfiyya* at any time. They could draw distinctions between properties, benefits and rights to the estate. For example, they could allow their spouses and daughters to benefit from the primary dwelling, while granting male children, descendants and other relatives the revenues from other properties, like shops and lands.

This chapter is based on an analysis of 61 *waqfiyyāt* from Mandatory Jerusalem as well as 100 *sharī'a* court decisions. The latter relate to disputes over the interpretation of family *waqfiyyāt*, most of which were drawn up during the Ottoman period. I also reviewed all earlier *waqfiyyāt* recorded over a period of 400 years in the *sijill* of Jerusalem, as well as *waqf*-related *sijill* documents since the end of the nineteenth century. In my view, the Mandate-era material reflects a long-standing pattern of transmitting *waqf* usufruct, a pattern that was present throughout the entire Ottoman period in Palestine and which persists until today.

Reliance on legal documents presents us with two methodological problems. First, in most cases we do not have enough information about the founder – for example, his social and economic perceptions or his family's relations with him – in order to account for the strategy he devised.

Second, we lack information on other properties owned by the founder. Was the endowed property only part of the founder's total assets? Through the *sijill* and some interviews, I tried to find some biographical details of the founders. Furthermore, one must assume that the founder told the *qāḍī* or the notary how he wanted to distribute the *waqf* revenues and that the *qāḍī* or the notary then couched his wishes in legal language. In doing so, he may have added or modified some nuances of which the founder was not aware.

Comparisons between *waqf* stipulations from one area with

those from another make it clear that there are regional and historical differences, as well as differences between the four schools of law.[8] The studies by Powers and Layish point to the differences between Mālikī *waqf*s in North Africa and Ḥanafī *waqf*s in the Fertile Crescent. Our corpus deals exclusively with Ḥanafī *waqf*s from Palestine.

BENEFICIARIES

Beneficiaries of the first series

In a family *waqf*, the first series of beneficiaries – those whose entitlements take effect immediately upon the founder's death – reflect the immediate, original will. Although most *waqfiyyāt* set forth specific entitlements for future generations as well, they usually begin by listing the benefits intended for their contemporaries, as a rule, persons who are close to them: children, spouses, parents, siblings and their respective offspring (see Table 4.1). The way the entitlement is distributed in the second series is less important to the founder, because he is rarely personally responsible for it. It is made up of individuals with which, for the most part, the founder has no personal relationship, or which he knows only as children (usually the offspring of the beneficiaries of the first series). They are seldom direct dependants. For this reason, founders usually allow their social outlook (rather than their personal likings) greater latitude with regard to the entitlements for succeeding generations. An analysis of the entitlements, especially for the first series, may help us answer the question of whether the family *waqf* was mainly intended to circumvent the *sharīʿa* inheritance law.

Sharīʿa law, based on qur'anic precepts, entitles a spouse to one-eighth of the deceased's estate if there are agnate descendants, and one-fourth in their absence.[9] By contrast, the number of cases in which a founder made his wife the sole beneficiary in the first series is relatively high: 10 out of 47. (This contradicts Layish's findings, based as they are on randomly selected endowment deeds.)[10] These include two cases in which the founders were man and wife. In both, the co-founders stipulated that after the death of either, the surviving spouse was the only beneficiary; only after his or her death would the entitlement pass on to their children.[11] In another six or seven cases where the wife was the sole beneficiary in the first series,[12] the couple had no children.[13] The childless founder thus used the *waqf* to prevent his or her estate, or part of it, from going to the state exchequer (*bayt al-māl*).

In half of the endowment deeds of married founders, they not only included the wife among the beneficiaries but sometimes gave her a larger share than the legal requirement. Only seven family endowment deeds (13 per cent) gave the founder's wife the precise one-eighth laid down by *sharīʿa* law.[14] It is, however, not always possible to say whether the *waqf* benefited the wife more than the *sharīʿa* law would have done. This is so, for example, when the founder pledged his wife a sum of money or a residuary entitlement. (The granting of a residuary entitlement is reminiscent of the concept in Jewish law of 'alimony from the estate'.)

Many founders were concerned about others obtaining a share of the family property by marriage. One-fourth of the founders who designated daughters and wives as beneficiaries stipulated that their entitlement would lapse or be diminished if and when they married outside the family. On the death of the 'outside' husband, or if he divorced the woman, the original beneficiary would regain her entitlement. In only one case did a founder (Yāsīn al-Dasūqī) state explicitly that his wife might continue to benefit from the entitlement if she remarried after his death.[15] Subsequently, he reconsidered, and amended the *waqfiyya* to read that her remarriage would revoke her entitlement altogether.[16] In a third and final *waqfiyya*, he changed his mind again and reverted to the original stipulation.[17] Another founder, Muḥammad al-Māliḥī, gave his wife, Farīda, a share equivalent to that of a son (a greater share than the legal requirement), but stipulated that her entitlement and that of her daughters should lapse when they married. He added that if his wife were to die and he were to remarry, the new wife would become entitled to the former's share.[18] Yet another founder gave his wife a share in his *waqf* revenues but, upon divorcing her, summarily amended the *waqfiyya* and crossed her off the list of beneficiaries.[19] Sometimes the founder left his wife an unusually small share of entitlement if she were to marry outside the family after his death, or allocated her half as the share of a male upon her remarriage.[20] Al-Hidmī, for example, left his wife a male's share if she did not marry after his death, but a smaller one if she did.[21] Waqf founders in Egypt are known to have acted similarly.[22]

A summary of all these cases shows that a relatively large number of founders (about 70 per cent) gave their wives a share of the entitlement. In nearly half the cases (13 out of 27) their share was larger than they would have received under the *sharī'a*. One-fourth stipulated that their wives would cease to benefit from the *waqf* if and when they remarried. Presumably, some of the founders were divorced or widowed at the time they made their dedication; therefore, in only a minority of cases were wives excluded from the beneficiaries. Departures from *sharī'a* law were usually biased in favour of wives, and the prevailing norm seems to have indicated generosity towards wives, or at least non-discrimination against them.

In two-thirds of the endowment deeds in Mandatory Jerusalem, the founder's children were the principal beneficiaries of the first series. This corroborates Layish's findings.[23] In the other cases (when relatives other than the founder's children were the first beneficiaries), the founder appears to have been childless.[24] In most instances, the *waqfiyya* explicitly includes future offspring, if any, with the children already listed. In this respect, the entitlements laid down by the *waqf* conform with *sharī'a* law.

In one-third of the above *waqfiyyāt* where children are named as the first series of beneficiaries, they share the benefits with other relatives, particularly the founder's wife. Only in three cases do they benefit alongside other agnate relatives, sharing the entitlements with orphaned grandchildren.[25]

When analysing entitlements in the children's series, special note should be taken of the share of founders' daughters. We find that most founders did include their daughters among the beneficiaries, granting them at least half of the share of a son. As stated above, however, in one-fourth of the dedications, the founder stipulated that his daughters would be eligible for benefits only as long as they did not marry out of the family. They would, however, usually regain their share if they were widowed

TABLE 4.1 BENEFICIARIES OF FOUNDER'S NUCLEAR FAMILY IN THE FIRST SERIES

No.	Gender	*Beneficiaries* *Shares of spouse*	*Sons*	*Daughters*	*Apportionment between males and females*	*Notes*
1	F	–	–	–		Childless widow
2	M	Pension	2	6	Preference	For his wife, until she marries
3	M	–	4	5	Preference	Daughters, until their marriage
4	M	All	–	–		Childless founder
5	M	All	–	–		Childless founder
6	M	–	–	–	Preference	
7	M	Like a daughter	1	1	Preference	Females, until their marriage
8	M	–	6	5	Equal shares	
9	Couple	All	–	–		After both die, to their 7 daughters
10	M	Like a daughter	3	5		For his wife, until she marries
11	M	1/8	3	3	Preference	
12	M	–	1	–		
13	M	–	6	2	Preference	
14	M	–	–	–		For two agnatic nieces
15	M	1/2	–	–		+ To a cognatic nephew
16	M	–				Generally for founder's offspring
17	M	–				Generally for founder's offspring
18	M	–				Generally for founder's offspring
19	M	–	–	1		After her death, to her daughters
20	M	1/4	–	–	Preference	+ To his nieces and cousins
21	M	Like a daughter	3	5	Preference	For his wife, until she marries
22	M	Like a daughter	6	5	Preference	
23	M	All	–	–		
24	Couple	All				After both die, to children if come
26	F	–	1	–	Equal with the granddaughters	+ To two orphaned granddaughters
27	M	All	–	–		Childless founder, then to foreigners
28	M	Like a son	2	3	Preference	Females, until marriage

29	M	–	'My children'		Preference	
31	M	Two wives	–	–	Preference	+ To brother, sister and remote relatives
32	M	1/3	2	–	Equal shares	
33	F	All	–	–	Equal shares	After her husband, to their 4 children
34	M	–	4	2	Preference	Daughters, until their marriage
35	M	1/8	5	1	Preference	
36	M	–	2	4	Preference	+ To an agnatic, orphaned grandchild
37	M	1/8	2	4	Preference	Until her marriage, + 1/3 to sister
39	M	–	'To descendants'		Preference	+ To his brothers' descendants
41	M	–	1	–		
42	M	Like a daughter	1	8	Preference	
44	M	–	'To children'			
46	M	All	–	–		After his wife's death, to her sister
47	F	–		–	–	To her husband's cousin's son
48	M	1/8	–	–	Preference	+ To his 8 orphaned grandchildren
49	M	1/8	1	3	Preference	For his wife until she marries
50	M	'To my wife and children'			Preference	No indication of shares
51	M	–	'To children'			Educating his and his brothers' children
52	M	–	–	–		To his grandfather's *waqf* beneficiaries
53	F	–	–	–	Preference	To her 4 agnate cousins
56	M	–	2	–		
57	M	All	–	–	Preference	After her death, to their children
58	F	–	–	–	Preference	To a remote relative's descendants
59	M	–	8	–		
60	M	–	'To children'		Preference	
61	M	1/8	5	5	Preference	

Note: The serial numbers correspond to those in Table 3.1 (p. 50).

or divorced. Some founders determined that one of the dwellings belonging to the *waqf* should serve to lodge their daughters and the daughters of their male offspring. A woman filed a suit in the *sharī'a* court demand housing rights in accordance with the founder's intentions as laid down in the *waqfiyya*. The *qāḍī* ruled that in limiting the eligibility of his daughters to the period preceding their marriage, the founder had intended to keep them and their husbands from usurping the shares of the founder's descendants.[26] This is one of the major instances highlighting the difference between the norms of the family *waqf* and *sharī'a* law. There are many known instances, especially in rural areas, where custom has a powerful influence, in which daughters received no portion at all in an inheritance or were forced to sign over their share. The entitlement patterns of the *waqf* thus often followed customary norms. In Egypt, too, there were cases of excluding daughters if they married an outsider.[27] Interestingly, the *waqf* entitlement patterns with respect to the founder's children were similar in Mandatory Jerusalem to the family *waqf* standards under the British Raj in India.[28]

In rare instances, a founder favoured, or discriminated against, some of his children. In one of them, the founder spelled out the reason for excluding some of his children from the entitlement: they had been given outright ownership of other business properties of his (*wādhālika muqābil mā akhadhūhu awlādī al-bāqīn bi-maḥallī al-tijārī tanāzaltu lahum 'anhu*).[29] In British India, cases were known in which founders deprived a child of the *waqf* entitlement because he had fallen into bad ways.[30] Riḍā al-Ṣalāhī, director of the Muslim orphanage in Jerusalem, earmarked the revenues from his family *waqf* for the education of two of his sons who showed promise. Only after all his children reached the age of 20 would the entitlement be distributed equally among them all. By doing so, the founder wished to foster education and promote learning among his children, and ultimately to enhance his family's standing.[31]

Summing up, most beneficiaries of the first, or principal, series after the founder himself were his children and/or his wife. Orphaned grandchildren and orphaned nephews were often included in the first series, too. Discrimination against members of the extended family (parents, siblings), as compared with the law of inheritance, occurred rarely and do not reflect the norm applied in the Mandatory period. However, childless founders or those who had no heirs of the first degree created *waqf*s in order to keep their property out of the hands of distant relatives or the public treasury (*bayt al-māl*), to whom it would otherwise revert under the law.

Beneficiaries of subsequent series

In most Jerusalem endowment deeds, the beneficiaries of the second series were the descendants of the first-series beneficiaries, whether some or all of them depended on the founder's preference. In the two cases in which the founder favoured only some of his children in the first series, he stipulated that his other children would benefit in the second series.[32]

In seven of the eight endowments in which the founder designated his wife the sole beneficiary in the first series, the couple seems to have been childless. This is attested by the naming of distant relatives in the second series. Such were children of a cognate uncle,[33] the founder's sister-in-law,[34] and an unrelated orphan. In the absence of even distant relatives, one founder designated north Africans in Jerusalem who hailed from the same city as himself.[35] In one case, the founder preferred an orphaned grandchild of his uncle over closer kinsmen.[36] In only two endowments, one of a woman in favour of her husband in the first series and another of a husband in favour of his wife, were the founders' children listed as beneficiaries of the second, rather than the first, series.[37]

In most *waqfiyyāt* from Mandatory Jerusalem, founders stipulated that daughters of male relatives would benefit but could not transmit entitlements to their own descendants as long as the founder's agnate descendants were alive. In several cases, *waqf* administrators did not honour the founders' stipulations for daughters of sons to benefit after the death of sons of sons, and tended to withhold entitlement from the females. The *qāḍī*s, however, usually ruled in favour of daughters of sons and in favour of cognate descendants. For example, Maʿtūq al-Quṭub al-Mawqit stipulated that females would not benefit during the lifetime of agnate male descendants and that the principle of representation (see below) would apply only if the deceased had actually benefited from the *waqf* entitlement. Zulaykha, who was both the niece and daughter-in-law of the *mutawallī*, Maḥmūd al-Mawqit, sued for a share in the entitlement even though it seemed, according to the *waqfiyya*, that females had no right to any share as long as male descendants of any of the founder's sons were alive. The *qāḍī* ruled that if only one(!) of the beneficiaries ('Alī) had died and left only female heirs, the principle of barring females should be rescinded with respect to all branches of the founder's descendants. This would apply even if male beneficiaries who were offspring of the founder still lived in other branches of the family, such as the *mutawallī* and his brother's two children (see Figure 4.1). Therefore, the claimant and three females in another branch of the family were awarded shares of the entitlement. This ruling had no precedent in the religious legal literature and would probably fail the test of a rigorous application of *sharī'a* law.

Because 'Alī predeceased his father, the principle of representation (or of quasi-representation, as explained below) did not apply to his descendants; the *qāḍī* ruled that the male descendants of this branch of the family had lost their right to a share. He reduced the share of the *mutawallī* from 1/2 to 1/3 and that of his nephews from 1/4 to 1/9. 'Alī's four children would be entitled to benefits from the *waqf* in their father's stead only after the *mutawallī* had died and the entitlement passed to 'Alī's series.[38]

The right of females to transmit entitlements

The family *waqf* distinguishes between those entitled to enjoy the usufruct and those entitled to transmit it to their descendants. The *waqfiyyāt* usually limit the right to transmit an entitlement from the first series to the next to male beneficiaries. Ḥājj Muḥammad al-'Alamī, for example, divided his properties into two endowments: one for male relatives and one for his sister, his two wives and his nephew's wife (as long as she remained married to him). He stipulated that upon the death of one of them, her share would be distributed among the remaining beneficiaries, because the

TABLE 4.2 FEMALE ENTITLEMENT IN SUCCEEDING SERIES

No.	*Gender of founder*	*Entitled: no limitations*	*Agnatic only*	*Agnatic until marriage*	*Agnatic, but only after extinction of males of all series*	*Not entitled at all*	*Male/female shares*
1	F				X		Equal
2	M		X				Equal
3	M				X		1/2
4	M	X					1/2
5	M						1/2
6	M					X	–
7	M			X			1/2
8	M			X			Equal
9	Couple	X					Equal
10	M			X			1/2
11	M		X				1/2
12	M					X	–
13	M		X				1/2
14	N	X					–
15	M		X				Equal
16	M						–
17	M						–
18	M						–
19	M						1/2
20	M		X				–
21	M			X			1/2
22	M			X			1/2
24	Couple						–
26	F		X				Equal
27	M						–
28	M		X				1/2
29	M		X				1/2
31	M		X				1/2
32	M		X				Equal
33	F		X				Equal
34	M		X				1/2
35	M						–
36	M		X				1/2
37	M		X				1/2
39	M	X					1/2
41	M						–
42	M						–
44	M						–
46	M						–
47	F						–
48	M		X				1/2
49	M	X					1/2
50	M		X				1/2
51	M					X	–
52	M						–
53	F					X	1/2
56	M		X				Equal
57	M						–
58	F		X				Equal
59	M						–
60	M	X					1/2
61	M		X				1/2

cognate descendants are barred from the entitlement (*awlād al-banāt maḥrūmūn*).[39]

Sixty-one per cent (24 our of 39) of the family *waqfiyyāt* in Mandatory Jerusalem stipulated that the descendants of female beneficiaries (*awlād al-ināth, awlād al-buṭūn*) were entitled to a share in the usufruct of the *waqf* only after all male descendants (*awlād al-dhukūr, awlad al-ẓuhūr*) of all generations had died. In two of these cases, the founder added that his female descendants might receive a share in the *waqf* revenues only after the death of the descendants of his brothers, his uncles and other male agnates. In 21 per cent of the *waqfiyyāt* (eight cases) female beneficiaries were explicitly barred from transmitting entitlement rights to their descendants. In such cases, the *waqfiyya* stated that as soon as the descendants of the male beneficiaries died, entitlement should go to a public charity.[40]

In only seven cases (18 per cent) of the endowments founded in Mandatory Jerusalem did the founder grant females the right to transmit their entitlements to their descendants.[41] In four of these,

FIGURE 4.1 DISTRIBUTION OF ENTITLEMENT IN THE AL-MAWQIT WAQF

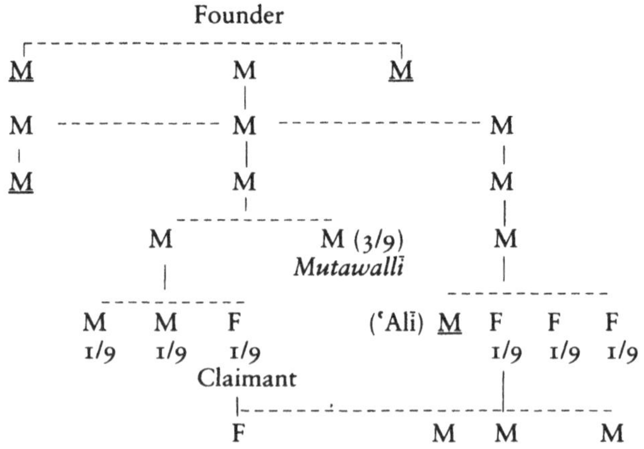

Legend:
M = Male
M = Male who died without share-entitled descendants
F = Female
F = Female who died without share-entitled descendants

the founder had no male children or none at all. In their absence, a founder may be interested in perpetuating his endowment through the transmission of entitlement to other family members and cognate descendants. One of the cases is exceptional in that the founder, ʿAlī al-ʿUmarī, listed his seven daughters as the exclusive beneficiaries of the first series and barred his agnate descendants from transferring entitlement to subsequent generations.[42] Possibly, al-ʿUmarī had previously made over parts of his estate to his sons by means of *inter vivos* gifts and now used the *waqf* to compensate those who had been excluded: daughters and cognate descendants.

It is noteworthy that the eight women in my corpus who established a family *waqf* all barred their female offspring from passing on their entitlements to their descendants. In four instances, the founder specified that the entitlement would pass to the females' offspring only after all male descendants had died.[43] In the other four, the exclusion was absolute.[44] Even where the founder granted his sons and daughters equal shares in the first series (unlike the inheritance law, which – as will be remembered – awards a daughter half the share of a son), daughters could not transmit entitlements to the next series, and their descendants were denied the right to benefit from the usufruct (see below).[45]

It is also interesting to note that 5 of the 25 founders who specified that agnate females were to benefit from the *waqf* stipulated that their entitlements would lapse upon marriage. This reflects the founders' concern over a *waqf* entitlement passing out of their agnate family forever. By getting married, the female beneficiary takes her benefits with her to her husband's family. According to the Islamic agnate family concept, her offspring (who, except for the above provision, would inherit her rights) belong to the husband's family.

The strong aversion to the possibility of cognate descendants taking family property to other families is particularly striking if compared with some other cases.[46] In these, the founders, after first barring their cognate descendants from entitlement, took pains to stipulate that if a beneficiary married within the family (that is, to a potential beneficiary among the founder's descendants) their descendants would be entitled to a double portion:

that of their deceased father as well as that of their deceased mother.[47] This kind of apportionment is based on a method similar to the principle of representation or quasi-representation in inheritance (see below).

Entitlement of orphaned grandchildren

Sunnī inheritance law does not recognize the right of orphaned grandchildren to a share of their grandfather's estate if the deceased has any living children.[48] As a result, an orphaned grandchild must be supported by members of the extended family until his maturity. *Qur'ān* 4:8 appears to recognize the tenuous position of orphaned grandchildren but leaves corrective action to the goodwill of the pious: 'If relatives, orphans and the poor are present when [the inheritance] is apportioned, give them of it and comfort them with gentle words.'[49] With the development of civil legislation in Muslim countries in the twentieth century, a remedy for this problem was discovered in a *sharīʿa* legal device. This was the principle of the 'obligatory bequest' (*al-waṣiyya al-wājiba*) established in the Egyptian probate law of 1946.[50] It requires testators to reserve a share for orphaned grandchildren, up to an aggregate maximum of one-third. This formalized a mode of behaviour that many founders had followed voluntarily for hundreds of years.

In Palestine, founders laid down that *waqf* revenues should be distributed separately for each generation, with a higher series excluding a lower. Next, they specified that upon the death of a parent, his/her children should receive his/her entitlement. The latter stipulation, which incorporates different generations in the devolution for *waqf* revenues, recalls the principle of representation known in European inheritance systems. But it differs from the European method, according to which the patrimony is devolved *per stirpes* (by family branches) in all generations, while the *waqf* entitlement is recalculated and reapportioned for each generation separately (see below).

This complex method caused occasional disputes between beneficiaries and *mutawallīs*. One founder, Muḥammad al-ʿAlamī, who mentioned both intergenerational devolution and representation in his *waqfiyya*, and also stipulated that a female should receive half the share of a male in the same generation, included the following hypothetical example in the deed: if a founder dies leaving two daughters, an orphaned grandson and an orphaned granddaughter (both the children of sons), these descendants would share the *waqf* revenues shown in Figure 4.2.[50]

Here, by virtue of the principle of representation, an orphaned granddaughter receives twice the share of her aunts (the founder's daughters), because she is her father's sole heir, and under the *waqfiyya*, her father was entitled to a share twice that of his sisters (as stipulated by the founder). Note that her share is equal to that of her orphaned male cousin who, according to the law, should receive a share twice as large as hers. From the founder's perspective, the matter would correct itself once the two aunts (daughters of the founder) had died, at which time revenues would be redistributed, with the female receiving half the share of the male, as shown in Figure 4.3.

When a founder stipulated that his orphaned grandchildren would step into the shoes of his deceased son, he actually caused all the descendants of his deceased son to advance one series. Figure 4.4 shows the distribution of entitlements in a *waqf* created by Yaḥyā al-Khalīlī, after the death of the founder's eldest son and two of his three grandchildren.[52]

After the death of the founder's eldest son, the entitlement was apportioned equally: each of the founder's three sons and his orphaned grandson received one-quarter. After the founder's middle grandchild died (no. 7 in Figure 4.4), the entitlement of 36 shares was redistributed among the second series of beneficiaries; his grandchild, the three children of another deceased grandchild, and the four children of a deceased great-grandchild. In other words: in the second series of beneficiaries, members of the third and fourth generations received a share alongside members of the second generation. Only one of the eight beneficiaries belonged to the second series of beneficiaries; the others were co-opted into it as representatives of a deceased father, or of a deceased father and grandfather. The distribution of the shares in the *waqf* is valid only for a specific span of time: whenever an actual or potential beneficiary dies, they must be reapportioned.

This pattern of distributing *waqf* entitlements has been practised for centuries, although Muslim jurists disagree in interpreting the intention of a founder who lays down these two principles simultaneously. A minority opinion holds that the second principle (representation) annuls (*yansakh*) the first one (the intergenerational barrier), and that entitlements are to be distributed *per stirpes*, with each son stepping into his father's shoes and receiving, together with his brothers (and his sisters, if they are beneficiaries), the share to which his father was entitled.[53] But most Ḥanafī jurists and the *qāḍī*s of Mandatory Jerusalem regarded these two stipulations as complementary rather than contradictory. They favoured a distribution based, first and foremost, upon quasi-representation, so that an orphaned grandchild may receive his father's share, but only until his father's generation expires, at which time the intergenerational barrier comes into force, and the *waqf* entitlement is redistributed among the beneficiaries of the subsequent generation, including orphans

FIGURE 4.2 HYPOTHETICAL DISTRIBUTION OF ENTITLEMENTS (Muḥammad al-ʿAlamī Waqf)

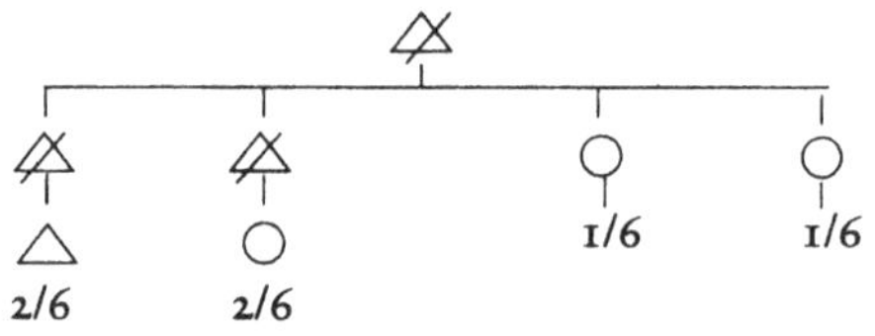

Note: △ a male; ○ a female; △ an expired male.

FIGURE 4.3 REDISTRIBUTION OF ENTITLEMENT AFTER THE DEATH OF THE BENEFICIARIES OF THE HIGHER SERIES

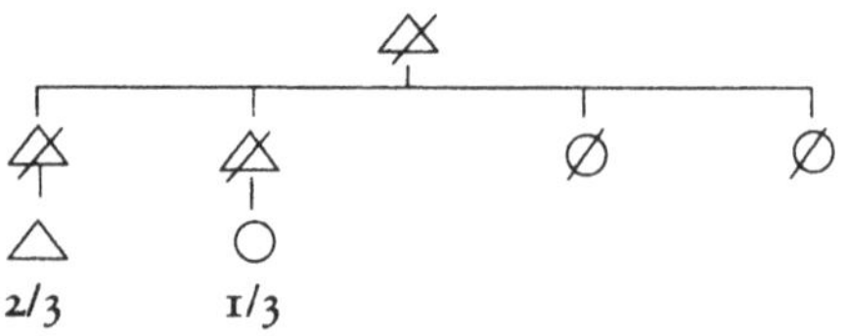

Note: △ a male; △ an expired male; ○ a female; ∅ an expired female.

from a lower generation, who represent, or substitute for, their deceased parents.[54] According to the latter method, the shares of orphans changes once the upper series of beneficiaries expires.

The method of quasi-representation as applied in Palestine differs from the taʿqīb described by Powers. He spoke of it as one option among others to allow the share of a deceased beneficiary to revert to all surviving beneficiaries, *per capita* or according to need.[55] In Palestine, however, quasi-representation of orphans is, at any given time, limited to one generation; the shares are then made proportional, and their apportionment changes each time the last beneficiary of a series dies. Once an entire series of beneficiaries has died, the existing distribution is no longer valid, and the *mutawallī* must redistribute the entitlement between the beneficiaries of the next series, without reference to the previous distribution. A traditional formula for this distribution is:

> When all members of the aforementioned series have died, the entitlement of this endowment will be distributed equally among members of the subsequent series [who are beneficiaries], be they alive or dead, if they have male children or grandchildren, however remote. Living children

FIGURE 4.4 DISTRIBUTION OF ENTITLEMENTS OF THE YAḤYĀ AL-KHALĪLĪ WAQF

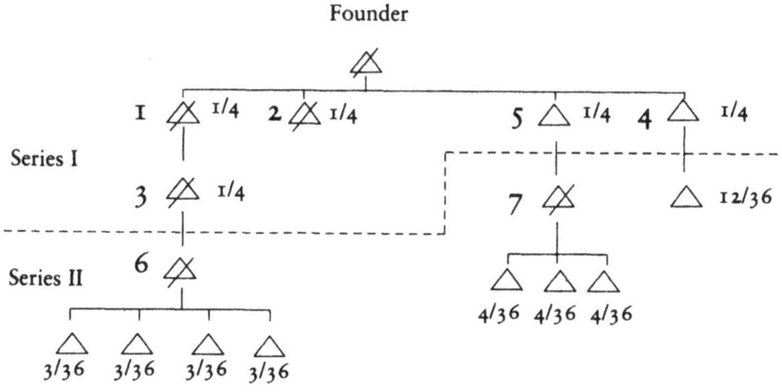

Notes: △ a male; ○ a female; an expired male.
The numbers to the left of the gender symbols denote the order of demise.
Dotted line separates first and second series.

> and grandchildren and subsequent descendants of the deceased will receive their share in person, while the share of the deceased [beneficiaries] will be transferred to their subsequent descendants . . . Children may not benefit from a share concurrently with their parents, but the parent excludes his own offspring only.[56]

According to a minority opinion among Shāfiʿī jurists – for example, al-Subkī and Ibn Ḥajar al-ʿAsqalānī – entitlements in subsequent generations should be distributed according to the *per stirpes* method: each separate branch of the family should receive the share granted to the founder's offspring from whom it derives.[57] According to a differing opinion, the previous distribution must be annulled after the death of each series, and entitlement redistributed equally among the beneficiaries of the subsequent series on a per capita basis.[58] The *qāḍī*s in Jerusalem, like their Egyptian colleagues, ruled in accordance with the second opinion, which most muftis also shared. In doing so, they were guided by their concern to prevent inequality among certain branches of the family because of the random number of beneficiaries at any given time. In the case of the *waqf* of ʿAlī al-Nammarī, one of the beneficiaries obtained a judgment from the *qāḍī* requiring the distribution of the revenues between 29 beneficiaries belonging to the fifth series. An orphaned son of a beneficiary of the fifth series who had not benefited from his entitlement during his lifetime because members of the fourth series were still alive appealed the case to the *sharīʿa* court. The *qāḍī* agreed, in an exceptional move, to allow witnesses who had testified in the previous hearing to amend their testimony in order to include another eight beneficiaries whom they had 'forgotten' to mention in their previous testimony.[59]

In an attempt to find the logic for this complex process of separation between generations and simultaneous quasi-representation or substitution, I conclude that this method aims at preventing inequality among beneficiaries of the same series. This emerges from the practice of the two interrelated stipulations mentioned above. Although the founder stipulated that any orphan enjoys his deceased parent's share, each distribution of *waqf* revenues is revoked (*tunqaḍ al-qisma*) once the last member of a series has died, and the entitlements are redistributed in such a manner that all beneficiaries in the next series receive equal shares. If a member of this series dies, his offspring 'represent' him and divide among themselves the share of the deceased. Looking again at the apportionment described in Figure 4.4, for example, we find that, were the founder's single living grandchild (a second-generation recipient) to die without leaving a descendant, there would be four beneficiaries of the third generation, one of them deceased. The three living beneficiaries were to receive a quarter each; the fourth quarter was to be divided among the four great-great-grandchildren (members of the fourth generation). This method gives preference to the older generation: the three living members of the third generation receive a quarter each, rather than the one-seventh they would have received were the shares apportioned per capita among the seven beneficiaries of all generations then alive. This complicated method was applied in Palestine, Egypt and elsewhere, and was chosen, so I conclude, to prevent inequality between cousins, that is, between offspring of different family branches.

The offspring of deceased beneficiaries who are 'promoted' to a higher series by quasi-representation are considered part of the series set up under the founder's terms (*al-daraja al-jaʿaliyya*), as against the original series (*al-ṭabaqa al-ḥaqīqiyya*).[60] The stipulation that allows an offspring to substitute for a deceased parent is therefore called *al-sharṭ al-jaʿalī*, except one case in which it is called *sharṭ al-ʿilāwa* (*ʿilāwa* means 'elevation', contrasting with the usual Arabic term for 'representation', '*tanzīl*', which means 'coming down').[61] Nowhere in the *sijill* or in the literature is the term '*tanzīl*', the standard term in the legal works on the principle of representation, used in this context.[62] This is probably so for two reasons: *waqf* laws are distinct from inheritance laws; and full representation implies that the entitlement is divided between the family branches (*per stirpes*) throughout all generations, not allowing for any redistribution that would separate one generation from the next.

The pattern is brought out clearly in a judgment relating to the ʿAbd al-Laṭīf al-Ḥusaynī Waqf, which specified the names of

FIGURE 4.5 ENTITLEMENT OF FOURTH SERIES –

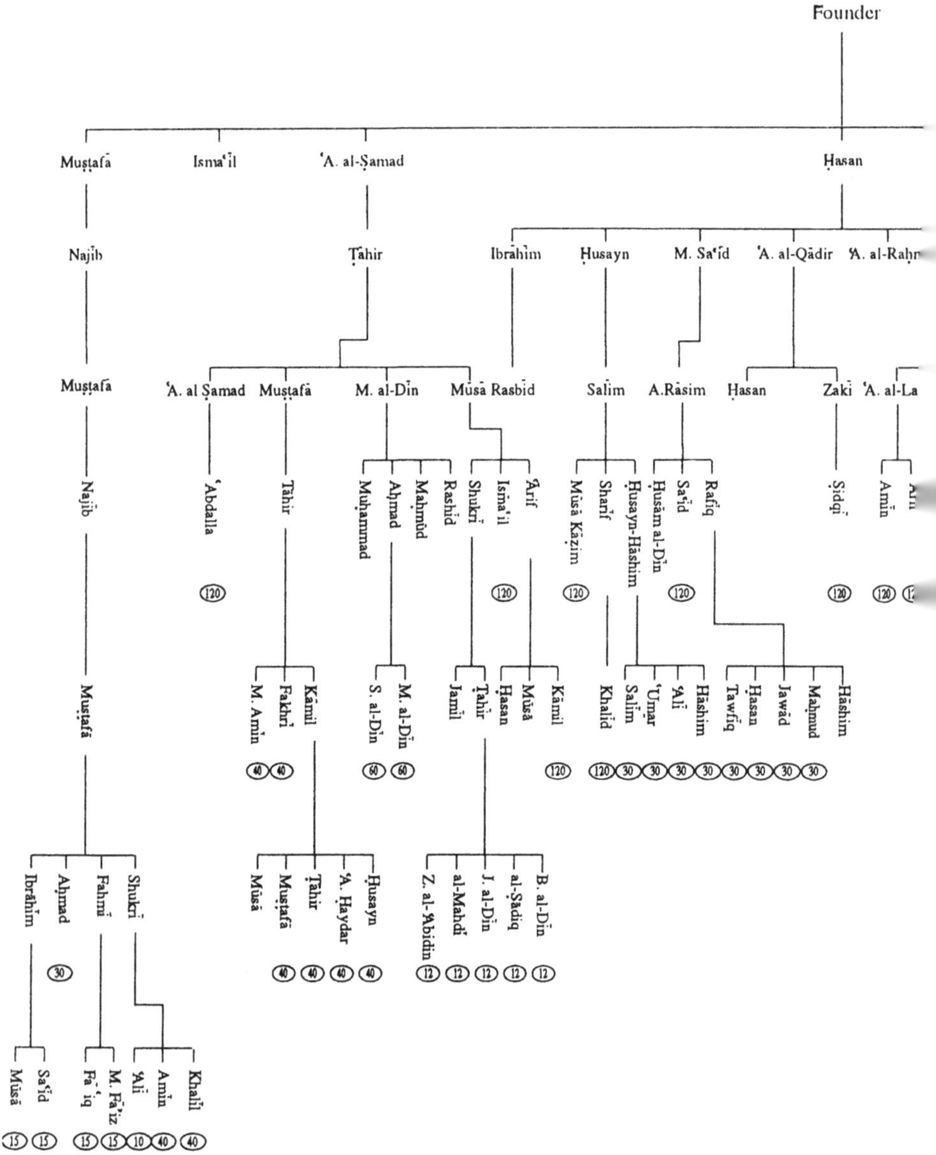

'ABD AL-LAṬĪF AL-ḤUSAYNĪ WAQF

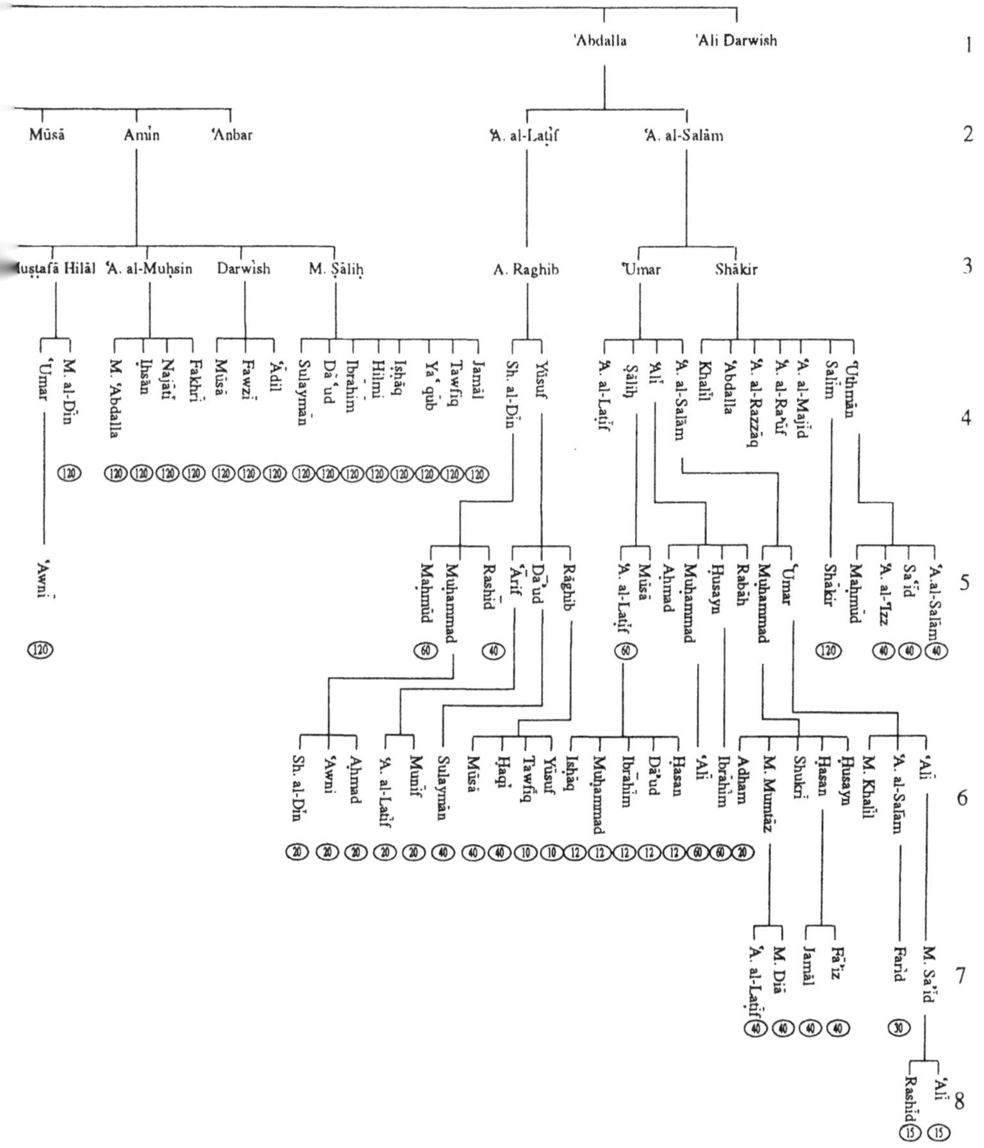

beneficiaries down to the eighth generation (the *waqf* was founded in 1766, the judgment given in 1931). The decision to ask the *sharīʿa* court to rule on the specific shares of each of the 87 beneficiaries arose from the need to obtain a detailed, authoritative calculation of the distribution of the entitlements, rather than from a dispute (see Figure 4.5). The *qāḍī* ruled that after the death of the last beneficiary of the third series, each of the 39 beneficiaries of the fourth series should receive 1/39 of the *waqf* revenues. Since 16 of these beneficiaries were dead, their share passed to their 64 offspring. Accordingly, by 1931, the revenues were divided among 23 beneficiaries of the fourth series and 64 offspring of the 16 beneficiaries of the third series who had died, bringing the total to 87.[63]

Most *waqfiyyāt* specify that offspring are to substitute for, or 'represent', deceased parents, even if the parents' turn to gain their share had not yet arrived and if the parent died without obtaining it:

> If one of [the beneficiaries] dies before actually receiving any share in the *waqf* revenues, leaving . . . a child, the child receives the share to which the father would have been entitled had he remained alive.[64]

This stipulation was made in order to ensure that orphans might exercise their right to the *waqf* at the appropriate moment, alongside their father's series. The founder wished to prevent the exclusion from entitlement of any descendant whose father had died too soon to benefit from his share. To do so improved the orphans' circumstances by elevating them to their parents' series.

The *sharīʿa* court records suggest that the principle of quasi-representation leads to disputes between beneficiaries of successive generations, each party interpreting the founder's stipulations in the way best suited to his or her interests. They compete with each other over the interpretation of the *waqfiyya*, and the inclusion or exclusion in *waqf* benefits according to the quasi-representation method caused disputes which formed the subject-matter of 68 per cent of the cases in our 30-year corpus. The rulings of the *qāḍī*s in Mandatory Jerusalem are guided by their understanding of the *waqf* as a charitable institution in which the founder's natural inclination is to act charitably towards as many descendants, especially orphaned descendants, as possible. They quote Ibn ʿĀbidīn, who wrote: 'It is better to give than to withhold' (*al-iʿṭā' awlā min al-ḥirmān*).[65] Allowing offspring of the deceased (or others) to benefit from their share even before their turn has come increases the potential number of beneficiaries in each series and reduces each beneficiary's share. Beneficiaries by quasi-representation (*al-daraja al-jaʿaliyya*) often came to outnumber the original beneficiaries (see Figure 4.5). The latter are called 'the living' (*al-aḥyā'*) or 'beneficiaries in their own right' (*al-mustaḥiqqūn bi-anfusihim*); beneficiaries promoted to this series are called 'the dead' (*al-amwāt*), because they 'substitute' for potential beneficiaries who are no longer alive. In cases in which both parents were beneficiaries but one died before enjoying his or her entitlement, children received a share alongside the living parent.

According to Islamic law, a custodian is appointed to look after orphans' interests during their minority until they are old enough to fend for themselves. The support of orphans was left to the private initiative of the family or to a charitable institution like the *waqf*.

Few founders granted first-series entitlements to orphaned cousins or other orphans who did not belong to the family at all. Granting shares to persons who, under the inheritance law, were not entitled to a bequest suggests a wish to act charitably toward the weaker elements of society. For example, in 1796, Ḥasan al-Ḥusaynī, Mufti of Jerusalem, created an endowment for two sons of his son, a son of his daughter, his brother's two wives (neither of whom were legal heirs) and his brother and sister, who might inherit only in the absence of children.[66] Although he had children, he wished to act generously towards others. This example – a cleric who created an endowment for people who were not his heirs – substantiates the religious motive of the endowment act: to be charitable towards the needy and to reap the attendant religious recompense. Apportionment by the quasi-representation method described above, which ensured fair shares to beneficiaries of different generations, may be looked at from this angle. Add to that the fact that most founders were advanced in age at the time they created their endowments. Older people are inclined to contemplate the fate of man after death and to cling to the belief that 'charity delivers from death'.

When the inter-generational barrier between series was revoked and a founder stipulated that a deceased beneficiary's share would pass to his descendants (rather than to his brothers' descendants), there arose the question of who would receive the share of a beneficiary who had died heirless. In the cases I examined, there was no instance of such a share being given to the poor. A few founders laid down that the share of an heirless deceased beneficiary should revert to the *waqf* for redistribution among the other beneficiaries.[67] Most founders awarded such entitlements to the deceased's brothers (or first to full brothers and, if there were none, then to brothers born of his father).[68] If he had no brothers, the share would accrue to the nearest kin.[69] This is the most common model, but there are variations.[70]

Most founders, for instance, allowed children of different generations to share the entitlement concurrently. They were not interested in seeing shares go to distant relatives of beneficiaries who had died; nor did they want the orphaned grandchildren of one beneficiary to benefit from the share of another. For this reason, they stipulated that the share of an heirless beneficiary should not be divided among *all* beneficiaries of the various generations but only among the deceased beneficiary's brothers; in the absence of brothers, the share was to go to the nearest kin.[71]

The *qāḍī*s of Jerusalem upheld this principle strictly. ʿAlī al-Nammarī, for example, stipulated that in the absence of descendants and brothers, the beneficiary's share should pass to his *awlād ʿumūmatihi al-dhukūr*', a semantically ambivalent expression signifying paternal cousins. The *mutawallī*s had an interest in interpreting this term to include all distant cousins, so that they, too, would be entitled to a share upon the demise of a beneficiary. In 1930, the *qāḍī* rejected this interpretation, because the founder had wished, as far as possible, for shares to go to the deceased's nearest of kin, that is, only to the descendants of the father's brothers.[72] Yet it is difficult to dismiss the *mutawallī*s' argument. Although the *qāḍī* found otherwise, their interpretation of the *waqfiyya* seemed reasonable and legitimate.

Several years later, a similar dispute arose over the distribution of the entitlements of this *waqf*. One beneficiary, a male, claimed the share of an aunt's daughter who, at the time of her death, had neither offspring nor brothers. The *mutawallī* argued that the claimant himself was not of the same degree of kinship as the deceased, not being one of her cousins, but rather one of her cousin's children. The stipulation of 'male' indicated that the children had to be offspring of the uncle, not of the aunt. The practical significance of the distinction was that benefits should accrue to the daughters of the deceased's uncle of the same series but not to cousins of a later generation. The claimant then argued that he was entitled to the deceased's share under the principle of representation, which allowed him to replace his deceased cousins in the succession. The *qāḍī*, however, turned down that argument, too, because the claimant's father and uncles had actually benefited before their death, whereas the *waqfiyya* had stipulated that a descendant might succeed a parent only if he or she had died before obtaining benefits from the *waqf*.[73]

DISTRIBUTION OF SHARES

The sharīʿa *norm: males receive twice as much as females*

The most prevalent method of apportioning *waqf* entitlements was the accepted norm of the *sharīʿa*, that is: a male was entitled to twice the share of a female (*lil-dhakar mithl ḥaẓẓ al-unthayayn*). This is also known as the 'method of preference' (*bil-tafāḍul*). In the twentieth-century Jerusalem *sijill*, it came to be called *ḥasba al-farīḍa al-sharʿiyya* (literally: 'the *sharīʿa* share' (as specified in the *Qur'ān*)),[74] because founders used language derived from the *sharīʿa* inheritance laws. However, the well-known Ḥanafī jurist Ibn ʿĀbidīn distinguishes between the inheritance laws and the laws of *waqf* entitlement. In his view, the *waqf* was a kind of gift *inter vivos*. Unlike other jurists, he interpreted the term *al-farīḍa al-sharʿiyya* as connoting equal apportionment. He derived his views from the opinions of earlier Ḥanafī jurists, chiefly Abū Yūsuf; he also cites Shāfiʿī and Mālikī jurists who ruled likewise.[75]

About 70 per cent of the founders of family *waqf*s in Mandatory Jerusalem stipulated that the above *sharīʿa* norm be applied after their death to all series.[76] But founders often distinguished between their own children and subsequent generations: in 87 per cent of the *waqfiyyāt*, the *sharīʿa* norm is applied to the series of the founder's immediate offspring, but in only 68 per cent to subsequent generations as well.

Even when the *sharīʿa* norm was observed as between males and females of the same class degree and strength of blood-tie, it was breached with respect to orphaned grandchildren. Most *waqfiyyāt* lay down that in contradistinction to Islamic law (subsequent) descendants of a deceased parent should benefit from the parent's share together with their uncles but that the entitlement should be apportioned among beneficiaries in each series in accordance with the preference the *sharīʿa* accords males over females.[77] This method was accepted even if the entitlement passed to the 'outer' family – cognate descendants or distant relatives of the founder – or non-relatives. Even if the founder awarded exclusive entitlement either to his sons or his daughters, he still laid down that the entitlement of future generations should be apportioned between the sexes as prescribed by the *sharīʿa*. Even women founders followed the norm more often than not.[78] This is an unequivocal example of a *sharīʿa* norm becoming accepted practice for *waqf*s.[79] Alternative methods of apportionment – inconsistent with the *sharīʿa* – were also used, albeit in a minority of cases.

Equal shares for males and females

About 30 per cent of founders in our corpus laid down that entitlements should be divided equally (*bi'l-tasāwī* or *bi'l-sawwiyya*) between male and female beneficiaries, without distinction (*min ghayr tafḍīl*). Although contrary to the law, this practice can be traced back to the second century AH, when Ḥanafī jurists ruled that if a founder failed to spell out the relative entitlement of male and female beneficiaries, it was to be assumed that he had intended to distribute entitlements equally.[80] Why did Muslim jurists devise a rule for the *waqf* different from, even contrary to, laws derived directly from the *Qur'ān*? Furthermore, why did they adopt an interpretation so far removed from customary law (under which women go without any inheritance)?[81] This can be accounted for if we realize that Muslim jurists saw no connection between the distribution of *waqf* entitlements and inheritance laws. The act of dedication, they held, is performed *inter vivos* and is perceived as a gift or grant (*ʿaṭiyya*). Their interpretation sprang from a *ḥadīth* relating to gifts: 'Share out gifts equally between your children, and if anyone is to be preferred, I would prefer women.'[82] A variant version states: 'Act fairly between your children in bestowing gifts.'[83] Family endowments – being a kind of gift – cannot be viewed as a charitable act intended to do justice and kindness to the founder's relatives and descendants. Most muftis have held that when a founder states explicitly that the *waqf* revenues are to be distributed among his children 'according to the compulsory *sharīʿa* inheritance rules' (*ḥasba al-farīḍa al-sharʿiyya*), his words are still to be interpreted as signifying an equal distribution between the sexes (*fa-lā tunṣaraf al-farīḍa al-sharʿiyya fī bāb al waqf illā ilā al-taswiyya*). This is because a *waqf* is a grant made during the founder's lifetime, and the norm in bestowing gifts is equality between males and females (*al-aṣl fī al-awlād bil-taswiyya fil-ʿaṭāya ḥāl al-ḥayyāt*). The first to apply this *ḥadīth* to *waqf*s was the Ḥanafī jurist Abū Yūsuf (d. 165/798).[84]

It is likely that *sharīʿa* and customary norms give preference to males over females for fear that the latter will transfer family property to their husbands. After all, Muslim women are entitled to acquire property, to keep their money and belongings separately from those of their husbands and to bequeath their wealth to their legal heirs – a freedom they may use in favour of their husbands. But *waqf* founders are not subject to such fears, since they may stipulate that the entitlement of a female beneficiary will not go to her offspring, or that it will lapse upon her marriage. Many founders in Jerusalem made exactly such stipulations. For example, Ḥājj Khalīl al-Hidmī, who endowed his property in three successive *waqfiyyāt*, first gave instruction for equal shares for the males and females for all series, but subsequently reviewed them to read that females who married would receive an allowance of only 1,50 piasters, certainly less than the males' share.[85] Since there was no fear that *waqf* revenues would go outside the founder's agnate family, there was less reason to prefer males over females, and it seemed reasonable to give women an equal share in the entitlement. By affording them better care – in accordance with the concept of the *waqf* as a charitable act – the founder felt he was earning a reward in the afterlife. By contrast, the inheritance norm is stricter and closer to the customary one, in which the brothers exert pressure on their sisters to renounce their rights in the patrimony.[86] It appears that the prevailing *sharīʿa* practice influenced 70 per cent of the founders in our corpus to grant women only half the share of a man, even though there was no formal barrier to granting them an equal share. The two norms co-exist and are in constant tension with one another.

There is little evidence of social opposition to granting males and females equal shares in *waqf* revenues. Apparently, this is so because, ordinarily, a married woman transfers her permanent share in the patrimony to another family, whereas if a *waqf* is founded, entitlements are permanently retained in the founder's family. The *waqf* administrator (the *mutawallī*) is, after all, usually a relative of the founder. Unlike inherited estate, which becomes the heir's permanent possession, *waqf* benefits derive from revenues, usually cash from rental payments. A woman who is entitled to a share in them usually benefits during her lifetime only. Her share does not go to her offspring; therefore, granting her a share equal to that of a man does not endanger the family estate in the event that she marries outside her family. And indeed, 30 per cent of the founders applied the *inter vivos* norm of equal shares.

Some *mutawallī*s and beneficiaries expressed dissatisfaction with founders who had given women equal shares. In the Qarqash case, for example, the *waqfiyya* had been lost, and the *waqf* beneficiaries were unable to find an entry in the *sijill*. They turned to the *sharīʿa* court, disputing the distribution of entitlements between males and females of the same series. To resolve the dispute, they agreed among themselves that the revenues should be redistributed according to the inheritance laws. Next, they petitioned the court to so record the *waqf* in the *sijill*, thus turning their agreement into a binding legal document.[87] The court did so, but subsequently, Fāṭima al-Qarqash, the *mutawallī*'s sister, appealed against the decision. The Appeals Court annulled the document on the ground that when the founder's intention was not known, distribution should be equal. The *mutawallī*, ʿAbd al-Raḥmān, was displeased and sent messengers to his sister to pressure her to make do with only half her share. When he refused to give her the full share, she lodged a complaint with the *qāḍī*, who had no alternative but to dismiss him.[88] However, in our example, Fāṭima was already married and probably supported by her husband, so her brother could not invoke any practical sanctions against her.

Economic apportionment

Another method of entitlement was the distribution of property among beneficiaries (individually or by groups) in complete economic units. This might be the rent of an entire dwelling or commercial building, or the whole yield of a farm, etc. But this type of distribution applied only to the first series; for subsequent series, the founder earmarked the shares to the beneficiaries' direct descendants, following the *per stirpes* principle (see below). This could be done under the preferential or the egalitarian method. Both were meant to prevent disputes between direct beneficiaries, as indicated by the custom to also award such a beneficiary the right to administer the property in question. In endowment deeds of this type, which are not common,[89] it is generally difficult to tell whether there was discrimination for or against a given beneficiary, because we do not know the value of the assets and the revenue they were expected to yield. In order to keep the property intact, the founder sometimes drew up several endowment deeds, one each for a separate group of properties and a distinct group of beneficiaries. For example, the ailing and childless ʿUmar Būja of Jerusalem established three successive endowments, at intervals of two months. In the first, he earmarked the first-series entitlement for his brother's two daughters, in the second for his wife and his sister's son, and in the third, for his wife (6/24), his brother's two daughters (4/24 each) and two cousins (5/24 each).[90] The entitlement of future generations passed to the descendants of each group of beneficiaries separately. No redistribution between the three *waqf*s was envisaged.

In another example, one Abū Khāṭir stipulated an economic apportionment of shares between his children from two different wives and their descendants for all following generations. He did so by means of a single entitlement deed, stating that within each group, the entitlement should be apportioned in accordance with the principle of preference (see above). One son who was not counted as a beneficiary was appointed *mutawallī*. The founder laid down that, if all the agnate descendants of one group of beneficiaries died, the entitlement would be distributed among the agnate beneficiaries of the other groups, and only after they, too, had died would it go to the cognate descendants.[91]

Muḥammad al-ʿAlamī divided the beneficiaries into two entitlement groups, one of males and the other of females.[92]

The per stirpes *method*

Some founders stipulated that the entitlement of first-series beneficiaries should be apportioned and passed on among them *per stirpes*, rather than by economic units – that is, in accordance with the principle of representation. No reapportionment should occur among beneficiaries of different branches upon the extinction of a series. Yāsīn al-Dasūqī, for example, required an equal share of the entitlements from his *waqf* to go, after his and his wife's death, to their three daughters, their son and their orphaned granddaughter. Each of them should eventually pass on his or her share to future descendants within the same family branch, applying the principle of double shares for males. Each group would benefit only from its original share (*yakhtaṣṣ kull farīq bi-ḥaẓẓihi al-aṣlī*).[93] ʿUmar Būja awarded varying proportions of entitlement to his two cousins and his sister's son, and required each of them to pass on his/her share to his/her children (*yaʿūd naṣīb kull minhum li-awlādihi*).[94] In another case, two brothers, founding a joint *waqf*, apportioned the entitlement among their descendants, half to each family branch.[95] The *per stirpes* method of distribution is considered a way of dividing the endowment into smaller units, corresponding to the number of the founder's children (*ja'ala hādhā al-waqf bi-manzilat awqāfan muta'addidatan bi-'adad awlādihi al-dhukūr*).[96]

TYPES OF ENTITLEMENTS

There are two main types of entitlement to *waqf* property. The first is an entitlement to revenue accruing from it (*ghilla wa-istighlāl*); the *mutawallī* lets the property or collects user's fees for it and apportions the rent, fees or other forms of income among the beneficiaries. The second is called 'direct benefit', such as a beneficiary's right to reside in the property (this includes subletting (*sakan wa-iskān*)) or other direct use. In such a case, the sole function of the *mutawallī* is the division of the property among the beneficiaries. He is not concerned with the collection of revenue; at most, he makes sure that the property is adequately maintained.

Most family *waqf*s in Mandatory Jerusalem allowed for benefits of both types. Only in one case did the founder lay down that the benefit should be exclusively of the direct (residential) type; he apparently wished to perpetuate direct relations between his family and the beneficiaries.[97]

FAMILY *WAQFS* SERVING PUBLIC PURPOSES

Immediate purposes

An example of a family *waqf* with an immediate public purpose is that of 'Umar 'Ābidīn, who dedicated a mosque and house (*waqf mushtarak*) and required that the revenue accruing from the ground floor of the house should go to any of his or his brother's descendants who would study Islamic law at al-Azhar (Cairo's prestigious religious college), provided there were no more than two students from their family at the same time. If none of their sons showed an aptitude for such study, students should be chosen from any other branch of the 'Ābidīn family. Each student's expenses would be refunded, and in addition, he would receive £P2 per month. The remainder (if there was one) would be forwarded to one particular office-holder at al-Azhar (Shaykh Riwāq al-Shawām) for the students' use.[98]

In another case, Jāʿūnī stipulated similarly that if any of his descendants wished to study at al-Azhar or some other Islamic college, he would receive a grant of £P50 per year. If there were more than one candidate, the most suitable would be selected by the *mutawallī*.[99] These examples reflect the founders' wish to use the *waqf* for upholding the family tradition of religious studies, thereby keeping certain religious appointments in the family, as well as enhancing its prestige for posterity.[100]

ʿAlī al-Turk (al-Qayṣarī) designated his wife and two sons as equal beneficiaries of his *waqf*. But he also required £P25 to be paid annually to three public charitable institutions: the Turkish Pilots' Association, the Red Crescent and the Muslim orphanage. Five years later, the founder passed away before he had managed to register the *waqf* in the Land Registry. His two sons and the wife rushed to the *sharīʿa* court and obtained an order of succession according to the law of inheritance.[101] Using this order, they contrived a fictitious sale among themselves in such a manner that the wife received one-third of their property (as the husband had stipulated in the endowment deed, but contrary to *sharīʿa* law). They then sold the property. They took court action for two reasons: to retain the option of selling the property, contrary to the (as yet unregistered) *waqfiyya*; and, perhaps more importantly, to invalidate the requirement to make the said charitable contributions.[102]

General purposes

In the Jerusalem endowment deeds in the Mandatory period, we find that the most common public (as distinct from family) motive was assistance to individual orphans or to orphanages (18 out of 57 cases), in particular to the *dār al-aytām* – the SMC Orphanage and School.[103] The next most frequent object was *al-Ḥaram al-Sharīf* (the Temple Mount) in Jerusalem (seven cases) or one of its two houses of worship, the Dome of the Rock (four cases) and al-

Aqṣā Mosque (nine).[104] Sometimes the founder preferred a neighborhood mosque to which he felt strongly attached (one case in Jericho, two in Hebron), a mosque built by himself (one), the Maghribī *zawiyya* (one), and the Nabī Dā'ūd *zawiyya*.[105] In two cases, after all members of the family had died, the entitlement was transferred to local indigents in the founder's place of residence. Sometimes two public institutions were specified before allowance was made for general purposes. The first was usually a specific one to which the founder was personally attached; the second was *al-Ḥaram al-Sharīf* or one of its two places of worship (nine).[106]

In charity *waqf*s for the poor, too, the founders laid down a scale of priorities. First came the poor within a certain specified group, for example, indigent *'ulamā'* or the poor from the Maghrib. Then came the Muslim poor in the founder's town: in Jerusalem, if the founder lived there, or of some other city, if he came from there but made the dedication in Jerusalem. After these, the Muslim poor of Palestine as a whole were sometimes specified, followed by the Muslim poor in some other region, and finally the poor in general. This lengthy list proceeds from the specific to the general; it was meant to keep the entitlement, to the extent possible, in the immediate vicinity of the founder.

The most conspicuous public endowment in Mandatory Jerusalem was (as already mentioned before) the *waqf* dedicated by Amīna al-Khālidī for the establishment of a hospital for indigent Muslims. There was a definite need for such an institution. Muslims envied the various Christian denominations their community hospital; that was why the Supreme Muslim Council itself set up a clinic in Jerusalem.[107] Amīna al-Khālidī had inherited vast properties from her parents, brothers and sister; she herself was childless. She decided to pledge her entire estate to the hospital, provided it would bear her name. She also required it to have a mosque for funeral services. A three-member committee, appointed by her, was to administer the endowment: two doctors (one from the Khālidī family, the other from the Dajānī family) and another member of the Khālidī family.[108] The administrators failed to realize the project for reasons not clear to the author. She also allocated annual sums for additional religious charitable purposes and stipulated that if she were to die before performing the *ḥajj*, the *mutawallī* was to set aside a sum of money for someone else to do so in her stead.

The endowment of Ḥājj Amīn al-Ḥusaynī, based on the aforementioned donation by Zakariyya al-Daghāstānī, was intended for the education of orphans and for religious instruction in general.[109] The founder himself was an orphan who had been schooled in an orphanage in Turkey, for which he set aside a separate donation.

It was also Ḥājj Amīn who convinced Prince Ḥaydarābād of India to make the above-mentioned donation for the establishment of an Islamic university in Jerusalem. It will be remembered that the donation was used for the purchase of land in the Tūlkarm area, which in turn was dedicated, under Ḥājj Amīn's auspices, as a *waqf* and its revenues pledged to the future university.[110] The donation was apparently made in the form of a *waqf* because both the founder and the recipient were interested in making sure that the university project be managed by the SMC. This is reminiscent of another modern *waqf* project, the Ḥijāzī railway, the administration of which was entrusted to the Ottoman Waqf Ministry in order to ensure Muslim management.[111]

SUMMARY

The patterns of *waqf* entitlement in Mandatory Jerusalem, as compared to Islamic inheritance law, show that 82 per cent of family *waqf*s excluded cognate descendants from enjoying usufructory rights. Although the desire to keep family property from passing to outsiders encouraged proprietors to have recourse to the *waqf*, the same end was more commonly achieved by other means grounded in custom.[112]

Only 30 per cent of founders granted males and females equal shares, as was the Islamic norm for gifts *inter vivos*. The rest gave females half the share of males in the same category of beneficiaries.

The main contradiction between family *waqf* patterns and Islamic law had to do with the right of orphans to obtain benefits through a special quasi-representation method. Layish wrote: 'The *waqf* mechanism makes it possible to bypass a social wrong anchored in the *sharī'a* which modern legislation has tried to amend in part via the device of the obligatory bequest.'[113] Powers, for his part, stressed the desire of *waqf* founders to establish a broader, lineal descent group. Both argued that their findings reflect the motivation of family *waqf* founders. The present study gives us an opportunity to raise that question once again. Did the family *waqf* reflect social dissatisfaction with the inheritance law? Or was circumventing the inheritance law a byproduct of other intentions, such as perpetuating the founder's name? It appears that many considerations combined in creating a family *waqf*. More case studies are needed in order to arrive at definite conclusions.

NOTES

1. D.S. Powers, 'The Islamic Inheritance System: A Socio Historical Approach', in Ch. Mallat and J. Connors (eds), *Islamic Family Law* (London/Dordrecht/Boston, 1990) pp. 11–29.
2. A. Layish, 'The Family *Waqf* and the *Shar'ī* Law of Succession,' in G. Baer and G. Gilbar (eds), *Studies on the Muslim Waqf* (Oxford: Oxford University Press) (forthcoming) p. 44.
3. D.S. Powers, 'The Islamic Inheritance System: A Socio Historical Approach', in Ch. Mallat and J. Connors (eds), *Islamic Family Law* (London/Dordrecht/Boston, 1990) p. 22.
4. D.S. Powers, 'The Mālikī Family Endowment: Legal Norms and Social Practices', *International Journal of Middle Eastern Studies*, 25 (1993) p. 401.
5. Approximately 2,000 *Waqfs* (including hundreds of Jewish and Christian endowments registered as *Waqfs*) in 480 years.
6. A. Layish, *Women and Islamic Law in a Non-Muslim State* (Jerusalem and New York: Israel Universities Press and John Wiley, 1975) pp. 290–2; idem, 'The Family *Waqf* and the *Shar'ī* Law of Succession', in G. Baer and G. Gilbar (eds), *Studies on the Muslim Waqf* (Oxford: Oxford University Press) (forthcoming) p. 42.
7. For a brief version of my arguments and findings with regard to the founder's motivation see Y. Reiter, 'Family *Waqf* Entitlements in British Palestine (1917–1948)', *Islamic Law and Society*, 2, 2 (1995) pp. 174–93.
8. For case studies, see G. Baer, *A History of Land Ownership in Modern Egypt: 1800–1950* (London: Oxford University Press, 1962) p. 165; O.L. Barkan and E.H. Ayverdi, *Istanbul Vakiflari Tahrir Defteri 953 (1546)* (Istanbul, 1970).; H. Gerber, *Economy and Society in an Ottoman*

City: Bursa 1600–1700 (Jerusalem: Magnes Press, 1988) p. 150ff.; H. Gerber, 'The *Waqf* Institution in Early Ottoman Edirne', *Asian and African Studies*, 17 (1983) pp. 29–45; R.C. Jennings, 'The Development of *Evkaf* in a New Ottoman Province: Cyprus, 1571–1640' in G. Baer and G. Gilbar (eds), *Studies on the Muslim Waqf* (Oxford: Oxford University Press) (forthcoming); G.C. Kozlowski, *Muslim Endowments and Society in British India* (Cambridge: Cambridge University Press, 1985); A. Marcus, 'Piety and Profit: The *Waqf* in the Society and Economy in Eighteenth Century Aleppo', in G. Baer and G. Gilbar (eds), *Studies on the Muslim Waqf* (Oxford: Oxford University Press) (forthcoming); R. Roded, 'The *Waqf* in Ottoman Aleppo', in G. Baer and G. Gilbar (eds), *Studies on the Muslim Waqf* (Oxford: Oxford University Press) (forthcoming). For general descriptions of the *waqf*, see W. Heffening, '*Waqf*', *The Encyclopaedia of Islam* (1st ed.) 4, pp. 1096–1103; R.J. Barnes, *An Introduction to Religious Foundations in the Ottoman Empire* (Leiden: E.J. Brill, 1987); E. Mercier, *Le code du habous ou ouakf selon la legislation musulmanne* (Constantine, 1899). For the *Waqf* laws, see D. Pearl, *A Textbook on Muslim Law* (London, 1979); O. Pesle, 'La theorie et la pratique des habous dans le rite malekite' (Casablanca, n.d.); R.C. Tute, *The Ottoman Land Code* (Jerusalem, 1927). J.N.D. Anderson,'Recent Developments in *Sharī'a* Law: The *Waqf* System', *The Muslim World*, XLII (1952) p. 257; E.Clavel, *Droit Musulman, Le wakf ou Habous* (2 vols, Cairo, Impr. Diemer, 1896); O. Hilmi, *A Treatise on the Laws of Evkaf* (trans. C.R. Tyser and D.G. Demetriades, Nicosia, 1899).

9. N.J. Coulson, *Succession in the Muslim Family* (Cambridge: Cambridge University Press, 1971) p. 41; A. al-Ḥuṣarī, *al-Tarikāt wal-Wiṣāya fī al-Fiqh al-Islāmī* (Amman, 1972) p. 320.
10. A. Layish, 'The Family *Waqf* and the *Shar'ī* Law of Succession', in G. Baer and G. Gilbar (eds), *Studies on the Muslim Waqf* (Oxford: Oxford University Press) (forthcoming) p. 6.
11. Nos. 9, 24 in Table 3.3.
12. *Sijill* 423/87/32 (vol. 423, p. 87, no. 32), 423/133/38, 441/31/41, 475/8/13, 454/19/109, 478/175/68.
13. *Sijill* 486/96/481, 423/133/38.
14. *Sijill* 467/99/47, 477/36/190, 479/104/265, 505/5/564, 427/174/173.
15. *Sijill* 427/174/173.
16. *Sijill* 467/99/47.
17. *Sijill* 479/104/265.
18. *Sijill* 455/6/296.
19. *Sijill* 446/100/49.
20. *Sijill* 439/122/107.
21. *Sijill* 427/132/136, 467/99/47.
22. G. Baer, *A History of Land Ownership in Modern Egypt: 1800–1950* (London: Oxford University Press, 1962) p. 166.
23. A. Layish, 'The Family *Waqf* and the *Shar'ī* Law of Succession', in G. Baer and G. Gilbar (eds), *Studies on the Muslim Waqf* (Oxford: Oxford University Press) (forthcoming) p. 6.
24. For example: *Sijill* 454/19/109.
25. *Sijill* 427/132/146, 423/133/38, 427/147/148, 462/36/4, 455/6/296,

421/74/21), 427/132/136.

26. *Sijill* 438/251/109.
27. G. Baer, *A History of Land Ownership in Modern Egypt: 1800–1950* (London: Oxford University Press, 1962) p. 166.
28. G.C. Kozlowski, *Muslim Endowments and Society in British India* (Cambridge: Cambridge University Press, 1985) p. 56.
29. *Sijill* 557/177/139; cf. A. Layish, 'The Family *Waqf* and the *Shar'ī* Law of Succession', in G. Baer and G. Gilbar (eds), *Studies on the Muslim Waqf* (Oxford: Oxford University Press) (forthcoming) pp. 19–21.
30. G.C. Kozlowski, *Muslim Endowments and Society in British India* (Cambridge: Cambridge University Press, 1985) p. 56.
31. *Sijill* 478/175/68.
32. *Sijill* 422/260/334, 427/86/17.
33. *Sijill* 423/87/3.
34. *Sijill* 475/8/13.
35. *Sijill* 441/31/41.
36. *Sijill* 423/133/38.
37. *Sijill* 461/26/40, 486/96/481.
38. *Sijill* 460/86/120, 466/134//59, 489/63/166, 483/200/164, 399/124/278.
39. *Sijill* 446/107/56.
40. *Sijill* 470/145/11, 427/245/245, 467/98/46, 474/133/212, 482/7/46, 427/141/142, 484/32/340, 490/10/16.
41. *Sijill* 423/87/3, 433/123/77, 446/60/11, 467/76/19, 504/90/551, 427/141/142.
42. *Sijill* 427/141/142.
43. *Sijill* 470/145/11, 484/32/340, 490/10/16.
44. *Sijill* 416/119/184, 454/1/81, 461/26/40.
45. *Sijill* 427/132/136.
46. Cf. A. Layish, 'The Family *Waqf* and the *Shar'ī* Law of Succession', in G. Baer and G. Gilbar (eds), *Studies on the Muslim Waqf* (Oxford: Oxford University Press) (forthcoming) p. 41; idem., 'The Mālikī Family *Waqf* according to Wills and *Waqfiyyāt*', *Bulletin of the School of Oriental and African Studies*, 46 (1983) pp. 1–32; G. Baer, *A History of Land Ownership in Modern Egypt: 1800–1950* (London: Oxford University Press, 1962) p. 168; D.S. Powers, 'The Mālikī Family Endowment: Legal Norms and Social Practices', *International Journal of Middle Eastern Studies*, 25 (1993) p. 389 ff.
47. See, for example, the *Waqfiyya* of Ḥājj 'Abd al-Wahhāb 'Abdallāh Shakīmakī: *wa-laysa li-wuld al- unthā fī hādhā al-waqf ḥaqq mā dāma mawjūdan wāḥidun min awlād al-ẓuhūr illā in kāna abūhu min ahl al-waqf wa-law kāna abūhu ḥayyan.*
48. N.J. Coulson, *Succession in the Muslim Family* (Cambridge: Cambridge University Press, 1971) p. 91; A. Fyzee, *Outline of Muhammadan Law* (London: Oxford University Press, 1964) p. 441.
49. *Qur'an* 4:8; see S.D. Goitein and A. Ben Shemesh, *Muslim Law in the State of Israel* (Hebrew, Jerusalem, 1957) p. 144.
50. J.N.D. Anderson, 'Recent Developments in *Sharī'a* Law: The *Waqf* System', *The Muslim World*, 42 (1952) pp. 45–7; N.J. Coulson, *A History of Islamic Law* (Edinburgh: University Press , 1964) pp. 203–206.

51. *Sijill* 446/107/56.
52. *Sijill* 432/464/228.
53. 'A. 'Ashūb, *Kitāb al-Waqf* (n.p., 1935) pp. 194–5; M. Abū Zahra, *Muḥāḍarāt fi al-Waqf* (2nd ed., Cairo: Dār al Fikr al-'Arabī, 1971) p. 283; M.A. al-'Umar, *al-Dalīl li-Iṣlāḥ al-Awqāf* (Baghdad, 1948) p. 54.
54. Ibid. This differs from the Mālikī case described and interpreted by D.S. Powers, '*Fatwās* as a Source of Legal and Social History: A Dispute over Endowment Revenues from Fourteenth-Century Fez', *al-Qanṭara*, 11,2 (1990) pp. 320, 340.
55. D.S. Powers, 'The Mālikī Family Endowment: Legal Norms and Social Practices', *International Journal of Middle Eastern Studies*, 25 (1993) p. 383; idem., '*Fatwās* as a Source of Legal and Social History: A Dispute over Endowment Revenues from Fourteenth-Century Fez', *al-Qanṭara*, 11,2 (1990) pp. 320.
56. *'Alā an 'inda inqirāḍ kull ṭabaqa min al-ṭabaqāt al mutaqaddimat al-dhikr yuqsam ray' hādhā al-waqf bil-tasāwī bayna ahl al-ṭabaqa allatī talīhā al-aḥyā' wal-amwāt idhā kāna lahum awlād wa-awlād awlād dhukūr wa-in safalū wa-mā aṣāba al-aḥyā' akhadhūhu bi-anfusihim wa-mā aṣāba al-amwāt fa-li-awlādihim wa-in safalū . . . la yushārik al-abnā' al-ābā' fi al-istiḥqāq bal al-aṣl yaḥjabu far'uhu faqaṭ* . . . ; *Sijill* 427/86/17. Some founders, after stipulating that a child may step into the shoes of his/her deceased parent and claim his/her share of the patrimony, specify that upon the termination of each series, the benefits are to be reapportioned among living and dead members of the succeeding series on a per capita basis (*'ala 'adad ru'ūsihim*). In two instances, the expression *'alā 'adad ru'ūsihim* is immediately followed by the expression 'the males [receive] double the portion that the females receive' (*li'l-dhakar mithl ḥaẓẓ al-unthayayn*). Therefore, the expression *'ala 'adad ru'ūsihim* should not be construed in the sense of full equality among all beneficiaries, male and female. Instead, it should be understood in the sense of 'per number of eligibles', i.e., a reapportionment according to number of beneficiaries in the succeeding series. *Sijill* 484/32/340, 436/45/52. See, for example, *Sijill* 436/45/52: *Yuqsam hādhā al-waqf fi jamī' al-ṭabaqāt 'ala 'adad ru'ūsihim al-aḥyā' wa'l-amwāt al-dhukūr al-mutawafin . . . li'l dhakar mithl ḥaẓẓ al-unthayayn fa-man kāna ḥayyan akhadha naṣībahu wa-man kāna mayyitan 'āda naṣībuhu li-wuldihi*. See also the entitlement distribution *'ala 'adad al-ru'ūs*, in which each beneficiary is entitled to a different share, in *Sijill* 444/43/121. Cf. A. Layish 'The Mālikī Family *Waqf* according to Wills and *Waqfiyyāt*', *Bulletin of the School of Oriental and African Studies*, 46 (1983) pp. 23–4.
57. M. Abū Zahra, *Muḥāḍarāt fi al-Waqf* (2nd ed., Cairo: Dār al Fikr al-'Arabī, 1971) pp. 283–4.
58. Ibid.
59. *Sijill* 444/51/28.
60. *Sijill* 483/175/119; M. Abū Zahra, *Muḥāḍarāt fi al-Waqf* (2nd ed., Cairo: Dār al Fikr al-'Arabī, 1971) p. 293; 'A. 'Ashūb, *Kitāb al-Waqf* (n.p., 1935) pp. 196, gives the proper term for a series of beneficiaries: *martaba*. The term *tartīb* is used in the *waqfiyyāt* for regulation of entitlement between generations. The terms *ṭabaqa* and *daraja* have other meanings in

inheritance law. Therefore, ʿAshūb names those orphaned from lower series: *al-martaba al-Jaʿaliyya*. Cf. Aḥmad Jamāl al-Dīn, *Al-Waqf Muṣṭalaḥātihi wa-Qawāʿidihi* (Baghdad: Maṭbaʿat al-Rābiṭa, 1955): *ṭabaqa = martaba min marātib al-mustaḥiqqīn*.

61. *Sijill* 460/160/194.
62. On *tanzīl*, see N.J. Coulson, *Succession in the Muslim Family* (Cambridge: Cambridge University Press, 1971) p. 91.
63. *Sijill* 452/187/23. Ḥājj Muḥammad-Amīn al-Ḥusaynī – president of the SMC – and ʿAbd al-Qādir Mūsā Kāẓim al-Ḥusaynī are included among the fifth series of beneficiaries.
64. *Wa-man māta minhum qabla istiḥqāqihi bi-shay'in min manāfiʿ al-waqf wa-taraka waladan . . . akhadha mā kāna yastaḥiqquhu aṣluhu in law kāna ḥayyan. Sijill* 437/78/90. See D.S. Powers, '*Fatwās* as a Source of Legal and Social History: A Dispute over Endowment Revenues from Fourteenth-Century Fez', *al-Qanṭara*, 11,2 (1990) p. 313.
65. Quoted by the *qāḍī* in *Sijill* 509/146/514. In some cases the *qāḍī* interprets the founder's stipulations as his desire to grant entitlement to as many descendants as possible, *Sijill* 478/210/136. See an interesting case in D.S. Powers, 'The Mālikī Family Endowment: Legal Norms and Social Practices', *International Journal of Middle Eastern Studies*, 25 (1993) p. 400.
66. This endowment was merely a portion of al-Ḥusaynī's considerable assets. See *Sijill* 241/112.
67. For example: *Sijill* 504/90/551.
68. *Sijill* 422/260/364.
69. *Sijill* 454/1/81, 461/26/40, 470/145/11, 477/36/190, 505/5/642.
70. *Sijill* 416/119/184, 504/90/551; 467/76/19; 467/53448; 479/104/265; 484/32/340, 486/96/482, 490/2635; 504/90/551.
71. ʿA. ʿAshūb, *Kitāb al-Waqf* (n.p., 1935) p. 200.
72. *Sijill* 456/151/137.
73. *Sijill* 483/175/119.
74. Cf. A. Layish, 'The Family *Waqf* and the *Sharʿī* Law of Succession,' in G. Baer and G. Gilbar (eds), *Studies on the Muslim Waqf* (Oxford: Oxford University Press) (forthcoming) p. 34.
75. M.A. Ibn ʿĀbidīn, *Khāshiyyat al-Durr al-Mukhtār* (2nd ed., Cairo, 1386/1966), p. 444.
76. A. Layish, 'The Family *Waqf* and the *Sharʿī* Law of Succession', in G. Baer and G. Gilbar (eds), *Studies on the Muslim Waqf* (Oxford: Oxford University Press) (forthcoming) p. 74.
77. Ibid.
78. For example: *Sijill* 484/32/340.
79. A. Layish, 'The Family *Waqf* and the *Sharʿī* Law of Succession', in G. Baer and G. Gilbar (eds), *Studies on the Muslim Waqf* (Oxford: Oxford University Press) (forthcoming) p. 34.
80. al-Khaṣṣāf, *Kitāb Aḥkām al-Awqāf* (Cairo: Diwān ʿUmūm al-Awqāf al-Miṣriyya, 1902) p. 9. Cf. D.S. Powers, 'The Mālikī Family Endowment: Legal Norms and Social Practices', *International Journal of Middle Eastern Studies*, 25 (1993) pp. 386.
81. *Qur'an* 4:12.

82. *Sāwwū bayna awlādikum fi-'l-'aṭiyya wa-law kuntu mu'aththiran aḥadan la'āththartu al-nisā' 'alā al-rijāl*. Quoted by M.A. Ibn 'Ābidīn, *Khāshiyyat al-Durr al-Mukhtār* (2nd ed., Cairo, 1386/1966), 444.
83. *Wa-idhā a'ṭā ba'ḍ wuldihi shay'an lam yajuz ḥatta ya'dila baynahum wa-ya'ṭī al-ākharīn mithlahu wa-lā yashhad 'alayhi wa-qāla al-nabī ṣalla allāh 'alayhi wa-sallam i'dalū bayna awlādikum fi'l 'aṭiyya*. 'A. 'Ashūb, *Kitāb al-Waqf* (n.p. 1935) pp. 188.
84. See M.A. Ibn 'Ābidīn, *Khāshiyyat al-Durr al-Mukhtār* (2nd ed., Cairo, 1386/1966) p. 444; 'A. 'Ashūb, *Kitāb al-Waqf* (n.p., 1935) p. 188.
85. *Sijill* 427/A132/A136.
86. A. Layish, *Women and Islamic Law in a Non-Muslim State* (Jerusalem and New York: Israel Universities Press and John Wiley, 1975) pp. 290–2; idem, 'The Family *Waqf* and the *Shar'ī* Law of Succession', in G. Baer and G. Gilbar (eds), *Studies on the Muslim Waqf* (Oxford: Oxford University Press) (forthcoming) p. 42.
87. *Sijill* 441/88/124.
88. *Sijill* 441/88/124, 452/329/183.
89. For examples see A. Layish, 'The Family *Waqf* and the *Shar'ī* Law of Succession', in G. Baer and G. Gilbar (eds), *Studies on the Muslim Waqf* (Oxford: Oxford University Press) (forthcoming) p. 38.
90. *Sijill* 433/123/77, 430/268/262, 433/131/82.
91. *Sijill* 467/53/448, 474/15/23.
92. *Sijill* 446/107/56.
93. *Sijill* 507/78/241.
94. *Sijill* 433/131/82.
95. *Sijill* 504/90/551.
96. *Sijill* 423/57/10.
97. Nos. 36–37 in Table 3.1.
98. *Sijill* 482/7/46.
99. *Sijill* 505/5/642.
100. G. Baer, 'The *Waqf* as a Prop for the Social System (16th–20th Centuries)', in G. Baer and G. Gilbar (eds), *Studies on the Muslim Waqf* (Oxford: Oxford University Press) (forthcoming).
101. *Sijill* 205/129/31.
102. *Sijill* 478/298/279.
103. One *Waqfiyya* included also the new orphans' school in Dayr Abū 'Amrū.
104. Other public purposes were: *Madrasat al-Aqṣā, madrasas*, religious students in Jerusalem, *Qur'ān* citers in Jerusalem and *al-Ḥaramayn al-Sharifayn*.
105. *Sijill* 422/260/364.
106. Some founders designated two institutions close to them.
107. U.M. Kupferschmidt, *The Supreme Muslim Council: Islam under the British Mandate for Palestine* (Leiden: E.J. Brill, 1987) p. 144. However, establishing hospitals was a purpose of *Waqfs* in the Middle Ages – see, as an example from 13th-century Central Asia, M. Khadr, 'Deux actes de *Waqf* d'un Qarahanide d'Asie central', *Journal Asiatique*, 215 (1967), p. 314.
108. *Sijill* 476/110/18, 476/89/8.
109. *Sijill* 475/25/42.

110. *Sijill* 467/142/109. On the attempts to establish an Islamic University see U.M. Kupferschmidt, *The Supreme Muslim Council: Islam under the British Mandate for Palestine* (Leiden: E.J. Brill, 1987) p. 207ff.
111. W.L. Ochsenwald, 'A Modern *Waqf*: The Hijaz Railway 1900–1948', *Arabian Studies*, 3 (1976), pp. 1–12.
112. G. Baer, *Population and Society in the Arab East* (London: Routledge and Kegan Paul, 1964) p. 39 and the sources mentioned there; A. Layish, *Women and Islamic Law in a Non-Muslim State* (Jerusalem and New York: Israel Universities Press and John Wiley, 1975) p. 290.
113. A. Layish, 'The Family *Waqf* and the *Shar'ī* Law of Succession', in G. Baer and G. Gilbar (eds), *Studies on the Muslim Waqf* (Oxford: Oxford University Press) (forthcoming) p. 42.

Part 3

5

The appointment of *mutawallīs*

When the *mutawallī* (administrator or executive director) of al-Ṣalāḥī Waqf in Jaffa died in 1933, a serious dispute broke out among his seven sons (its sole beneficiaries) over who was to succeed him. The oldest, Mūsā, claimed the post by virtue of primogeniture. Only two of his brothers backed him and, at his request, petitioned the *qāḍī* on his behalf. The other five feared that their entitlements would be adversely affected if Mūsā took over, and favoured the candidacy of one of their own number, Muḥammad. They, too, petitioned the *qāḍī*, who had thus to decide between Mūsā and Muḥammad. He submitted them to a ten-question test on the rules of *waqf* administration; both passed. Mūsā, however, was illiterate and had to be examined orally. Muḥammad's three backers told the *qāḍī* that they were prepared to deposit a financial guarantee, to be forfeited in case Muḥammad abused *waqf* funds. The *qāḍī* approved the proposal, backed as it was by a majority of the beneficiaries, and the appointments committee (see below) acted accordingly. The loser, Mūsā, then accused Muḥammad's supporters of having a personal monetary stake in the appointment; this, he stated, explained their offer of a guarantee.

This incident in Jaffa (no such dispute in Jerusalem is documented in similar detail) demonstrates the importance of the office of *mutawallī* for the fate of a *waqf*. The *mutawallī* has broad powers and is subject to no more than lax supervision (see Chapter 8). If he possesses administrative ability and economic vision, he can develop the *waqf*'s assets, increase the revenues, and secure its future. An inept or corrupt *mutawallī* may ruin the property and destroy the endowment. His broad discretionary powers allow him to prefer certain beneficiaries and to enjoy extra benefits himself, beyond his officially recognized status. Beneficiaries, therefore, often hasten to succeed a *mutawallī* who has died, resigned or been dismissed by the *qāḍī*. This is particularly evident in family endowments with considerable assets and revenues. The *qāḍī* used to have much latitude in the choice of *mutawallī*s, but in 1913 the Ottoman government revoked his exclusive power to appoint *mutawallī*s and, through that year's Ottoman Appointments Law, laid down procedures intended to ensure the appointment of capable candidates.

APPOINTMENT OF *MUTAWALLĪ*S UNDER *SHARĪʿA* AND CIVIL LAW

The Appointments Law, an Act of civil legislation, required candidates for any *waqf*-related position, including the *mutawallī*, to pass a test devised by an appointments committee. The latter was headed by a *qāḍī* or mufti, and the test had to be taken in the presence of the *ma'mūr al-awqāf* and of three *ʿulamā'*. Although the *qāḍī* sometimes chaired the committee, the new rules curtailed the previously exclusive rights which the *sharīʿa* had given him. Under *sharīʿa* law, the founder was entitled to list present and future *mutawallī*s in the endowment deed. Founders could appoint specific people to administer the *waqf* personally or *ex officio*, or set criteria for the future appointment of *mutawallī*s by the *qāḍī*. He might, for example, lay down that the eldest child should succeed the incumbent.[1] In such cases, the position of *mutawallī* was transferred directly to the person designated by the founder, and there was no need for a letter of appointment.[2]

The *sharīʿa* stipulates that a *mutawallī*, even if he is the founder himself, must meet four criteria: he must be legally a major (*bāligh*), intelligent (*ʿāqil*), reliable and trustworthy (*amīn*) and administratively competent (*qādir ʿalā al-qiyām bi-umūr al-waqf*). Women, the blind, slaves and non-Muslims may all serve as *mutawallī*s.[3]

Jurists of the Shāfiʿī school of law held that a *mutawallī* must not only have capability (*kifāya*) but also have an honourable religious record (*ʿadāla*) and innocent even of minor wrongdoing (*fisq*). Ḥanafī jurists consider these qualities desirable but not a *sine qua non*. According to Abū Zahra, a contemporary Egyptian *ʿālim*, it is hard to find anyone who not only observes all religious commands but is also an expert in finance and administration, and unlikely to succumb to corruption. Therefore, he settles for *mutawallīs* who are reliable and trustworthy in the care of money and property.[4]

Jurists disagree about the considerations that should guide the *qāḍī* in appointing *mutawallīs*. Most recommend, but do not require, that the *qāḍī* should give preference to a family member or descendant of the founder over a non-relative.[5] Mālikī and Shāfiʿī jurists, who believe that abstract ownership of the *waqf* reverts to the beneficiaries, also assert that in cases where the founder has not made a choice, the beneficiaries should choose the *mutawallī*.[6] According to another opinion, the administration of a family *waqf* should be entrusted to one of the beneficiaries, since a beneficiary's very interest in the *waqf* rules out embezzlement. Abū Zahra criticized this opinion, asserting that the beneficiaries were likely to harm the *waqf* because their interest was to seek an immediate maximum profit rather than the long-term maintenance and preservation of the property.[7] Jurists had a rule of thumb: anyone seeking the appointment should not be made *mutawallī*, since he presumably had a vested interest and might not resist the temptation of preferring his particular interests over those of the *waqf* and the other beneficiaries.[8]

One of the issues in the appointment of *mutawallīs* in family *waqfs* was how to interpret the founders' request that the *mutawallī* be 'the most capable of the beneficiaries' (*al-arshad fal-arshad* or, for short, *al-arshad*; the superlative of *rashīd*). Ordinarily, the term '*rashīd*' has a religious connotation and means 'upright'. In *waqf* affairs, it tends to denote economic and administrative proficiency, as defined by the Egyptian author of the collection of Ḥanafī *waqf* laws of the end of the nineteenth century, *Qadrī Pāshā*: 'The meaning of *rushd* here is the sound administration of money or property' (*wal-murād bil-rushd hunā ḥusn al-taṣarruf bil-māl*).[9] Shaykh Asʿad al-Imām, a contemporary

Jerusalem *'ālim*, also defines *arshad* as 'a good administrator who acts honestly'.[10] Assume that a founder has two children who are both suitable; one is more God-fearing, the other a better and more trustworthy administrator. Then, al-Imām holds, the second should be appointed.[11] If both are equally capable, some believe the appointment should go to the elder,[12] while others insist that they should be appointed jointly (with no gender distinction made).[13]

Under the *sharī'a* laws pertaining to the *waqf*, if a founder failed to name his successor as *mutawallī*, or to stipulate that the position should go to the 'most capable' (*arshad*) of the beneficiaries (or his offspring), the *qāḍī* alone is authorized to make the appointment. Only he is to select the most competent and suitable of the beneficiaries.[14] The Ottoman Law of Appointments established a statutory committee (*lajnat tawjīh al-jihāt*) to verify the candidates' suitability. This created some tension between two authorities: the appointments committee, an administrative authority that determined suitability, and the *sharī'a* court, which watched over the observance of the founder's wish to apply the principle of *al-arshad*. Theoretically, the appointments committee might deem a certain candidate suitable on the basis of the test, while the *qāḍī* might turn him down because of the presence of more competent beneficiaries. Nevertheless, civil law enjoined the *qāḍī* not to appoint a *mutawallī* who had failed the committee's test. *Arshad* was determined in the presence of the *qāḍī* following *sharī'a* procedure, requiring testimony by witnesses that the candidate was indeed the most competent of all beneficiaries.[15]

FOUNDERS' ARRANGEMENTS FOR THE ADMINISTRATION OF FAMILY *WAQFS*

In all Jerusalem endowments established during the Mandate period in which the founder designated himself as beneficiary during his lifetime, he also appointed himself as the *mutawallī*. In cases where he designated other beneficiaries, he required the immediate beneficiary to act as *mutawallī*.[16] Where he named his wife as the next beneficiary, he also appointed her as *mutawallī*.[17]

In most *waqfiyyāt*, the founder named one or several of his children to take over the *waqf* administration at the time the entitlement would pass to the first series of beneficiaries.[18] (On the composition of series, see Chapter 4.) On almost all deeds, the founder laid down that future *mutawallī*s (after the death of the first-series beneficiaries) should be the *arshad al-mustaḥiqqīn*, the most competent of the actual beneficiaries within each series. In two exceptional cases, the founder stipulated that the *mutawallī* should be the *arshad al-mawqūf ʿalayhim*, the most suitable from among the broader circle of beneficiaries of all series – including those whose share in the entitlements was deferred to some later stage.[19]

Some founders did not make do with the characteristic of *arshad*, regarding this as a merely administrative attribute; they required the *mutawallī* also to excel in the quality of *ṣalāḥ* – to be the most God-fearing of their relatives.[20] One founder stipulated that if more than one person were qualified as *arshad*, the more reliable (*amāna*) of the two should be appointed.[21] Another founder stated that the *tawliyya* (the appointment to the position of *mutawallī*) should accrue to a beneficiary chosen by the others through consent (*li-man yastaḥiqq fī hādhā al-waqf wa-yutafaq ʿalā tawliyyatihi*). If the beneficiaries could not reach agreement, the eldest beneficiary should be appointed, provided he was qualified. He also banned the appointment of non-relatives as long as one of his own descendants was alive, and insisted that the *tawliyya* should on no account be transferred to the *mudīr al-awqāf*. If the entitlement later came to be transferred to the poor, the *qāḍī* would appoint the person whom most inhabitants of the founder's town (Nablus) considered competent.[22] Most founders preferred to designate *mutawallī*s in later series, by specifying beneficiaries whom them knew, such as their children. This was meant to prevent disputes over the appointment, and place the job in the most suitable hands.

Most founders of family *waqf*s preferred to appoint one administrator only. Yūsuf Ḥabrumān, for example, while stipulating that his two sons should jointly administer the *waqf* after his death in order to prevent discrimination and contention between them, required that in the subsequent series, only a single *mutawallī*, the most competent of his descendants, should administer the *waqf*.[23]

A review of the *sijill* of the late Ottoman period shows that *waqf* founders during the Mandate era perpetuated Ottoman appointment patterns.

PROCEDURES FOR THE APPOINTMENT OF *MUTAWALLIS*

The practices of *waqf* administration have not yet been researched.[24] There are no studies to tell us who managed the non-*maḍbūṭ waqfs*, by what criteria they were appointed in practice and who determined their candidacy. In the Mandatory period, the Jerusalem *sharīʿa* court appointed 214 administrators for local non-*maḍbūṭ waqfs*. They proceeded in three stages:

1. nomination by means of petition on the part of the beneficiaries;
2. review of the candidates by the appointments committee;
3. verification by the *qāḍī* of the extent to which the candidate met the founder's condition for him to be *arshad*.

Petition by beneficiaries

When a *mutawallī*'s position fell vacant, a petition for a new appointment was submitted to the *qāḍī*. In the case of a public *waqf*, it was signed by local *mukhtārs* and notables in the candidate's neighborhood; in the case of a family *waqf*, the beneficiaries, too, signed it. The Shāfiʿī and Mālikī view, according to which the beneficiaries may name the *mutawallī* where the founder failed to do so in the endowment deed, was also accepted by the Ḥanafī school. This practice was a consequence of the rule against candidates who came forward themselves. Yet, in most cases, candidates named in the petition had actually taken the initiative themselves. The requirement for the beneficiaries of a family *waqf* to sign the petition shows that they had a great deal to say in the matter. There is clear evidence in the *sijill* that the *qāḍī* would not appoint a *mutawallī* unacceptable to the beneficiaries. Two female beneficiaries in the Tahbūb Waqf, for example, demanded the dismissal of the *mutawallī*, claiming, *inter alia*, that he had been appointed illegally without being **selected** with the consent of a **majority** of beneficiaries (*lā yuqām 'alayhi mutawallin illā bi-intikhāb wa-muwāfaqat aghlab al-mustaḥiqqīn ḥālan wa-ma'ālan*). The *qāḍī* rejected this argument and also pointed out that the claim had been improperly submitted. In this fashion, he signalled that the beneficiaries had an alternative: to present a candidate more suitable than the incumbent (see below under 'Determining the *arshad*').[25] A similar view was implied in statements by beneficiaries to the effect that they 'chose' (*intakhabū*) the *mutawallī* or proposed his candidacy (*miman yurashshiḥuhu al-mustaḥiqqūn*).[26]

The practice of the 'election' of *mutawallīs* by the beneficiary had already existed in the Ottoman period. For example, in appointing the *mutawallī* of the Shihāb al-Dīn Aḥmad al-Yamānulī Waqf in 1897, the beneficiaries came before the *qāḍī* and announced: 'Now we have elected one of our own' (*wa-innā al-ān qad intakhabnā aḥadinā*).[27]

Scrutiny of the wording of the petitions (as subsequently summarized by the *qāḍī* in his letters of appointment) shows that in each case, only some of the beneficiaries – almost certainly the minority – had signed. Only 22 per cent of the letters of appointment stated that the candidate had been proposed by a majority of the beneficiaries. In other cases, the *qāḍī* used ambiguous phrases such as: 'a large portion of the beneficiaries', 'many of the beneficiaries', 'some of the beneficiaries', 'a group of beneficiaries' or simply: 'beneficiaries'.

If the petition recommended a single candidate, the *qāḍīs* did not bother to ascertain whether the signatories represented a majority among the beneficiaries. The fact that the nomination was unopposed satisfied them. Several letters of appointment affirmed that the appointee had 'no opponents among the beneficiaries'.[28] All the same, occasional requests by beneficiaries to revoke an appointment (six cases during the Mandatory period) show that not all beneficiaries had been kept informed; some may not have known of the petition. If the petition met the requirements set forth in the *waqfiyya*, the *qāḍī* would forward it to the *ma'mūr al-awqāf*. The latter would, in turn, summon the candidate for examination by the appointments committee.

The examinations

The Jerusalem appointments committees, formed during the late Ottoman period, continued their work under the British military administration. When committee members died, others were appointed to take their place. After the SMC (see Chapter 2) came into being, the appointments committee continued to operate under the 1913 Ottoman Appointments Law. Since the SMC had much of the power formerly belonging to the Ottoman government, it also claimed prerogatives in all matters touching on the appointment of *mutawallīs*. Members of local or district appointments committees were named by recommendation of the local *ma'mūr al-awqāf*, who was subordinate to the SMC.

In the early Mandate years, the Jerusalem Appointments Committee was chaired by the *Qāḍī* of Jerusalem, Shaykh Mūsā al-Budayrī. The *ma'mūr al-awqāf*, Badr Yūnis al-Ḥusaynī, was *ex officio* co-ordinator of the committee's work. Its members were three high-ranking *'ulamā'*: Ḥussām al-Dīn Jārallah (the inspector of the *sharī'a* courts), Amīn al-Sa'ūdī and Ḥasan Abū al-Sa'ūd.[29] Yūnis participated regularly in the meetings of the committee and supervised its correspondence. But the *qāḍī* did not, as a rule, participate in committee meetings at which candidates were given their examinations. Rather, the correspondence in the *sijill* shows that the *ma'mūr al-awqāf* notified him in writing of the committee's decision.

The examination was held in writing only, and its objective was to ascertain the candidate's familiarity with the *sharī'a* rules for administering a *waqf*. Written rather than oral tests were given for two reasons: to verify the candidate's literacy and to provide evidence against a possible subsequent charge of favouritism.[30]

The test questions show that the committee examined the candidate's overall knowledge of *sharī'a* rules of management but not his administrative abilities. There was no assurance that the committee's considerations were always pertinent. At least one piece of evidence suggests that they were not. In 1934, the appointments committee in Acre turned down the candidacy of Burhantīn Būlant Bey, son of Sa'īd Pāshā, the only male beneficiary in the 'Alī Pāshā Waqf, in favour of his sister, Sa'ādat

Khānum. Bulant appealed the decision to the inspector of the *sharīʿa* courts, claiming that two committee members – its chairman, the local *mufti* and the *ma'mūr al-awqāf* – had an interest in the endowment because they were respectively a *mudarris* and a *khaṭīb* in its institutions. The other two members, for their part, had been litigants in another case involving Bulant and should therefore be barred from administering the examination. He demanded (in vain) that the SMC name a special ad hoc appointments committee to test him once again.[31] On the whole, however, the *sijill* and other documents provide hardly any evidence of alien considerations on the part of an appointments committee. Shaykh Asʿad al-Imām, interviewed for this study, confirmed the existence of such considerations by stating that if the appointments committee had prior knowledge that the candidate was not honest, it would ask him particularly difficult questions in order to ensure his failure.[32] In other words: the committee adjusted the test to suit the candidate.

The *qāḍī* was not alone in taking the beneficiaries' attitudes into account; so, evidently, did the appointments committee. It usually accepted their choice. Outright rejection of their recommendations was rare, even when the candidate was illiterate (written examination notwithstanding) or woefully deficient in administrative competence (see below under 'Qualifications'). The rule of thumb in Jerusalem was that an ignorant *mutawallī* related to the founder was preferable to a knowledgeable non-relative.

Few candidates failed the test.[33] A candidate had to pass only once; that would then suffice for any future appointment as *mutawallī* as well; he would never have to sit the examination again and demonstrate his suitability a second time. This supports our conclusion that the examination was designed to test general knowledge of administrative procedure, not administrative ability.[34] Those with legal training, such as lawyers or judges, were exempt from the examination, their suitability being 'a known fact'.[35]

Determining the arshad

Having been informed by the appointments committee that a candidate was qualified, the *qāḍī* had to determine that he was the *arshad*, as defined by the *sharīʿa* code. If the appointment was uncontested, the *qāḍī* settled for two reliable witnesses who affirmed that the candidate was the most competent person to administer the endowment.

A study of letters of appointment during the Mandatory period shows that witnesses explicitly referred to the candidate as the *arshad* in only one-third of *mutawallī* appointments (68 letters). Most of the letters did not say that the nominee was the *arshad*, but only stated that he possessed the necessary qualities and aptitude to administer the endowment (*lahu al-dirāya wal-ilmām al-tām bi-idārat umūr al-waqf*). Failure to prove the *arshadiyya* of the candidate, when it was common knowledge that this was required by most founders of family *waqf*s, was a breach of *sharīʿa* law and a contravention of the founder's wishes.[36] The *qāḍī*s devised vague formulae that circumvented the *arshadiyya* issue. Some letters of appointment asserted that the candidate was deemed suitable 'according to the founder's stipulations', with no reference to the imperative of *arshadiyya*. Other letters described the candidate as 'one of the most competent of the beneficiaries' (*min arshad al-mustaḥiqqīn*), but not necessarily the most competent.[37] One letter depicted the nominee as *rashīd* but not as *arshad*.[38] The *qāḍī*s' laxity on this point expedited the appointment process, satisfied the beneficiaries, or at least some of them, and may have pleased the *qāḍī* himself, who wished to promote the person in question. The overriding significance of the *qāḍī*s' attitude towards this aspect of the process, however, is that they waived their authority under the *sharīʿa* and allowed the appointments committee to appoint the *mutawallī*. Even in the few cases where more than one candidate was proposed, the *qāḍī* customarily consulted the findings of the appointments committee, even though it was for witnesses rather than for the committee to determine the *arshad*. It has to be borne in mind that the titular chairman of the appointments committee was the *qāḍī* himself, although he rarely attended its meetings. In the case of the al-Bashītī Waqf, for example, the committee found that only one of the two candidates was qualified. The *qāḍī*, understanding that he might cause a dispute within the family by ruling in accordance with the decision of the appointments committee, appointed the suitable candidate as *mutawallī* and the other as supervisor (*nāẓir*) of the *waqf* – a higher position![39] In this unorthodox manner, the *qāḍī* circumvented the *sharīʿa* restrictions, since the *sharīʿa* established no criteria for the post of *nāẓir*. In one case, when the committee found that two candidates proposed by the beneficiaries of the al-Anṣārī Waqf were both qualified, the *qāḍī* perused the test forms and chose one of the candidates according to his personal impression.[40] In this case, he preferred familiarity with the rules of administration over proof of *arshadiyya*.

Unlike the test administered by the appointments committee, decisions on an *arshad* were not permanent; they remained in effect only as long as there was no other beneficiary whose qualities might surpass those of the incumbent. If such a claimant existed, he had to file a suit with the *sharīʿa* court against the *mutawallī*, proving through witnesses that he was more competent and suitable than the present *mutawallī*.[41] Under *sharīʿa* law, such a suit was admissible only after sufficient time had elapsed for the characteristics of the principals to have changed. The *qāḍīs* in Jerusalem set one year as the minimum period.

Only three suits of this kind were filed during the Mandatory period. In one of them, two beneficiaries of the Quṭayna Waqf claimed that they were more competent than the *mutawallī* who had been appointed towards the end of the Ottoman period. The *qāḍī* persuaded them to compromise and, with their consent, appointed one of them *nāẓir*.[42] In another suit, two cousins had competed for the post of *mutawallī* of the Muḥammad Saʿīd al-Khālidī Waqf. When one of them won, his cousin filed an *arshadiyya* before a year had passed. Undeterred by the court's refusal, he waited another year and sued again, arguing that he had become the *arshad* under new circumstances that had arisen (*wa-hādhā amr tajaddada lī*). The court rejected his claim.[43]

The time sequence of the procedure for appointing family *waqf* *mutawallīs* points to a basic flaw: the fact that an administrative committee examined the candidate and approved his appointment, and only then did the *qāḍī* determine his *arshadiyya*, undermining the *qāḍī*'s authority. Once the appointments committee had endorsed a candidate, the *qāḍī* could do no more than rubber-stamp the move. His hearing the testimony of the two witnesses who affirmed the candidate's *arshadiyya* became a mere formality. Often enough, this was not even done by the *qāḍī*, because the witnesses testified only that the candidate was knowledgeable and suited to the task. Beneficiaries were able to appeal such a decision only by filing an *arshadiyya* suit that the *qāḍī* had no choice but to adjudicate. The very filing of such a suit signalled a measure of distrust in the *qāḍī*'s appointment; naturally, therefore, the chances of reversing his previous decision were very slight. This may account for the paucity of *arshadiyya* claims (six cases) compared with the large number of demands for the dismissal of *mutawallī*s (82 cases).

CHARACTERISTICS OF THE *MUTAWALLĪ*

Family lineage

All of the 214 persons appointed as *mutawallī*s of Jerusalem *waqf*s in the Mandatory period were relatives of the founder. We studied the *mutawallī*s' family lineage by comparing their full names with those of the founders, which usually mentioned their fathers' and grandfathers' names. It turned out that many persons appointed as *mutawallī*s were direct descendants of founders.

A similar comparison shows that many newly-appointed *mutawallī*s were sons of the last, deceased *mutawallī* (17) or of earlier ones. Sometimes the deceased appointee's brother or his brother's son was appointed (5 and 3 cases, respectively).[44] This trend perpetuated traditions prevalent in the Ottoman period.

An examination of *waqf* entitlements shows that the *mutawallī* was always a member of the series closest to the founder. In other words: he was among those who received the largest entitlement; indeed, his was usually the very largest. Shaykh Asʿad al-Imām, describing his personal experience as *mutawallī* during the Mandatory period, explains that 'those who had the largest portions of the entitlement were the most eager to be appointed as *mutawallī* in order to safeguard their rights more effectively.'[45] The *qāḍī*s respected this consideration. For example, Muḥammad al-Budayrī, discharged as *mutawallī* of the al-Budayrī family *waqf*, was subsequently reinstated as *nāẓir* because, as possessor of the largest entitlement, he was thought incapable of acting contrary to *waqf* interests or of misusing its assets, as had been alleged against him.[46]

Gender

In contrast to the sizeable proportion of women founders of *waqf*s, the number of female *mutawallī*s was rather small. According to Baer's analysis of *waqf*s in sixteenth-century Istanbul, only 22.5 per cent of the administrators of family *waqf*s and 10 per cent of the administrators of all endowments were women, whereas they accounted for 36.8 per cent of founders.[47] In Jaffa during the Mandatory period, only 5 per cent of administrators were women.[48]

In Mandatory Jerusalem, the only woman *mutawallī* appointed was Bakriyya ʿAqaba, who became the sole administrator of a *waqf* founded by her father and brothers, since she was the founders' only descendant.[49] Another seven women managed *waqf*s under appointments dating back to the Ottoman period; each of them shared her position with another *mutawallī* who was, naturally, male.[50]

Thus, the balance among *mutawallī*s in the Mandatory period was eight women to approximately 400 men.

The following case illuminates the attitude of the *sharīʿa* court toward the appointment of women to *waqf* positions. A woman who was the only descendant of a founder whose *waqf* included a building for *Qur'ān* readings (known as *madrasat al-qurā'*) sought to be appointed as *mutawallī*. One of the best-known Jerusalem *ʿulamā'*, Shaykh Asʿad al-Imām, represented her in court. The *qāḍī* opposed her appointment because the *waqfiyya* laid down that the *mutawallī* must be a *Qur'ān* reciter. The woman insisted that she was competent to recite the *Qur'ān*, but the *qāḍī*, citing the Appointments Law, dismissed the possibility of her being a *Qur'ān* reciter. Consequently, she could not be the *mutawallī* either.[51] Instead, the *sharī'a* court appointed a man as acting (*qā'imaqām*) *mutawallī*. Subsequently, it transpired that the *qā'imaqām* was illiterate, and the *qāḍī* was forced to dismiss him and to transfer administration of the *waqf* to the *ma'mūr al-awqāf*.[52] Shaykh As'ad al-Imām, though pleading for the woman in court, was himself less than fully reconciled to her appointment. Asked in an interview in 1990 why there were so few women administrators, he replied: 'Because in order to get the appointment, a woman has to fraternize with men.' Also, he added, 'a married woman is busy with housework and child-rearing'.[53]

In cases in which the beneficiaries were one man and several women, the man always received the appointment, irrespective of his suitability. In one such instance, it was explicitly stated that the candidate had been given the job because he was 'the only male beneficiary', even though the founder had not stipulated that the *arshad* must be male.[54] In another case, five sisters and their cousin asserted of their own volition that their brother, the only male beneficiary, was the most competent to administer the endowment.[55] In yet another case, a sole male beneficiary was given priority over his mother and two sisters.[56] In yet another case, the female beneficiaries of the Balūkbāshī Waqf asked to appoint Shaykh Yaḥyā al-Anṣārī, who was neither a member of the founder's family nor one of the beneficiaries, as *qā'imaqām*. This should be done, he argued, because 'there was no male beneficiary'. This example illustrates the women's own attitude towards female *mutawallī*s.[57]

Qualifications

The procedures described above did not always assure the correct appointment. Although most *mutawallī*s were indeed suitably qualified for the position, there were exceptions. For example, the *mutawallī* of the al-Bashītī Waqf, who occupied his post for 28 years, was illiterate. When the beneficiaries sought his dismissal, he asserted that he paid several beneficiaries to help him keep the books. But taking all the circumstances into account, the *qāḍī* dismissed him.[58] In a similar case, the appointments committee found that the candidate knew no arithmetic. Nevertheless, the *qāḍī* appointed him because he was the only offspring of the founder, and ordered him to seek the assistance of someone who knew how to count.[59] In the case of the Muḥammad Abū al-Faḍl al-ʿAlamī Waqf, a beneficiary passed the appointments committee examination, was declared *arshad* by the *qāḍī* and was appointed to the post of *mutawallī*. Five months later, one of the female beneficiaries filed suit, claiming that he was old, illiterate and incompetent, and that he had withheld her portion of the entitlement. In the course of the proceedings, he was forced to resign.[60]

In ten Mandate-period lawsuits brought by beneficiaries to secure the dismissal of *mutawallī*s, the administrators were accused, *inter alia*, of incompetence or unsuitability for the job, even though most of them had held their post for many years.[61]

Rectitude

As stated above, the cardinal test in the appointment of *mutawallī*s was their trustworthiness in the eyes of the beneficiaries who had proposed them as candidates. Of particular importance was the suspicion that a given candidate might deprive some beneficiaries of their entitlements for the benefit of others. The examination, in itself, was no test of the candidates' ethical standards, because most of the beneficiaries could produce a candidate favouring them by conspiring against a minority. Indeed, of the 400 *mutawallī*s in Mandatory Jerusalem, including the 214 who were appointed during the Mandatory period itself, 35 were dismissed for corruption or abuse of *waqf* funds. (For details, see Chapter 8.) In several cases, *mutawallī*s already thus dismissed were reinstated. *Sharīʿa* law permits reinstatement if the wayward administrator repents (*tawaba*) and mends his ways.[62] To re-appoint such an administrator, the beneficiaries had to appear before the *qāḍī* within one year of his dismissal and testify that he had reformed.[63] In one case, a *mutawallī* about to be reinstated by the beneficiaries was required to provide a financial guarantee.[64]

Sometimes the only way to wrest administration of a *waqf* from the *ma'mūr al-awqāf* (who was always disliked and feared by beneficiaries) was by reinstating a *mutawallī* who had been dismissed; he was, apparently, the only beneficiary for whom suitability could be claimed.[65] Some corrupt *mutawallī*s exploited this situation to threaten beneficiaries with their resignation, and in some cases even carried out their threats.[66]

Wealth

The rule in large *waqf*s was that indigents were ineligible as *mutawallī*s. A person who owned no property could hardly be expected to know how to administer *waqf* assets. Moreover, he would be more easily tempted to enrich himself. In at least one case, it was argued that a candidate was not suitable because he was *miflis*: he owned no property.[67] In several instances involving large endowments, *mutawallī*s were required to proffer a financial guarantee through a third party.

Tenure and reasons for dismissal

In *waqf*s not temporarily administered by the *ma'mūr al-awqāf*, *mutawallī*s were appointed because of the death, dismissal or resignation of the incumbent. Occasionally, a vacancy arose for some other, unknown reason.

One hundred and eighty-nine *mutawallī*s and 25 acting *mutawallī*s (*qā'imaqām*) were appointed during the Mandatory period to administer the assets of 150 from among approximately 200 active *waqf*s established before the Mandatory period and not administered by the SMC. For roughly 50 *waqf*s, no new *mutawallī* was appointed throughout the 30 years of British rule. In other words, about a quarter of the *waqf*s in Mandatory Jerusalem were either administered by the same *mutawallī* for over 30 years, or else some *mutawallī*s were replaced without recourse to the *qāḍī*.

Death accounted for 39 per cent (74 cases) of new appointments, dismissals for 5 per cent (10 cases) and resignations for 10 per cent (19 cases). In 46 per cent of the appointments (86 cases) the letter of appointment did not state why the vacancy had arisen. The apparent reason was the death of the previous *mutawallī*, usually some time earlier. During the interim, no formal appointment was made. The *sijill* shows that most *mutawallīs* kept their positions until their death; only a minority were dismissed or resigned.

Shaykh Asʿad al-Imām confirms that most *mutawallīs* remained at their posts until their death. People of advanced age, he explains, do not tend to forfeit their authority. The *mutawallī*'s concerns were threefold: to keep his job; to look after his interests and prerogatives, and to continue to receive his fee. *Mutawallīs* were therefore disinclined to resign, though some unofficially entrusted the daily running of the *waqf* to their sons.[68] This sometimes led to conflicts between beneficiaries and *mutawallīs*. A female beneficiary of the Khalīl Abū Jibna Waqf, for example, claimed that her brother, *mutawallī* for the last 30 years, had become ill and unfit. The *mutawallī* acknowledged this and resigned because of old age and infirmity; his nephew was appointed instead.[69] In another case, a beneficiary of the Muḥammad Shitayya Waqf alleged that the *mutawallī* was too old, lived outside Jerusalem and did not administer the *waqf* himself. The *qāḍī* dismissed him on grounds of mismanagement.[70]

APPOINTMENT OF *MUTAWALLĪS* FOR PUBLIC ENDOWMENTS

When the management of a public endowment not administered by the SMC fell vacant, two or more *mutawallīs* were appointed. The rules governing the administration of such *waqfs* usually dated back to the Ottoman period; *firmāns* had promised the position to members of a specific family, and it was handed down from the father to the eldest son.

The four largest public endowments in Jerusalem were those of Nabī Mūsā, Nabī Dā'ūd, Shaykh Aḥmad al-Dajānī and Abū Midyan. In the first three, the post of *mutawallī* was entrusted to families of notables (Nabī Mūsā to the Yūnis and al-Ḥusaynī families, Nabī Dā'ūd and al-Dajānī to the al-Dajānī family); the fourth was managed by a *mutawallī* proposed by the Maghribī community in Jerusalem.

In the late Ottoman period, the government transferred the tithes of these endowments to the Waqf Ministry, which forwarded them directly to the beneficiaries. The British agreed to channel them through the SMC, thus giving it control of the *waqf*s.[71] The SMC had a special interest in controlling the Nabī Mūsā Waqf, because the annual celebrations at the shrine there were a source of country-wide prestige. Although this *waqf* was not of the *maḍbūṭ* type, the SMC controlled it closely because of its dependence on the tithes of which it had become the repository. The *mutawallī*s were required to provide the SMC with a draft budget, and the SMC, exploiting its status, decided on the details of the budget. Another reason for the SMC's particular involvement in this *waqf* was that the *ma'mūr al-awqāf* in Jerusalem, Badr Yūnis al-Ḥusaynī, was himself one of the *mutawallī*s, representing the Yūnis family. In 1926, after a dispute had broken out between the *mutawallī*s, the administration of the Nabī Mūsā Waqf was transferred to the SMC's administrator of *waqf*s.[72] Even after the curtailment of the SMC's powers in 1937, the *waqf*'s transaction swere closely supervised by the SMC. In a draft letter submitted on April 6, 1945, the *mutawallī*s stated that the Nabī Mūsā Waqf was not of the *maḍbūṭ* type, that the Waqf Department's intervention in Nabī Mūsā had been voluntary and that the *waqf* budget had been entrusted to the SMC merely as a deposit. For some reason, this sentence was deleted from the final, official version of the document.[73] The endowment had originally been entrusted by the Ottoman *Sulṭān* to three *mutawallī*s of the Yūnis and al-Ḥusaynī families, and was administered during the Mandatory period by their 12 descendants, who divided the duties and revenues among themselves.

The Nabī Dā'ūd Waqf, which had *mulḥaq* status, was actually administered as a family *waqf* of the al-Dajānīs, who were responsible for the *zāwiyya* (Sufi lodge) on Mt Zion because the family home was located nearby. Other Sufi lodges were administered in a similar manner – for example, al-Zāwiyya al-Fakhriyya, administered by the Abū al-Sa'ūd family, and Zawiyyat Shaykh Jarrāḥ, administered by the al-Dissī family. Most of the *zāwiyya shaykhs* were appointed by the SMC, including those of the al-Hunūd, Nabī Samwīl, al-Qādiriyya, al-Afghān, al-Majīdiyya, al-Naqshabandiyya, al-Mawlawiyya, al-Adhamiyya, al-Fakhriyya, al-As'adiyya, al-Rifā'iyya, the Abū Midyan and the Nabī Dā'ūd *zāwiyyas*. The SMC provided the *shaykhs* with a budget that took into account the number of people visiting.[74] The *mutawallī* of the Khāṣṣikī Sulṭān Waqf was also appointed by the SMC; his position was defined as *qā'imaqām al-takiyya*. After 1938, Shaykh Sa'id al-Khaṭīb, the preacher at al-Aqṣā mosque, was appointed to administer the *takiyya*. He was dismissed in 1938 and replaced by Shaykh Ḥasan 'Izz al-Dīn al-Khaṭīb. Al-Khaṭīb held this post until 1945, when he was succeeded by Isḥāq Yūnis.

The appointment of *mutawallīs* for large public *waqfs* resembled those for family *waqfs*, except that instead of the *waqfiyya*, there was a *firmān* requiring the post to be transferred from father to son. In these cases, the members of a family only had to confirm that the candidate was the eldest son of the deceased *mutawallī*.[75]

The Maghribī endowments were administered by various beneficiaries, grouped according to origin. The al-Takrūrī Waqf, for example, was managed by three *mutawallīs*, each representing a group of beneficiaries from his country of origin. The Abū Midyan Waqf was administered by two *mutawallīs*, one of Algerian the other of Moroccan origin. Later, when Maghribī beneficiaries presented petitions for several candidates, the appointments committee chose one as the most competent (*tafawaqa 'alā al-bāqīn*); the *qāḍī* accepted the committee's choice.[76]

The *mutawallīs* of large family *waqfs* or of public endowments had to be more competent than those of small family *waqfs*, since the pool of beneficiaries in the former was larger, and because the large holdings of the *waqfs* made it necessary to exclude all but the best candidates. In small family *waqfs*, by contrast, the group of beneficiaries from whom a candidate could be drawn was usually small. Thus the *qāḍī* tended to compromise in order to uphold the principle of preferring a member of the founder's family over an outsider.

REMUNERATION OF *MUTAWALLĪS*

That *mutawallīs* should be paid at all was not taken for granted. Most *mutawallīs* in Egypt and Palestine served with no remuneration, and this was the norm.[77] According to Shaykh Asʿad al-Imām, unpaid service as *mutawallī* was considered an act of altruism that carried its recompense in the next world. Because the *mutawallīs*' main motivation was to ensure their privileges by direct means, rendering unpaid service did not perturb them.[78] When a founder did not explicitly stipulate that a *mutawallī* should be remunerated, the *qāḍī*'s approval was required for him to charge a fee. In one case, a beneficiary sued for the dismissal of a *mutawallī* on the grounds that he was drawing a fee without authorization. The *mutawallī* hastily gathered together a majority of the beneficiaries to sign a petition approving a fee of ten per cent of the benefits for him. The *qāḍī* disapproved of such tactics and dismissed the *mutawallī*, arguing that the *mutawallī*, having been appointed to an unpaid position in the first place, must not now charge a fee.[79]

The norm in Jerusalem evidently required that *mutawallīs* should not demand a fee, unless the *waqf* they managed exceeded a certain level of revenue and activity. Thus 74 letters of appointment unequivocally required the *mutawallī* to serve 'out of altruism' (*ḥisbatan li-wajhi allāh majānan*). Four letters authorized the *mutawallīs* to take ten per cent of *waqf* revenues for their efforts, as the beneficiaries themselves had demanded in a petition to the court.[80] The other letters of appointment make no mention of this matter.

According to the *sharīʿa*, the *mutawallī*'s fee (*maʿlūm*) must be 'proper recompense' (*ajar al-mithl*).[81] The SMC established a standard charge of ten per cent of *waqf* revenue for the *ma'mūr al-awqāf* who managed an endowment temporarily.[82] Over time, this became the accepted 'proper recompense' for the *mutawallīs* of small family *waqfs*.[83] The 1930s saw a wave of petitions for fees by *mutawallīs*; Shaykh Asʿad al-Imām attributes this to an increase in the cost of living.[84] Most petitions were approved, and the *mutawallīs* began to charge fees after having served with no remuneration for many years. The *qāḍī* approved a ten per cent fee only for the *mutawallīs* of *waqfs* with small revenues. (The documents give the impression that the limit was £P200 per year.) In some of the larger *waqfs*, the *mutawallīs* were given a fixed sum as a fully fledged salary, on the reasonable grounds that they were doing a full-time job;[85] in other cases, a commission of less than ten per cent was specified.[86]

ACTING *MUTAWALLĪS*

According to the *waqf* laws, the *qāḍī* is entitled to appoint an acting *mutawallī* (*qā'imaqām mutawallī*) – an appointment meant, as the name implies, to be temporary – in one of six situations:[87]

1. if the *mutawallī* takes a lengthy trip (of at least one year) or has been missing for long and has failed to name a stand-in (*wakīl*);[88]
2. if the endowment deed designates a person who is a minor at the time;
3. if the *waqf* is found to have no *mutawallī*;
4. if a complaint against the *mutawallī* is in the course of being investigated – in this case, the *qāḍī* appoints a temporary administrator and makes him join the plaintiff(s), because only an acting *mutawallī* has the judicial standing to sue a *mutawallī*;
5. if several individuals claim the *arshadiyya* – the *qāḍī* appoints a *qā'imaqām* until the claim is settled and a permanent appointment made;
6. if the *mutawallī*, though still trustworthy, has become incapacitated – the *qāḍī* appoints a *qā'imaqām* to help him until he can again administer the endowment by himself.

However, of the 25 *qā'imaqām* appointments in Mandatory Jerusalem, only six were based on the grounds listed above. In the other cases, the *qāḍī* was not satisfied that the appointees had proved to be the most competent (*li-'adam taḥaqquq arshadiyyat aḥad al-mustaḥiqqīn*).[89] In only one case was it stated that the *qāḍī* had named the stand-in because the most competent (*arshad*) beneficiary was away.[90] The *qāḍī*s used the practice of appointing substitutes to circumvent the need to name the *arshad*. The *sijill* shows that such appointments, ostensibly temporary, actually turned out be permanent, for most *qā'imaqām*s served until their death. Through this method, the *qāḍī*s found a way to bypass the *sharī'a* provisions concerning the qualifications of the *mutawallī*; they used it to appoint persons whom they favoured or whom the beneficiaries had pressed upon them, thus barring outsiders. In one case, where none of the beneficiaries in the founder's family could demonstrate that he was the *arshad*, the *qāḍī* appointed the founder's grandson simply to prevent an outsider or the *ma'mūr al-awqāf* from taking over the *waqf*.[91]

QĀḌĪS, *MUTAWALLĪS* AND THE *MA'MŪR AL-AWQĀF*

Under the 1913 Appointments Law, when the position of *mutawallī* fell vacant for any reason whatever, the *ma'mūr al-awqāf* was to be appointed as *qā'imaqām* until a permanent *mutawallī* was named. According to the *sharī'a*, such vacancies should have been filled without delay.[92] The Ottoman regime seems to have exploited this as a pretext to impose central control over as many *waqf*s as possible, claiming that its Waqf Division, an agency under official supervision, was suitably equipped to administer the *waqf*s. Consequently, it was the practice for the *sharī'a* court to name the *ma'mūr al-awqāf* as the *qā'imaqām* for *awqāf ghayr maḍbūṭa* (non-*maḍbūṭ* *waqf*s) as soon as a *mutawallī* was dismissed or had resigned. As stated, the SMC exploited this practice to gain control of public-purpose non-*maḍbūṭ* endowments and had the *qāḍī*s' co-operation in this regard (see Chapter 6). However, the SMC took little interest in family *waqf*s, and the *qāḍī*s actually helped family members who wished to appoint one of their number as *mutawallī*, thus keeping the *ma'mūr al-awqāf* out. The Muslim population of Jerusalem seems to have been displeased when *ma'mūr*s were appointed, one reason being that they deducted a sizeable administration fee. The Jerusalem *sijill* provides many examples of beneficiaries quickly petitioning the court to appoint a *mutawallī* from among themselves, in order to restore administration by the family.[93] One such case in particular reflects the fear of even temporary administration by the *ma'mūr*: when the *mutawallī* of the Qāsim Bey Waqf died, the beneficiaries hastened to sign a petition that very day, asking to appoint a *mutawallī* from among themselves on the grounds that he was the most competent; the appointment went into effect three days after the *mutawallī*'s death.[94]

Qāḍīs evidently had to resign themselves to appointing the *ma'mūr* as temporary *qā'imaqām* of family *waqf*s until an *arshad* was located among the beneficiaries. But as soon as the founder's relatives turned up, the *qāḍī* did not hesitate to name any one of them who had passed the appointments committee examination. For example, a candidate who had not even proved *arshadiyya* was named *qā'imaqām* by the *qāḍī* in lieu of the *ma'mūr*, who had been appointed only two weeks earlier.[95] In another case, the *qāḍī*, believing that the *ma'mūr* had been negligent in the administration of a family *waqf*, replaced him with a *mutawallī* who had previously been dismissed for embezzlement. To justify the reinstatement, he noted in the letter of appointment that the *mutawallī* had mended his ways by watching over the *waqf*'s two shops.[96]

To sum up, the *qāḍī*s in Mandatory Jerusalem failed to exercise the supreme authority given to them by the *sharī'a* in the appointment of *mutawallī*s; instead, they entrusted much of this authority to the *ma'mūr al-awqāf*, who applied civil rather than religious law. In so doing, they failed to honour the founders' wish that the candidate appointed be the most competent of the possible candidates. In so doing, the *qāḍī*s may have been prompted by a desire to deflect on to the appointments committee possible pressures from those who had been offended in the process. Beneficiaries displeased with a *mutawallī* contested the choice by suing for his dismissal on grounds of incompetence. This was tantamount to shifting the burden of the dispute to a technical matter more easily dealt with by the *qāḍī*. In none of the six *arshadiyya* suits filed during the Mandatory period did the *sharī'a* court repeal the appointments made earlier. As for the appointment of women, the examples we have cited show that the court constituted an obstacle. The *qāḍī*s helped the SMC take over the administration of public-purpose non-*maḍbūṭ* *waqf*s but helped beneficiaries of family *waqf*s regain management from the *ma'mūr al-awqāf* (a position subordinate to the SMC), even when they regarded their candidate unsatisfactory.

The Ottoman appointment procedures survived during the Mandatory period. The conventional pattern was for the oldest son to take over from his father, assuming he was capable. This gave the beneficiaries much latitude in choosing the *mutawallī*. The *sijill* points to a large measure of correlation between the series of administrators named by the founder and the series of beneficiaries. The founder's wishes were even given preference with regard to obviously unqualified candidates. Most founders wanted the most competent to succeed to their *waqf*'s administration. In practice, however, the *mutawallī*s appointed were those who had the largest entitlement – those who belonged to the series closest to the founder – a choice not always compatible with selecting the most competent. Rather than thinking in terms of a generational hierarchy, the founders laid down a representational format that enabled members of lower series, too, to participate in the administration of the *waqf* if one beneficiary was better qualified than the others. Thus neither the founders' wishes nor the *sharī'a* were implemented literally. Acceptability to the family as a whole usually ranked above competence. The above case descriptions show that it was actually the beneficiaries who chose the administrator. The appointments committee and the *qāḍī* were simply executors of their wishes, and the *qāḍī*'s overriding consideration was to prevent, as far as possible, struggles over *waqf* management.

NOTES

1. The founder can also nominate a person to execute his stipulation after his death, who will success him in appointing the *mutawallī*. M. Qadrī Pāshā, *Kitāb Qānūn al-'Adl wa'l-Inṣāf li'l-Qaḍā' 'alā Mushkilāt al-Awqāf* (Cairo, 1902) art. 147.
2. According to O. Hilmi, *A Treatise on the Laws of Evkaf* (trans. C.R. Tyser and D.G. Demetriades, Nicosia, 1899) art. 301, there is no need for a *qāḍī* approval of a *mutawallī* who was defined by the founder by name, or definite description like 'the eldest son'. However, most *mutawallī*s applied for

the *qāḍī* approval.

3. M. Qadrī Pāshā, *Kitāb Qānūn al-ʿAdl wa'l-Inṣāf li'l-Qaḍā' ʿalā Mushkilāt al-Awqāf* (Cairo, 1902) arts. 144–145, O. Hilmi, *A Treatise on the Laws of Evkaf* (trans. C.R. Tyser and D.G. Demetriades, Nicosia, 1899) art. 290.
4. M. Abū Zahra, *Muḥāḍarāt fī al-Waqf* (2nd ed., Cairo: Dār al Fikr al-ʿArabī, 1971) pp. 318–23.
5. Ibid., art. 306.
6. Ibid., art. 311.
7. Ibid., art. 312.
8. Ibid.; O. Hilmi, *A Treatise on the Laws of Evkaf* (trans. C.R. Tyser and D.G. Demetriades, Nicosia, 1899) art. 294.
9. M. Qadrī Pāshā, *Kitāb Qānūn al-ʿAdl wa'l-Inṣāf li'l-Qaḍā' ʿalā Mushkilāt al-Awqāf* (Cairo, 1902) art. 154.
10. Interview dated 24 March, 1990.
11. M. Qadrī Pāshā, *Kitāb Qānūn al-ʿAdl wa'l-Inṣāf li'l-Qaḍā' ʿalā Mushkilāt al-Awqāf* (Cairo, 1902) art. 154.
12. Ibid.
13. O. Hilmi, *A Treatise on the Laws of Evkaf* (trans. C.R. Tyser and D.G. Demetriades, Nicosia, 1899) art. 301.
14. Ibid., art. 304.
15. Ibid.
16. *Sijill* 461/2640. Nos. 31, 33 in Table 3.1.
17. *Sijill* 423/87/3; 423/133/38; 427/147/148; 446/107/56; 475/25/42; nos. 4,5,10,31,45 in Table 3.1.
18. Nos. 1,2,3,5,7,8,9,13,20,24,37,55,60 in Table 3.1.
19. *Sijill* 474/233/212; 477/361/90.
20. *Sijill* 474/100/155 (no. 43 in Table 3.1).
21. *Sijill* 446/107/56.
22. *Sijill* 455/13/303.
23. *Sijill* 418/259/14.
24. A. Layish, 'The Muslim *Waqf* in Jerusalem after 1967: Beneficiaries and Management', in *Le Waqf dans le monde musulman contemporain (XIXe–XXe siecles)*, ed. Faruk Bilici, *Varia Turcica* (Istanbul: Institut Français d'Etudes Annatoliennes) 26 (1994) pp. 145–68.
25. *Sijill* 502/1/199.
26. *Sijill* 456/2447/231, 471/82/47, 474/79/124, 496/382/191, 471/82/47.
27. *ISA, Land Court*, B/774, file 101/36, *Sijill* record 93/712.
28. *Sijill* 417/355/357, 417/354/356.
29. *CIH*, 13/25/5,2/60.
30. Interview with Shaykh Asʿad al-Imām. For a questionnaire see *CIH*, 1192, 13/53/5,39/60.
31. *CIH*, 13/34/5,18/60.
32. Interview dated 23 April 1990.
33. *Sijill* 451/113/174.
34. *Sijill* 484/58/388.
35. *Sijill* 485/14/144.
36. For examples see *Sijill* 416/105/156, 421/315/27, 441/49/68, 442/87/90, 485/115/29, 495/71/287.
37. *Sijill* 469/135/171, 471/23/29, 471/29/27, 471/82/47.

38. *Sijill* 417/365/365.
39. *Sijill* 484/65/399.
40. *Sijill* 457/48/203.
41. M. Qadrī Pāshā, *Kitāb Qānūn al-'Adl wa'l-Inṣāf li'l-Qaḍā' 'alā Mushkilāt al-Awqāf* (Cairo, 1902) art. 155.
42. *Sijill* 473/396/420.
43. *Sijill* 483/49/255, 483/377/235.
44. In six cases a resigned or fired *mutawallī* was reappointed to the office.
45. Interview dated 24 April 1990.
46. *Sijill* 489/314/65.
47. G. Baer, 'Women and the *Waqf*: An Analysis of the Istanbul *Taḥrīr* of 1546', *Asian and African Studies*, 17 (1983) p. 13.
48. Ibid., p. 14.
49. *Sijill* 418/1/386.
50. *Sijill* 427/521/204, 460/96/126, 489/63/166, 438/362/222, 486/17/355, 474/57/87.
51. *Sijill* 502/226/92.
52. *Sijill* 515/110/456.
53. Interview dated 24 May 1990.
54. *Sijill* 464/92/140.
55. *Sijill* 417/205/212.
56. *Sijill* 426/100/30, 417/135/145.
57. *Sijill* 465/5/200.
58. *Sijill* 478/393/150.
59. *Sijill* 512/99/12.
60. *Sijill* 456/119/103.
61. *Sijill* 515/110/456..
62. M. Qadrī Pāshā, *Kitāb Qānūn al-'Adl wa'l-Inṣāf li'l-Qaḍā' 'alā Mushkilāt al-Awqāf* (Cairo, 1902) art. 248.
63. *Sijill* 474/5/6.
64. Ibid.
65. *Sijill* 474/5/6, 475/48/79.
66. Examples: *Sijill* 445/48/159, 477/19/168.
67. *Sijill* 483/239/246.
68. Interview dated 20 April 1990.
69. *Sijill* 478/96/127, 479/90/241.
70. *Sijill* 478/291/267.
71. *CIH*, 13/23/5,3/55, minutes of 6 June 1923.
72. See below.
73. *CIH*, 13/32/1,8/2/45, 13/40/1,31/40, 13/39/2,4/45.
74. *CIH*, 13/32–31/1,5/2/45, 13/33/1,9/2/45, 13/38/1,1/24/40, 13/42/1,39/40.
75. *Sijill* 439/149/182.
76. *Sijill* 439/36/46.
77. *Sijill* 478/343/65.
78. Interview dated 20 April 1990.
79. *Sijill* 478/343/65.
80. *Sijill* 474/79/124, 500/36/15, 482/100/203, 484/60/391.
81. M. Qadrī Pāshā, *Kitāb Qānūn al-'Adl wa'l-Inṣāf li'l-Qaḍā' 'alā Mushkilāt al-Awqāf* (Cairo, 1902) arts. 169, 173.

82. *Sijill* 473/129/44.
83. Examples: *Sijill* 484/60/391, 498/36/448, 498/110/564, 498/111/565, 500/36/15, 500/48/31, 504/115/589, 505/122/77, 512/13/26, 474/79/124, 484/60/391.
84. *Sijill* 439/36/46, 461/1/2, 479/111/269, 517/8/459, 471/46/2, 484/79/419.
85. *Sijill* 461/122/170, 416/105/166, 481/107/405.
86. Interview dated 20 April 1990.
87. O. Hilmi, *A Treatise on the Laws of Evkaf* (trans. C.R. Tyser and D.G. Demetriades, Nicosia, 1899) art. 303–304.
88. *Mutawallī* may appoint an agent, see example in *Sijill* 455/67/385.
89. *Sijill* 441/36/33, 498/104/555, 510/19/591, 446/55/8, 495/71/287, 513/96/374.
90. *Sijill* 484/8/297, 475/60/97.
91. *Sijill* 418/259/14.
92. *Sijill* 458/23/364.
93. *Sijill* 486/48/407, 475/95/49, 475/48/49.
94. *Sijill* 480/138/244.
95. *Sijill* 513/96/374.
96. 498/19/468.

6

Current *waqf* administration

Researchers disagree about how *waqf* property was administered in comparison with private property. G. Baer, among many others, believes that *waqf*s did not administer their assets from the perspective of the market economy. This seems to follow from the restrictions which the *sharīʿa* places on *waqf* properties, such as banning their sale or long-term rental, and requiring investments beyond what was strictly necessary in economic terms. The occasional discoveries of corruption also helped spread the view that the *mutawallī*s were more concerned with personal gain than with managing the *waqf*s soundly and efficiently. G. Gilbar holds the opposite view, arguing that *waqf* properties contributed to the Islamic economy and that it cannot be proved that they were administered less profitably than non-*waqf* properties.[1] No empirical research capable of resolving the issue has been undertaken thus far. This chapter, dealing with transactions in *waqf* properties, may answer part of the question: that of the *sharīʿa* restrictions and their application. As will be seen presently, it is harder to come by an answer with respect to ongoing *waqf* management.

The available documents, such as rental contracts, financial statements and public bids – insofar as these were disclosed – do not necessarily show the true picture. The *sijill* contains accurate records of complaints alleging mismanagement of *waqf*s, but these are methodologically difficult to assess. For example, few complaints to the *sharīʿa* court charged *mutawallī*s with neglect. However, it is impossible to tell whether this reflected the overall realities or whether there were many other such instances that never led to litigation. It may have been difficult to prove corruption or economically ineffective administration, or the *mutawallī* may have succeeded in silencing his adversaries in various ways. Furthermore, information on the management of non-*waqf* private or public property, which one would need in order to establish a standard of comparison, is generally unavailable.

This chapter contrasts examples of sound economic management of *waqf* properties with cases of neglect and mismanagement, as reflected in the *sijill* and in administrative documents. It also compares *waqf* management by the *mutawallī*s with the administration of *maḍbūṭ waqf* properties by the SMC.

Ongoing management of a *waqf* includes the following:

1. letting the property and collecting the rent;
2. keeping the property in good repair, including renovations and preservation when necessary, and paying property taxes;
3. keeping the property fully under *waqf* control – preventing trespass and usurpation;
4. faithful compliance with the founder's instructions dealing with the allocation of sums for charity;
5. drawing up regular financial statements and having them audited.

This chapter will discuss the first four points; the fifth is discussed in Chapters 4 and 8.

MANAGEMENT BY THE *MUTAWALLĪS*

Letting property and collecting revenue

According to the *sharīʿa* laws, a *mutawallī* may let *waqf* property for short periods only: one year for urban assets and three for agricultural property.[2] This rule was designed to deny tenants the possibility of asserting possession rights. It also enabled the *mutawallī* to raise the rent periodically and keep it up to the market level. However, in cases where renovation of a *waqf* property was urgently needed, the *mutawallī* could apply to the *qāḍī* for permission to let the property for a longer period.[3]

The most important test of the *mutawallī* as administrator was his ability to obtain maximum revenues from the property he managed. Until rent restriction laws were enacted in the mid-1930s, the one-year term of rental was a serious constraint. Tenants had no motivation to keep the premises in good repair when they held them for such a short time. However, they had an interest in inducing the *mutawallī* to extend their tenancy. They could do so by proving that they had maintained the property, by agreeing to a rent increase, or by paying the *mutawallī* under the table.

In the mid-1930s, a substantial problem arose: the Rent Restrictions Law, later known as the Tenant Protection Law, established a rent ceiling and prohibited the eviction of tenants.[4] The possibilities of extracting maximum revenues were thus curtailed. Moreover, in being applied to *waqf* properties, it seemed to clash with *sharīʿa* laws limiting rental to one year. It might, therefore, have been supposed to elicit opposition on the part of the Muslim urban establishment, but there are no written indications of protest or resistance. On the contrary: the public, including members of the Muslim religious establishment, was apparently pleased with this law, which – even during an economic recession – was meant to keep rents down and give tenants security. This is the explanation given by Shaykh Asʿad al-Imām, who also believes that there is no essential contradiction between this law and the *sharīʿa*.[5]

One way to overcome the obstacle of short-term rentals was to simultaneously draft separate contracts for several successive years, usually three. *Mutawallī*s had to ask the *qāḍī* for permission to do so. The rationale for most of these requests was the need to renovate the property and the prospect that, if let for a longer span of time, it would command rental fees in excess of market value. The latter point was made even though it was common knowledge that rents for longer than one year brought in less income, because they could not be raised annually.

The *sharīʿa* court issued 27 permits for long-term rentals. Nine were given to *mutawallī*s who wished to dwell in the property themselves, and several of them received such permits consecutively for a lengthy period (see below).[6] Presumably, there were

TABLE 6.1 LONG-TERM RENTAL OF *WAQF* PROPERTIES

	Waqf	*Period of rental (years)*	*Reason given for long-term rental*	*Reference*
1	al-Hidmī	9	Renovation	416/184/000
2	ʿAqaba	10	Renovation	416/389/000
3	Ḥasan al-Ḥusaynī	6	Renovation	419/90/20
4	ʿAlama Abū Sharīf	3	Renovation	419/135/65
5	Aḥmad Bey Rajab	3	Renovation	419/363/91
6	al-Tarahī	10	Renovation	419/391/1
7	al-Turjamān	4	Renovation	424/58/51
8	Aḥmad Bey Ibn Rajab	2	Renovation	427/376/48
9	al-Ḥarīrī	3	Renovation	454/49/153
10	Maḥbūba al-Khālidī	3	Renovation	455/66/36
11	al-Jāʿūnī	3	Renovation	455/108/101
12	Dā'ūd al-Anṣārī	3	Renovation	458/78/56
13	Abū Sabitān	6	Renovation	463/62/111
14	al-Jāʿūnī	*	Renovation	481/94/389
15	al-Sāfūṭī	10	Rent increase	481/128/15
16	Tahbūb	2	Renovation	500/31/7
17	al-Jāʿūnī	12	Renovation	505/134/97
18	al-ʿAnabūsī	5	Property development	512/49/86

Note: * Unlimited

other such cases that did not come before the *sharīʿa* court for prior approval.

In several cases (nos 1, 2, 3 and 6 in Table 6.1), long-term rental was achieved by drawing up in advance annual rental contracts for a total of three years. Most permits stipulated that the rent should be increased after renovations were completed, and that this increase would be passed on to the beneficiaries. In a few cases (nos 13, 15 and 18 in Table 6.1), it is clear that the purpose of the rental was economic development of the property rather than renovation. The *mutawallī* of the Abū Sabitān Waqf, for example, requested permission to let the *waqf* premises for six years to obtain money for renovations estimated at £P600. Rent, however, was set at £P225 per year, so that three years' rent would suffice.

It did not seem difficult to obtain permission from the *sharīʿa* court to let *waqf* property for terms exceeding the legal norm. In one case, the *qāḍī* authorized a two-year rental *post facto*. When the beneficiary sought the dismissal of the *mutawallī* for having let the property for two years, the *qāḍī* ruled that post-factum approval was 'equivalent' to *a priori* approval (*al-ijāza al-lāḥiqa ka'l-idhn al-sābiq*).[7] The custom of renting out *waqf* properties for three years became so prevalent that a former *qāḍī* (Shaykh Asʿad al-Imām) believed that for urban properties, *mutawallī*s were allowed to do this without applying to the court. According to al-Imām, those who requested the *qāḍī*'s permission did so in ignorance of the extent of their powers.[8] Drawing on his lengthy experience as *qāḍī*, *sharīʿa* lawyer, *mutawallī* and SMC official, Shaykh Asʿad asserts that most lessors of flats, whether owned by *waqf*s or by private individuals, usually allowed tenants to extend the rental term in return for a reasonable increase in rent, if the tenants were found to have kept the property in good repair.[9]

In ten suits against *mutawallī*s during the Mandatory period, they were accused of having let *waqf* property for lengthy terms without the *qāḍī*'s permission. In only a single case (that of the al-ʿAnabūsī Waqf) was a *mutawallī* dismissed for this reason.[10] The evidence in the *sijill* shows that the *qāḍī*s tended to take into consideration the stated reasons for prolonging the rental term. A beneficiary of the Mūsā al-Raṣṣāṣ Waqf, for example, demanded the dismissal of a *mutawallī* on the grounds that he had let two *waqf* buildings in the Jewish Quarter to Jews for two years. The *mutawallī* claimed that the *waqfiyya* said nothing about the rental terms, and no wrongdoing had therefore been committed. The *qāḍī* accepted his argument, even though it had no support in *sharīʿa* law.[11] The Court of Appeals overruled him, but when the case returned to the first instance, the *qāḍī* again protected the *mutawallī* from dismissal, now arguing that the long-term rental had been for the benefit of the *waqf*.[12]

Sufficient data are not available to compare rental terms for *waqf* as against private property. It was the personal impression of those interviewed by the author that *waqf* dwellings were usually rented for longer periods than privately owned ones. The private owners were more careful to limit rentals of dwellings to one year in order to raise rents as often as was feasible. *Mutawallī*s, by contrast, agreed to longer terms when they considered the tenant a reliable person likely to maintain the property, or when they needed immediate cash.[13]

It is very hard to estimate the extent to which the economic potential of *waqf* properties was realized. The law did not require public bidding for the rental of *waqf* properties, although the Ottoman Waqf Ministry introduced this custom for *maḍbūṭ waqf*s. Failure to realize the full potential of properties was reflected, *inter alia*, in complaints brought against *mutawallī*s. In 17 Mandate-era suits for the dismissal of *mutawallī*s, it was alleged that they had let property much below the going rate. This was not, however, the main charge in these cases, and one gets the impression that the claimants added it in order to reinforce other allegations (see Chapter 8). In only two cases did beneficiaries accuse the *mutawallī* of letting property at an uneconomical rate. In one, the *mutawallī* of the Shams al-Dīn al-Yamānulī Waqf admitted that he had lowered the rent but claimed to have done so under duress, as part of a compromise agreement with a tenant who was in debt to the *waqf*. Eventually, after receiving his entitlement, the beneficiary withdrew the charges.[14] In the second case, the *nāẓir* of the Muḥammad al-Budayrī Waqf accused the *mutawallī* of letting property to people who were in debt and therefore unlikely to pay their rent, and of having set the rent at an unreasonably low level. In this case, however, the *qāḍī* dismissed the *nāẓir* (rather than the *mutawallī*) because he had failed to prove his claims.[15] The existence of unfounded complaints makes it difficult to estimate the number of genuine charges against *mutawallī*s.

In only two complaints during the Mandatory period were *mutawallī*s accused of failing to let the property and of thereby leaving assets idle. The *sharīʿa* court did not investigate the complaints in depth.[16] Ten other complaints during this period allege that *mutawallī*s had failed to collect rent. Most of the complaints were trivial. In some instances, according to Shaykh Asʿad al-Imām, both the Waqf Department and family *mutawallī*s let property to relatives without insisting on the maximum rent and on effective upkeep by the tenant.[17]

Renovation and maintenance

One of the basic functions of the *mutawallī* was to ensure that the *waqf* property was properly maintained and to make sure that the necessary renovations were carried out at the proper time. Because founders considered their *waqf* a living memorial to themselves, all *waqfiyyāt* included a binding order for the *mutawallī*s to attend to renovations and sound maintenance (*ʿimāra*), and to pay property taxes, before apportioning entitlements. According to the *sharīʿa* concept of the *waqf*, concern for the property itself was more important than concern for the purpose of the endowment. This principle was applied even for endowments whose founders had not explicitly laid down the condition of *ʿimāra*.[18] (*ʿImāra* was understood to mean suitable upkeep, renovation and maintenance of the property, with a view to preserving it as it was when the *waqf* was founded.) Development of a property beyond its original condition and renovations meant to enhance its value were absolutely prohibited.[19] Where a *waqf* property did not generate revenue but needed renovation and maintenance in order to prevent collapse, the *mutawallī* had to ask the *qāḍī* for permission to take out a loan (*istidāna*) for the necessary work.[20]

*Mutawallī*s often vacillated between their desire for maximum short-term revenues for immediate distribution among the beneficiaries and the need to let the property lie idle for a certain period in order to renovate it at *waqf* expense (thus affecting, even if only for a while, the beneficiaries' entitlements).

Some researchers believe that this conflict of interest kept *waqf* properties in a worse state of repair than others and made them much more likely to collapse. This, they hold, was one reason for the economic inferiority of the *waqf*, alongside the prohibitions barring sale or exchange. Also, loans for upkeep or renovation were hard to obtain. Moreover, the *mutawallī* was unlikely to look after *waqf* property as he would his own.[21] This is also the conventional opinion in the Muslim community. According to Shaykh Asʿad al-Imām, private property was better maintained than *waqf* property, because private persons were naturally more concerned owners. *Mutawallī*s who had a relatively large share of the entitlement were more conscientious. If, however, their main benefit from the *waqf* was the fee rather than a share in the entitlements, they were less motivated.[22]

Disputes between beneficiaries and *mutawallī*s, and demands by the former to dismiss the latter, provide evidence of neglect. When *mutawallī*s accused of neglect denied the charges, the *qāḍī* appointed a committee of building and renovation experts to inspect the site and report to the *qāḍī* on its physical condition. Not every claim of this type was found to be justified. We found no evidence of the findings of the investigating committee being challenged, and the overall impression is that they did their job faithfully. It should, however, be noted that not all charges of neglect were fully examined; at times, the court found reasons for dismissing the *mutawallī* which could be substantiated more easily than by sending out a team of experts. Having recourse to an investigating committee made litigation lengthier and costlier.

In one case, a beneficiary of the Sanʿallāh al-Khālidī Waqf sought the dismissal of a *mutawallī* for a series of offenses, the main one being neglect. The beneficiary demanded that an expert committee inspect the property, so the *mutawallī* could be discharged and the property renovated before the rainy season began. (The ruling was given in mid-October.) Rain, it was argued, would threaten the property with total collapse. The expert committee – a municipal engineer, two other experts and a representative of the *qāḍī* – stated that 15 buildings belonging to the *waqf* had become dilapidated and needed basic repairs to prevent their collapse. It found that the *mutawallī* had carried out no renovations for five years. Moreover, the municipality had warned the *mutawallī* and, when nothing was done, had condemned some of the buildings as dangerous and had served the tenants with an eviction order. The *mutawallī* argued that he could not afford the renovation work, but this argument fell flat because he had distributed revenues to the beneficiaries. The *qāḍī* therefore dismissed him.[23] Similarly, the *mutawallī* of the Yūsuf al-Jāʿūnī Waqf was dismissed for having neglected renovation and maintenance work for eight years, instead dividing all revenues among the beneficiaries.[24] In a similar suit against the *mutawallī* of the ʿAbdallāh al-Anṣārī Waqf, the *qāḍī* noted that a *mutawallī* must set aside some revenues for urgent renovations rather than distribute all earnings to the beneficiaries.[25]

Of the 82 suits for dismissal of *mutawallīs* in the 30 years of Mandatory Jerusalem, 29 alleged, *inter alia*, that the defendants had neglected the properties of which they were in charge. Only ten were dismissed on this count, after the charge had been investigated and verified. Court cases of this kind were relatively few, but it must be borne in mind that their number only indicates those reaching the stage of litigation. The fact that beneficiaries could have a *mutawallī* dismissed for failing to maintain *waqf* property deterred them from doing so.

In comparison with the above instances of neglect, there is much evidence of preservation and renovation, and even of economic and physical amelioration. Because, as stated, renovation and maintenance were the *mutawallīs*' principal duties, they did not need the *qāḍīs*' authorization to use *waqf* income or to take out loans for these purposes. It was thus surprising to discover that the *sijill* contains records of many requests by *mutawallīs* for precisely this kind of authorization. It took effort, time and expense to obtain the approval of the *sharīʿa* court. When the *qāḍī* received the request, he would appoint a committee of contractors experienced in preservation and renovation. The committee was chaired by the chief clerk of the *sharīʿa* court (*ahl al-sharʿ al-sharīf*), whose job it was to look at the work from the *sharīʿa* perspective. That meant ensuring that it would not be more expensive than required to keep the property in sound repair and would not constitute improvement and development. The task of the experts (*ahl al-khibra*) was to estimate the cost of renovation and draft the specifications. The committee visited the property and submitted a detailed report, including an opinion on how essential the requested work was. It also drew up a detailed cost estimate.[26]

The *sharīʿa* court in Mandatory Jerusalem authorized 41 renovations of *waqf* properties by *mutawallīs*. There were 15 permits for the use of *waqf* money for the work required, 10 entitling *mutawallīs* to take loans and 16 for long-term rentals, with the rent for the entire period being paid in advance for use in the renovation.

Under the law, only requests of the last two types required the *qāḍī*'s consent. Renovations of the first kind could not only be carried out without recourse to the court; they were actually defined in law as the *mutawallī*'s basic obligation.[27] Why, then, were such requests made at all? As we have seen, the beneficiaries usually wanted to benefit from their entitlements in the short term and to postpone, for as long as was feasible, basic renovations likely to reduce or suspend their benefits for some time. Generally speaking, the interests of the *mutawallī*s, even though most of them were themselves beneficiaries, were different. As administrators, they were responsible for keeping the property in good repair and were more alert to the long-term economic aspects of their conduct as managers of the properties. Furthermore, dishonest *mutawallī*s could exploit renovation work for personal gain, because it was hard to monitor the costs effectively. (Renovations of non-*maḍbūṭ waqf* properties did not require competitive bidding or the selection of the lowest bid.) This seems to explain why *mutawallī*s petitioned the *qāḍī* of their own volition for authorization to make the repairs after an inspection by experts, even though the procedure involved considerable efforts as well as disbursements from *waqf* revenue. In this fashion, the *mutawallī*s protected themselves from future gossip or lawsuits on the part of the beneficiaries.

It appears that in most instances, the *qāḍī*'s approval was sought. This had become the accepted (but not the compulsory) procedure in the late Ottoman period. We infer this from cases in which beneficiaries demanded the dismissal of *mutawallī*s for having renovated *waqf* property without the *qāḍī*'s prior approval. As was to be expected, the *qāḍī* ruled against the applicants, pointing out that no permission was needed to perform essential renovations: to do so was the *mutawallī*'s duty in any event.[28] But the *qāḍī* usually set up a committee to ascertain that the renovation had been carried out at the stated prices.[29]

Another possible reason for asking prior approval was the wish to use the renovation work to develop and upgrade the property. The *qāḍī*s sometimes actually predicated their approval on the expectation that the requested work would lead to greater revenues in the future.[30]

In five cases in which beneficiaries sought the dismissal of a *mutawallī* during the Mandatory period, one of the allegations was that the renovations he had carried out went beyond what was actually required. In none of these cases did the *qāḍī* rule against the *mutawallī*. In another instance, the *mutawallī* of the Muḥammad Shitaya Waqf attempted to explain his investment of *waqf* moneys in building a new house for the *waqf* as the fulfilment of his duty of *'imāra*, thus investing this term with the literal meaning of 'construction'. The *qāḍī* rejected his interpretation and dismissed him.[31] In the other cases, however, the *qāḍī*s backed *mutawallī*s who had improved *waqf* properties.[32] In another suit, a woman beneficiary of the al-Khaṭīb Waqf sued the *mutawallī* for having installed a large display window in a *waqf*-owned shop without the beneficiaries' consent. The *mutawallī* claimed that his action had increased the annual rent from £P25 to £P40. The *qāḍī* dismissed the suit, because the *mutawallī* had acted in good faith and had the *waqf*'s best interests in mind, even though his decision contradicted the letter of *sharī'a* law.[33]

The *qāḍī* was aware that renovation provided *mutawallī*s with opportunities to line their own pockets. Even after an expert committee had submitted a detailed estimate, it was obvious that he did not always rely on the *mutawallī*s. Therefore, in some of his permits the *qāḍī* ordered the *mutawallī*s to submit an itemized report on the costs of the work, together with receipts (*ḥisāb munaẓẓam bi-wuṣūlāt rasmiyya 'alā al-uṣūl*) for the *sharī'a* court.[34] Invoices were not considered sufficient. The *qāḍī* also obliged the *mutawallī*s to defray the cost of a second committee of experts, to be called in at the end of the work, and to check whether the receipts corresponded to the work performed. A note confirming that the audit had been completed was added to the *qāḍī*'s permit.[35]

One way to gauge the physical and economic viability of *waqf* properties was to enquire whether the properties had been renovated even when their current revenues were insufficient to do so. In such cases, the *mutawallī* had two possibilities: to take out a loan or to find a long-term tenant willing to pay the entire rent in advance. The *qāḍī*s of Jerusalem preferred long-term rentals over loans. Twenty-seven permits for long-term rentals with rent paid in advance were given during the Mandatory period.[36] In one-fourth of all renovation permits in the Mandatory period, the *mutawallī*s took loans. Five of the ten loans came from the *mutawallī*'s own money, and the *qāḍī* permitted him to repay himself in the future, when the *waqf* would again generate income. Loans to the *waqf* were always interest-free.[37]

One of the problems of the *mutawallī*s was how to make the necessary renovations in buildings where, under the terms of the *waqfiyya*, beneficiaries were actually living themselves. In order to finance the renovation, the *mutawallī* had to let the building, thus requiring the residents to vacate it, sometimes for several years. They were not eager to do so, and if they refused outright, the *mutawallī* asked the *sharīʿa* court to order them out.[38]

An essential point in looking after *waqf* properties was the payment of property taxes. In only one lawsuit was a *mutawallī* accused of failing to pay the tax (for five consecutive years). The Land Registry Office (*ṭābū*) had therefore placed a lien on the property. For this and other reasons, the *mutawallī* was dismissed.[39] The existence of a lien in favour of the Land Registry points to the contradiction between *sharīʿa* and civil law. It is quite possible that under civil law, one could attach a *waqf* property in this fashion or even sequestrate it, although this is not known to have occurred.

Safeguarding waqf *rights*

One of the *mutawallī*'s major duties was to safeguard the *waqf* status of its assets and prevent encroachment. Attempts to acquire rights to *waqf* properties could be made by claiming possession or any other means. A *mutawallī* who knew of an attempt at encroachment and failed to take legal action to stop it was deemed to have breached the trust vested in him. He was therefore liable to dismissal. A beneficiary of the Zāwiyya al-Fakhriyya Waqf, for example, sued the *mutawallī* for not having applied in time for the eviction of Jews who had squatted on *waqf* land in the Jerusalem neighbourhood of Talpiot. The claimant alleged that the trespassers had paved a road across *waqf* land. The *qāḍī*, accompanied by the several *mukhtārs* from the neighbourhood, visited the site and concluded that the *mutawallī* had been eight years late in suing the trespassers in the district court. The claimant further alleged that the beneficiaries (members of the Abū al-Saʿūd family) had urged the *mutawallī* to sue; he turned them down, however, arguing that litigation in the land court was costly. The *qāḍī* considered this to constitute negligence, and dismissed the *mutawallī*.[40]

In 14 suits for the dismissal of *mutawallī*s, litigants argued, *inter alia*, that the *mutawallī*s had failed to take action against trespassers. In only three of these suits was the accusation proven and the *mutawallī* dismissed. The *qāḍī*s took a tough stand toward *mutawallī*s who neglected to safeguard *waqf* rights. The archives of two courts, the district land court in Jerusalem and the *sharīʿa* court, however, contain records of many suits filed by *mutawallī*s themselves against persons who, in their opinion, had jeopardized the rights of the *waqf*. For example, the *mutawallī* of the Darwīsh Waqf sued his brother who, while living in a *waqf*-owned dwelling, laid personal claim to it as an inheritance from his father. The *qāḍī* ruled that the usurper be evicted.[41] In an opposite example, a beneficiary who kept other beneficiaries from taking control of *waqf* properties and registering them as their own was appointed by the *qāḍī* as *mutawallī*.[42]

Charitable obligations

The conditions contained in a *waqfiyya* are binding and have the status of *sharīʿa* rulings (*sharṭ al-wāqif ka-naṣṣ al-sharʿ*).[43] This includes instructions to earmark portions of *waqf* revenues for specific purposes. Most such allocations were for charity, such as feeding the poor on festivals and during the month of Ramaḍān, or for acts of religion, such as prayer and reciting of qur'ānic verses in the founder's memory.

It is an intriguing question whether the founders' stipulations were honoured by succeeding generations. In Mandate-era lawsuits for the dismissal of *mutawallī*s, non-fulfilment of the founder's instructions was considered to add to other grounds for dismissal, but did not in itself justify dismissal. The few suits of this type that reached the *sharīʿa* court prove that failures to honour charitable stipulations did occur, but give no indication of their frequency.[44] For example, a *mutawallī* was sued for having failed to distribute 150 piasters to the poor as laid down in the endowment deed. (The claimant ignored the change in currencies and their values between the time of dedication and the Mandatory period.)[45] In another case, a beneficiary of the Sanʿallāh and Mūsā al-Khālidī Waqfs sued the *mutawallī* for having failed all along to honour the founder's wishes for the supply of water to the fountain (*sabīl*) in the al-Silsila neighbourhood of the Old City of Jerusalem, for the distribution of bread to the poor near the *sabīl* and for the provision of candles at the Mūsā dome and the Sulṭāniyya building in the Old City in the month of Ramaḍān. The charge was never examined, because the *qāḍī* dismissed the *mutawallī* on different grounds.[46]

It is evident that not all cases of disregarding charitable obligations were recorded in the *sijill*. Beneficiaries were more concerned with obtaining their own share; quite possibly, they were not interested in charitable payments being made which were bound to reduce their share. Moreover, the *mutawallī* and the beneficiaries had a common interest in maximizing their share. They attributed little importance to charitable stipulations, and the beneficiaries would invoke them as additional grounds in suing for the dismissal of a *mutawallī*. Shaykh Asʿad al-Imām claims that in modern times, only a few *mutawallī*s honoured founders' wishes to perform charitable works.[47]

Administration of waqfs *by the SMC*

The management of *waqf* properties by the SMC has not yet been thoroughly researched. There are only two sources for doing so: the self-serving publications of the SMC and the critical memorandum of Abū al-Hudā and Mukhliṣ, written in 1923. Kupferschmidt, in his study on the SMC, attributes the paucity of our knowledge to the lack of records; many of the transactions were concluded orally, some over the telephone. The SMC archives abound with bureaucratic documents on every financial transaction, small or large, that was approved according to SMC procedures.[48] They give the superficial impression of great concern for sound administrative principles. However, administrative regulations do not eliminate every possibility of corruption and mismanagement. The reorganization of SMC documents in the archives rules out a methodical and quantitative study. Therefore, the findings presented below are based on a sample perusal and are a general impression evoked by the documents.

Rentals and rent collection

Letting *maḍbūṭ waqf* property through public competitive bidding had been the practice in Jerusalem since the late Ottoman period.[49] When the SMC took over that function, its Waqf Department issued annual invitations to bid. These were posted on the bulletin board at the Waqf Department offices and sometimes in mosques as well. Newspaper advertising was also used. The bidding period was 20 days, and bidders had to fill out a special form (*waṣlat muzāwada*) at the Waqf Department. The winner had to sign a standard rental contract and register it with the municipality. The contract laid down that the Waqf Department would bear the cost of repairing leaks; the tenants would pay municipal taxes, business licensing fees and other expenses. Tenants presented a financial guarantee or paid one-third of the yearly rental in advance. Rent was paid in three instalments: when the bid was won, two months later, and after another month. Tenants who failed to vacate the premises on time were fined.[50]

The bids were examined by the local *waqf* committee, which decided which to accept. The aforementioned memorandum by Abū al-Hudā and Mukhliṣ, two senior Ottoman Waqf Department officials whom the SMC dismissed soon after it went into operation, shows that the rules were sometimes flouted. They alleged that big merchants had won most of the bids and paid rent at levels lower than warranted. There is no way of knowing whether these were exceptions that were subsequently remedied or whether this was, and remained, the norm.[51]

It is also impossible to determine, on the basis of the available archive material, whether the SMC obtained the maximum revenue from the properties it administered. The following example illustrates this difficulty. Khān al-Khatrūr, a caravanserai on the road to Jericho, was let in 1921 for 4,000 piasters. When the time came to bid for 1922, the highest bid was 3,500 piasters. The local *waqf* committee decided to extend the deadline by another week. During this time, another eight bids were tendered; the highest, offering 4,700 piasters, came from the previous tenant.[52] The SMC archives contain some few pieces of evidence that the SMC officials felt free to act in this fashion because the decision to accept a bid or postpone the deadline was in their discretion. The existence of fixed administrative and bureaucratic procedures within the SMC did not, therefore, guarantee sound economic administration, and left room for irregularities.

In 1940, the SMC appointed a rental transactions committee made up of a member of the SMC (Shaykh Kamāl Ismāʿīl, chairman), the *ma'mūr al-awqāf*, and one ʿUthmān al-Nammarī. Its function was to replace the local *waqf* committee in handling bids. It was empowered to refuse letting the property to the highest bidder if this was in the *waqf*'s interest (*ʿalā an takūn lahā al-ṣalāḥiyya bi-ʿadam al-taqayyūd bil-mazīd al-akhīr idhā ra'at maṣlaḥat al-waqf mu'ammana fī ghayrihi*).[53] It is not clear why the SMC transferred this function from the local *waqf* committee to a new body.

Invoking a provision of the Ottoman Land Law,[54] the SMC set a rent of 2.5 per cent of the value of the land for lessees who improved and developed the property by building on it. The government instructed the property tax (*wergo*) office to inform the Waqf Department of any improvement made and to help it appraise the land.[55]

The Waqf Department sent out its own officials to collect leasing fees, and paid them six per cent of the sums they brought in.[56] An SMC report of 1939 shows that the 211 *maḍbūṭ* properties administered by the SMC in Jerusalem were expected to yield a revenue of £P4,604; actual collection amounted only to £P4,007 (87 per cent). For 121 family *waqf* properties provisionally administered by the SMC, its clerks collected £P439 instead of £P764 (57 per cent!). The SMC admitted that revenues were lower than warranted but blamed this on legal problems rather than the rent collectors. Consequently, the SMC concluded an agreement with the government for its tax collectors to collect rents as well.[57]

In setting fees for large tracts, the SMC took economic circumstances into account. In 1937, for example, it decided not to raise *waqf* rents in view of the economic conditions and the general strike declared that year, which had caused some lessees to vacate *waqf* properties.[58] In 1942, it decided to help lessees who had planted orchards on leased *waqf* land because, under wartime conditions, they had made no profits. With this in mind, the SMC lowered rents from £P1.25 per dunam to £P0.25 for the years since the outbreak of the war, and allowed the lessees to pay earlier arrears in instalments.[59] It was apparently motivated by political considerations related to the Jewish–Arab struggle over land.

The rate of collecting rents seems to have been high during most of the Mandatory period. Internal SMC guidelines indicate that it strove to maximize the efficacy of collection. The improvement was felt mainly in the 1940s. In 1943, the debts of lessees of *mundaras waqf* properties amounted to £P777. The new *ma'mūr al-awqāf*, appointed in 1941, proposed that the SMC make a settlement with the lessees and cancel all outstanding claims. His predecessors, he claimed, had been negligent, while during his own tenure, the collection rate had reached 100 per cent.[60] A report by the SMC auditor, George Asʿad Khaḍir, shows rent collection rates of 97–100 per cent in 1946.[61]

Maintenance and renovation

All renovation and construction work on *waqf* land required public bidding. Contractors who wished to bid filled out a form at the Waqf Department (*waṣlat munāqaṣa*). The bids were examined by the *waqf* engineer and the local *waqf* committee;[62] the latter also approved participation by the SMC in the renovation of village mosques.[63]

SMC budget data show that the SMC placed greater emphasis on renovation and maintenance of *waqf* properties after 1937. In 1934, for example, the SMC spent £P3,272, or only three per cent of its annual budget, on such works throughout the country (even though it was in excellent financial condition due to the tithes agreements). In 1946, by contrast, the SMC spent £P15,000 (12 per cent) on renovations.[64]

The SMC's greatest enterprise in this regard was the renovation of al-Aqṣā Mosque and other religious buildings on the Temple Mount (*al-Ḥaram al-Sharīf*), including old religious colleges, some of which were converted into modern schools, cultural institutions or offices.[65] In its publications, the SMC claimed to have renovated 313 mosques and built 21 new ones. In reality, according to Kupferschmidt, the SMC renovated only about 100 mosques.[66] The renovation files in the SMC archives shows that the SMC's contribution towards the renovation of rural mosques was negligible, yet it described such works as its own.[67] According to its own publications, the SMC also renovated some 300 non-devotional buildings in order to improve their state of upkeep and thus their ability to generate revenue. The SMC took a great deal of pride in this. Thirty-five shops destroyed in the 1927 earthquake were rebuilt and renovated with revenue from long-term tenants who paid the rent in advance.[68]

Safeguarding waqf *prerogatives*

One of the first actions taken by the SMC was an attempt to wrest from the British the control of *waqf* assets that had been confiscated by the Ottomans.[69] Where the SMC failed to obtain satisfaction in the first place, most of its demands were met later, after the Webb Commission had concluded its work. In 1929, Amīn al-Tamīmī was sent to Istanbul in order to collect documents that might support SMC guardianship of various *waqf*s. Correspondence between Tamīmī and Ḥājj Amīn makes it evident that his mission accomplished little. The SMC claimed that Tamīmī returned with 500 documents, and that these were used by the Webb Commission as well as in ten lawsuits meant to prove *waqf* ownership, but this was merely a belated attempt to justify his expensive mission.[70] The SMC's overall efforts to assert its right to manage *waqf* assets paid off in the agreements of 1932 and 1934 with the British administration.

The SMC also vigorously defended its rights against squatters and trespassers, as is attested to by the large number of lawsuits filed for this purpose. The SMC hired a prominent lawyer to represent it in these cases.[71]

Honouring charitable stipulations

The management of endowments by a central administration, such as the Ottoman Waqf Ministry or the Mandate-era SMC, virtually neutralized the founders' *waqfiyyāt* and their painstaking guidelines on the disposition of revenues. Although the statutes of the SMC required it to adhere to the founders' stipulations, the SMC regarded itself as exempt from this obligation for *maḍbūṭ waqfs* under its administration. In a famous lawsuit, some Hebron residents claimed that the entitlement of the Khalīl al-Raḥmān Mosque in Hebron was intended, above all, for renovating the Hebron *ḥaram* (the Cave of the Patriarchs) and only then for the benefit of Hebron citizens. The SMC replied that **civil law** absolved it from having to comply with the founder's stipulations in the case of a *maḍbūṭ waqf* (*al-awqāf al-mabḥūth ʿanhā maḍbūṭa wa-inna lā luzūm qānūnan li-murāʿāt shurūṭ al-waqfiyya fī al-awqāf allatī hiya min hādhā al-nawʿ wal-awqāf al-maḍbūṭa ism tuliqa ʿalā al-amwāl al-mawqūfa allatī yudīruhā wazīr al-awqāf raʾsan*). The SMC thus based itself on the Ottoman civil code and ignored *sharīʿa* law.[72] The (civil) Supreme Court, before which the claim against the SMC was brought, ruled for the claimant, asserting that the relevant clause in the SMC statutes referred to new *waqfs* only.[73] The position of the SMC on this issue, however, did not dissuade it from accepting grants from the Egyptian Waqf Ministry, originating in the Cairo-registered Sinān Pāshā Waqf, for the purpose of remunerating *Qurʾān* reciters at al-Aqṣā Mosque.[74]

The SMC applied a selective policy in funding social welfare projects from the income of *waqfs* it administered. Its most significant charitable enterprise in Jerusalem was the soup kitchens, the *ʿimāra* in the *takiyya* (Sufi lodge) of the Khāṣṣikī Sulṭān Waqf. The founder had wished to provide two daily meals for 400 indigents as well as staff and wayfarers who stayed at the *takiyya*, to distribute 2,000 loaves of bread daily to the eligible poor and to provide special festive meals for the entire population of the city on Muslim holidays.[75]

In 1927/28, the SMC allocated £P2,779 for operations at the *takiyya* and put six employees on the payroll there (and eight at the Hebron *takiyya*).[76] However, like its Ottoman predecessor, the SMC had trouble listing those eligible to eat at the *takiyya*. In the 1930s, the SMC received many complaints to the effect that the head of the *takiyya* was disregarding the old Ottoman list of eligibles and let anyone whom he favoured eat there.[77] Others complained of the quality of the soup that was served. Although the principal was eventually replaced, the SMC was no less responsible for the prevalent disorder. The local *waqf* committee, which received numerous requests for assistance from indigent locals, sent the applicants to the *takiyya*, where they received a sum of money or some basic foodstuffs. Some of the needy took the food and then peddled it. The director-general of the Waqf Department wrote to the SMC, stating that if the Hebron *takiyya* was to go on meeting every request for help, twice the current budget would not even cover the cost of bread.[78] In the late Mandatory period, 275 eligibles from the Ottoman period received an aggregate of £P107 and 65 eligibles from the Mandatory period received another £P43.[79] In 1934, the SMC spent £P1,353 on welfare, in addition to £P2,665 for operating the *takiyyas* in Jerusalem and Hebron.[80] In 1946, the sum of £P2,366 was spent on welfare and the distribution of flour in Hebron, £P6,079 for food at the two *takiyyas*, and £P299 for *zāwiyya* allotments.[81] Although the operation of the *takiyya*s was part of the founder's stipulations, the welfare stipends were granted by a central administrative body and were unrelated to any specific deed. The *zāwiyya* also served a small number of families who operated it and benefited from allocations; *zāwiyya* visitors did not, however, benefit as they had done in the past.

In 1930, faced with a budget crisis, the SMC slashed payroll and welfare expenditure by 20 per cent, and in 1931 by a further 15 per cent. Subsequently, staff salaries were restored, but allocations to 15 *zāwiyya*s were not.[82] In 1938, the SMC stopped funding the Adhamī *zāwiyya* on the grounds that no more worshippers were coming to visit it.[83]

Welfare apart, the SMC took charge of the traditional ceremonies of Nabī Mūsā and Nabī Rubīn at which food was distributed to the celebrants. Approximately £P700 was spent for this purpose in 1945.[84] Similarly, Palestinian students at al-Azhar in Cairo were given scholarships.[85] These activities were, however, marginal. Clearly, the SMC engaged in some charitable acts (provided they were not overly expensive) in order to gain popularity. Most of the founders' stipulations were not honoured.[86] In 1946, the SMC paid £P2,027 to *Qur'ān* reciters. This item had not appeared in the 1934 budget; it seems that the SMC began allocating *waqf* revenues for *Qur'ān* recitations only after 1937, in an effort to meet the *waqfiyyāt* terms.[87] Kupferschmidt, for one, does not believe that the SMC should be faulted, because it did no more than follow Ottoman practice.[88]

The most significant question concerning the observation of founders' instructions was whether the revenue of *al-ḥaramayn waqf*s was forwarded to Mecca and al-Madīna. There were many endowments in Jerusalem whose primary purpose was to support the two holy cities in the Ḥijāz. In others, this was the stated purpose meant to take effect after the deaths of the family beneficiaries. The records show that the SMC forwarded some moneys to the *ḥaramayn* on an ad hoc basis, at irregular intervals and irrespective of the current revenue of the properties pledged. In 1941, for example, the SMC set aside £P1,000 for Mecca and al-Madīna.[89] In Algeria, by contrast, the French regime negotiated an agreement with Ibn Saʿūd in 1932 for the transfer of the *awqāf al-ḥaramayn* revenues.[90]

To sum up: the SMC adhered strictly to bureaucratic procedures in its ongoing management of *waqf*s, but these did not always prevent corruption or mismanagement. There were occasional allegations that *waqf* properties had been leased on preferential terms to relatives of Ḥājj Amīn or other employees of the *waqf* administration. Revenue collection was relatively efficient, but rents were low (for reasons to be explained in Chapter 7). Places of worship seem to have been renovated regularly, and after 1937, efforts were stepped up to maintain non-devotional buildings. The SMC took pains to uphold the *waqf* status of properties it managed. As for observing the founders' stipulations, the SMC regarded itself as the successor to the central Ottoman administration and deemed itself free of the shackles of the dedication deeds, even though its own statutes ordered it to respect them. It provided welfare services that corresponded in a general way to some of the founders' wishes, but disregarded specific terms set forth by them.

COMPARATIVE CONCLUSION

Mutawallīs let *waqf* properties to the same tenants for periods longer than those allowed under *sharī'a* law. Properties of *maḍbūṭ waqfs*, by contrast, were let on a yearly basis through competitive bidding. This should have secured a higher level of rent, but there is no assurance that this was so, because – so it was said – the same bidders were chosen each time. In the collection of rent, family *waqfs* were usually more successful than the SMC. SMC collection percentages from family *waqfs* under its temporary care were especially low. Its clerks seem to have had little interest in the matter.

With respect to maintenance, *waqfs* under the SMC evidently fared better. Contracts drawn up by the SMC required tenants to provide adequate maintenance. Renovations of places of worship had first priority, but others were dealt with as well, especially after 1937, when the SMC was less preoccupied with high-visibility enterprises. There were, however, several instances of neglect.

The SMC paid much attention to safeguarding *waqf* prerogatives and covered the legal expenses involved. So, as a matter of fact, did the *mutawallīs* themselves. But they were not always able to cover legal expenses or provide the necessary documentation. Some cases therefore went by default. In others, *mutawallīs* gave their *waqfs* loans from their own money to cover court expenses.

On one point, both the *mutawallīs* and the SMC displayed a similar degree of neglect: the founders' wishes for funding charitable works were often disregarded by both. The SMC did indeed operate welfare projects such as soup kitchens in Jerusalem, Hebron and Sidnā 'Alī, and handed out charity to the needy, but it did so irrespective of the precise terms laid down in endowment deeds. The *mutawallīs*, though bound to honour the founders' terms, had an interest in cutting down on charitable spending, and so did the beneficiaries. This common interest resulted in few complaints being lodged against *mutawallīs* on this count.

NOTES

1. See Sh. D. Goitein and A. Ben Shemmesh, *Muslim Law in the State of Israel* (Hebrew) (Jerusalem, 1957) pp. 169–70; Avraham Granovski, *The Land Regime in Palestine* (Hebrew, Tel-Aviv, 1949), 127–30.; G. Gilbar, 'The *Waqf* and Economic Growth' in G. Baer and G. Gilbar (eds), *Studies on the Muslim Waqf* (Oxford: Oxford University Press) (forthcoming); idem, 'Muslim *Waqf* and Distribution of Capital and Income, Towards a Quantitative Analysis' in G. Baer and G. Gilbar (eds), *Studies on the Muslim Waqf* (Oxford: Oxford University Press) (forthcoming).
2. M. Qadrī Pāshā, *Kitāb Qānūn al-ʿAdl wa'l-Inṣāf li'l-Qaḍā' ʿalā Mushkilāt al-Awqāf* (Cairo, 1902) art. 276.
3. Ibid., art. 277.
4. Interview with Shaykh Asʿad al-Imām on 12 May, 1990.
5. Examples: *Sijill* 445/10/118, 445/44/156, 461/6/9, 471/110/84, 479/69/21, 451/78/120, 455/117/115, 455/109/102, 461/5/8.
6. *Sijill* 502/1/199.
7. See note 4 above.
8. Ibid.
9. *Sijill* 452/381/246, 456/178/161, 478/393/150, 502/1/199, 502/232/101.
10. *Sijill* 449/7/68.
11. *Sijill* 452/43/120.
12. M. Qadrī Pāshā, *Kitāb Qānūn al-ʿAdl wa'l-Inṣāf li'l-Qaḍā' ʿalā Mushkilāt al-Awqāf* (Cairo, 1902) art. 277.
13. *Sijill* 473/313/69.
14. *Sijill* 483/182/136.
15. *Sijill* 483/182/136, 449/98/187.
16. Examples: *Sijill* 478/359/93.
17. M. Qadrī Pāshā, *Kitāb Qānūn al-ʿAdl wa'l-Inṣāf li'l-Qaḍā' ʿalā Mushkilāt al-Awqāf* (Cairo, 1902) art. 277.
18. Ibid., art. 180.
19. Ibid., art. 196.
20. Ibid., art. 180.
21. Sh. D. Goitein and A. Ben Shemmesh, *Muslim Law in the State of Israel* (Hebrew, Jerusalem, 1957) pp. 169–70; G. Baer, *A History of Land Ownership in Modern Egypt: 1800–1950* (London: Oxford University Press, 1962) p. 169; A. Granovski, *The Land Regime in Palestine* (Hebrew, Tel-Aviv, 1949) pp. 127–30.
22. Interview with Shaykh Asʿad al-Imām on 12 May 1990.
23. *Sijill* 424/208/170, 449/98/187.
24. *Sijill* 456/347/337.
25. *Sijill* 489/5/47. Other examples: *Sijill* 466/9/179, 502/156/423, 483/378/6, 489/163/348, 419/27/642, 449/26/91, 449/7/68.
26. The experts were the engineers Yāsīn al-Dasūqī and ʿĀrif al Zamāmīrī. Each

committee was chaired by the municipality engineer – Thuraya al-Budayrī.

27. M. Qadrī Pāshā, *Kitāb Qānūn al-ʿAdl wa'l-Inṣāf li'l-Qaḍā' ʿalā Mushkilāt al-Awqāf* (Cairo, 1902) art. 180.
28. *Sijill* 452/357/214, 502/1/199.
29. *Sijill* 452/357/214, 478/359/63, 502/1/199.
30. Examples: *Sijill* 500/36/241, 481/134/21, 458/78/46, 454/49/153, 485/124/220.
31. *Sijill* 478/291/267.
32. *Sijill* 502/1/199.
33. *Sijill* 509/61/399.
34. *Sijill* 508/125/81, 469/120/153.
35. *Sijill* 427/171/170.
36. *Sijill* 458/78/46, 455/108/101.
37. *Sijill* 419/395/5, 427/171/170, 427/343/15.
38. *Sijill* 481/94/38, 436/111/20, 432/262/376, 455/108/101.
39. *Sijill* 466/9/179.
40. *Sijill* 456/247/231, 466/9/175.
41. *Sijill* 452/126/218, 516/123/7.
42. *Sijill* 502/15/217.
43. M. Qadrī Pāshā, *Kitāb Qānūn al-ʿAdl wa'l-Inṣāf li'l-Qaḍā' ʿalā Mushkilāt al-Awqāf* (Cairo, 1902) arts. 102, 182.
44. For a case of the dismissal of a plaintiff from his position of *nāẓir* see *Sijill* 483/182/136.
45. *Sijill* 449/98/187, 478/359/93.
46. *Sijill* 424/208/170. Other examples: *Sijill* 438/362/222, 489/5/47, *CIH*, 13/42/1,39/40.
47. Interview with Shaykh Asʿad al-Imām on 12 May 1990.
48. The *ma'mūr al-awqāf*, the inspector of *Sharīʿa* Courts, the *waqf* engineer, the general director of the *waqf* department, the local *waqf* committee and the SMC.
49. H. Gerber, *Ottoman Rule in Jerusalem 1890–1914* (Berlin: Klaus Schwarz Verlag, 1985) p. 190–1.
50. *CIH*, 330, 13/23/6,15/20.
51. U.M. Kupferschmidt, *The Supreme Muslim Council: Islam under the British Mandate for Palestine* (Leiden: E.J. Brill, 1987) p. 158.
52. *CIH*, 330, 13/23/6,15/20.
53. *CIH*, 13/40/1,31/40.
54. Paragraph 32 of the Ottoman Land Law. See letter from the president of the SMC to the Chief Secretary dated 31 July 1930, *CIH*, 920, 13/29/1,13/40.
55. *CIH*, 920, 13/29/1,13/40.
56. In 1942, the collection fee was raised to 7 per cent, *CIH*, 920, 6/42/1,36/40. For *awqāf mundarasa* the fees were 12 per cent of the total collected, *CIH*, 921, 13/41/1,34/40.
57. Al-Majlis al-Islāmī al-Sharʿī al-Aʿlā, *Majmūʿat al-Balāghāt li-sanat 1345, 1346h*, p. 1.
58. Letter of al-Tamīmī dated 3 March 1937, *CIH*, 3/52, 13/38/2,48/10.
59. *CIH*, 921, 6/42/1,36/40.
60. *CIH*, 13/42/5,27/60.
61. *ISA, SMC*, P/988, 38.

62. See for example *CIH*, 330, 13/21/6,1/20.
63. Ibid.; and files 13/22/6,8/20, 13/22/6,2/20, 13/22/6,2/20, 13/22/6,4/20, 13/22/6,5/20.
64. *ISA, SMC*, P/988, 37,38.
65. The Maghribī Mosque became a museum, four *madrasas* became schools, *al-madrasa al-manjaqiyya* were made the office of the SMC and a *zāwiyya* was turned into the *Sharīʿa* Court.
66. *CIH* 13/38/2,4/4/45.
67. *CIH*, 13/33/2,24/10.
68. Al-Majlis al-Islāmī al-Sharʿī al-Aʿlā, *Bayān al-Majlis al-Islāmī al-Sharʿī al-Aʿlā*, 1929, p. 10.
69. See Chapter Two.
70. Al-Majlis al-Islāmī al-Sharʿī al-Aʿlā, *Bayān al-Majlis al-Islāmī al-Sharʿī al-Aʿlā*, 1931, p.31.
71. Attorney Avcarius Bey. *ISA, Land Court*, B/772, 41/36; B/749, 56/28; B/763, 19/35; B/747, 55/28.
72. See Chapter Two for District *Awqāf* Administrators' Regulations and the Ottoman Budget Law, *Dustūr* (2nd series), 6, p. 1036; *Palestine* (newspaper) 10 May 1932; *ISA, SMC*, P/988, 2; Y. Arnon-Ohana, *The Internal Struggle within the Palestinian Movement 1929–1939* (Hebrew, Tel Aviv, 1981) p. 100.
73. U.M. Kupferschmidt, *The Supreme Muslim Council: Islam under the British Mandate for Palestine* (Leiden: E.J. Brill, 1987) p. 163.
74. *CIH*, 13/40/1,31/40.
75. For the *Waqfiyya* see *Sijill* 270/18; al-Imām al-Ḥusaynī, p. 78; O. Peri, 'The Ottoman State and the Waqf Institution in late Eighteenth Century Jerusalem' (unpublished M.A. Thesis in Hebrew, Jerusalem: The Hebrew University, 1983) p. 3.
76. *CIH*, 13/27/2,1/3/45, 0/44/2,2/2/45.
77. *CIH*, 13/38/2,4/3/45.
78. Ibid.: *Idhā sirnā ʿalā al-istijāba li-kul maṭlab la yakfi ḍiʿf mukhaṣaṣāt al-takiyya li-ta'mīn al-ḥubz faqaṭ*.
79. For list of benefectors see *CIH*, 13/45/2,9/3/45.
80. *ISA, SMC*, P/988, 37.
81. Ibid., 38.
82. Ibid.
83. Ibid.
84. *CIH*, 13/22/1,8/2/45, 13/40/1,31/40.
85. *CIH*, 921, 13/38/1,24/40.
86. See Aḥad Fuḍala' al-Muslimīn, *Bayān wa-Radd ʿAlā Bayān al-Majlis al-Islāmī al-Aʿlā muwajjah li-Kull Muslim fī al-ʿĀlam al-Islāmī ʿĀmmatan wa-fī Filasṭīn Khāṣṣatan* (Jerusalem, 1924).
87. *ISA, SMC*, P/988, 38.
88. U.M. Kupferschmidt, *The Supreme Muslim Council: Islam under the British Mandate for Palestine* (Leiden: E.J. Brill, 1987) p. 164.
89. *CIH*, 921, 13/411/34/40.
90. G. Busson de Janssens, 'Contribution a l'etude de habous public algeriens' (Ph.D. dissertation, 1950) p. 1.

7

Transactions and economic development

It is widely held in the relevant literature that the restrictions imposed on *waqf* properties by religious law prevented their economic improvement.[1] This is particularly true of the ban on the sale of such property, as implied in its very name (*waqafa*: 'to stand').[2] Baer, speaking of *waqf* lands, summarizes this opinion as follows:

> Everybody agrees that *waqf* land was always neglected, its income always lower than that of other land. There are two reasons for this: first, since it cannot be sold, it cannot serve as collateral for a loan that would be invested in the development of such land. Second, it is impossible to sell parts of the property and invest the proceeds in the development of the other parts.[3]

Gilbar, too, while challenging Baer's thesis and defining the *waqf* as a major motor of economic advancement (on the grounds that the very dedication and earmarking of property is tantamount to creating economic resources), thinks of the prohibition of selling *waqf* property as an economic drawback, albeit one that existed only in the past 150–200 years. Gilbar's important assertion is that the overall characteristics of the *waqf* vary from place to place and from period to period; thus only a series of case studies can give us a proper understanding of its economic function of the *waqf* in Muslim society.[4]

In this chapter, findings from the *sijill* about *waqf*-property transactions in Jerusalem during the British Mandate period are presented, analysed and compared, both with findings from earlier (Ottoman) periods and with what little the literature tells us about other parts of the Muslim world.

The *waqf* is characterized by the contradiction between two of its basic principles, both stemming from the sacrosanct obligation to respect the founder's wishes: (1) the wish to perpetuate the endowment's **purpose**, a charitable act that, in itself, lends it the characteristic of sanctity, and (2) the desire to perpetuate the **properties** so dedicated as a living memorial, so to speak, to the founder and his lifework.

Any asset, of course, depreciates over time, and it is not always possible to preserve and maintain properties by means of *waqf* revenues only. Consider, for example, a person who dedicated a date plantation for a specific charitable purpose. Gradually, the palms bear less and less fruit, and the land loses its fertility. Under the prevalent constraints, the *waqf* administrator cannot develop the property; the *waqf* is therefore doomed. The endowment proves to be less than eternal, and the founder's wishes cannot be honoured in perpetuity. Founders had to choose between keeping the property in its original state, even at the cost of forfeiting the *waqf*, or safeguarding its purpose at the risk of having to make changes to the property.

Muslim jurists have debated this problem since the dawn of Islam. Abū Yūsuf, the Ḥanafī jurist of the second Islamic century (d. 798CE), who was chief *qāḍī* in Baghdad under the caliphs al-Mahdī and Hārūn al-Rashīd, ruled that founders are entitled to provide for the future exchange (*istibdāl*) of *waqf* properties for others, or even for their sale and the purchase of an alternative property.[5] In practical terms, founders made little use of this. More than that: in most endowment deeds, the founders went out of their way to state that the property must not be exchanged. The Ḥanafī jurist al-Khaṣṣāf (d. 874/5CE), whose book on *waqf* law is one of the oldest extant, cites the above example of the date plantation to show that it is more desirable and efficient to sell the property through *istibdāl* and purchase another instead, perhaps smaller but more fertile and productive, provided that the purpose of the *waqf* is honoured.[6] The way in which al-Khaṣṣāf sets forth his ideas allows one to draw three conclusions:

1. There were jurists who, as early as the formative period of Muslim law, preferred to perpetuate the purpose rather than the original property of the *waqf*. Consequently, they permitted sales of *waqf* property, subject to approval by the *qāḍī*, when it ceased being productive and could no longer serve its purpose. The proceeds of the sale were then to be invested in an alternative property, to which the founder's original stipulations would continue to apply.
2. Such sales had become part of material law by the second Islamic century – during the lifetime of Abū Yūsuf (although it is not certain that other jurists of the Ḥanafī school accepted his views).
3. The intention of *istibdāl* was to preserve the purpose of the *waqf*, even if this meant purchasing property of lesser value and revenue potential than of the original property.

Istibdāl was permitted when the founder himself stated in the endowment deed that he, or any succeeding administrator, was to have the right to apply it. If the founder failed to say so explicitly, and even in most cases in which he expressly prohibited it, the *qāḍī* was empowered to overrule him, provided the property had lost its value and become unproductive. As we have noted, Abū Yūsuf permitted *istibdāl* if the new property was smaller than the first one, as long as it brought in income. Qadrī Pāshā, the Egyptian author of a collection of *waqf* laws, whose late nineteenth-century work summarizes preceding Ḥanafī literature, lists duress (*ḍarūra*) as the principal consideration (*musawigha*) for Ḥanafī jurists to permit *istibdāl*. Duress is present when a building has been destroyed, or is mostly in ruins (*takharraba muʿaẓamuhu*) or is about to collapse, and has become totally unproductive. It also applies to landed property no longer generating sufficient revenue to cover expenses (taxes, rent collection expenses and the like).[7] Before a *mutawallī* proposes *istibdāl*, he must attempt to save the property: first, by using *waqf* money to rehabilitate it; next, if there is no revenue, by taking out a loan (*istidāna*). If the *waqf* is a building, and if these options are not feasible, the *mutawallī* must seek a tenant willing to sign a long-term contract and pay the rent for the entire term in advance.

Where duress is not present, the *qāḍī* will not approve *istibdāl* unless convinced that the *waqf* will benefit from it (*manfaʿa, maṣlaḥa*). In other words, *istibdāl* is predicated on the existence of two fundamental preconditions: duress and advantage.[8] In ordinary exchange transactions (property for property), the alternative property must not be in a location of inferior 'reputation'. Qadrī cites two other circumstances in which *istibdāl* is permitted even if the *waqf* property is not in disrepair: when an outsider has damaged the property, or when the *mutawallī* cannot prove that the property belongs to the *waqf*. In such a case, he is permitted to reach a financial compromise with the trespassers.[9] Abū Yūsuf also acknowledged the principle of selling original *waqf* properties, provided that doing so promoted the interest of the *waqf*. This presumed that the *mutawallī* would be able to replace the sold property with other assets of greater value and income.[10] Abū Yūsuf's opinion differs from that of most jurists in two regards:

1. The later juridical literature allows the sale of the original property, with the proceeds to be used for the purchase of another in its stead. This form of *istibdāl* is called *istibdāl bil-nuqūd*, or *istibdāl bil-darāhim* (exchange for money or *dirhams*).
2. As for sale on the grounds of economic utility only, that is, irrespective of duress or the physical condition of the original property, Qadrī notes that most jurists do not accept Abū Yūsuf's opinion.

One of the reasons why most jurists rejected *istibdāl* was that it might lead to corruption on the part of *qāḍī*s, rulers and others. Al-Maqrīzī tells of a late fourteenth-century Ḥanbalī *qāḍī* in Egypt, Kamāl al-Dīn ibn al-ʿAdīm, who permitted liberal use of *istibdāl* and accepted the testimony to the effect that the property needed replacement, even if it was known to be prosperous. Anyone who wished to buy and sell *waqf* property could do so by offering a bribe or obtaining the sultan's authority.[11] The Ḥanafī jurist al-Tarsūsī (d. 1357) warned of this type of behaviour in his work on *fatwā*s.[12] Ḥanafī jurists were even more adamant in opposing *istibdāl bil-darāhim*. In the sixteenth century, Ibn al-

Nujaym proscribed *istibdāl* for financial remuneration and permitted in-kind exchange only, explaining that, in practice:

> The *mutawallī*s squander the proceeds of the sale and seldom use them to purchase alternative properties. We have not seen any *qāḍī* supervising this, despite the abundance of *istibdāl* transactions today. I even alerted several *qāḍī*s to this fact; they began to take an interest in supervision but stopped doing so subsequently.[13]

It was the lack of suitable supervision that fuelled the jurists' objections to *istibdāl*, particularly to *istibdāl bil-darāhim*. Therefore, several jurists made *istibdāl* conditional on the approval of a *qāḍī* who merited the title '*qāḍī* of paradise' (*qāḍī al-jannah*)[14] – one who not only possessed theoretical knowledge but was also an active and upright individual who supervised the *mutawallī*. The major problem in permitting use of *istibdāl* was how to ensure appropriate supervision.

Istibdāl was not the only device developed in an attempt to circumvent the fundamental constraints of the *waqf* system. In the Ottoman period, there emerged several methods of long-term rental and lease (discussed in greater detail below). The relevant legal literature seems to reflect a socio-economic norm and legitimizes customary leasing methods.

There is no information on the number of *waqf* transactions before the Ottoman period. *Sijillāt* do not seem to have been kept until then, and written sources have little to say on the subject. The fact that the Muslim legal literature mentions no transactions other than *istibdāl*[15] implies that new devices to circumvent the known constraints on the *waqf* were not developed until the Ottoman period.

The circumstances under which the *qāḍī* could permit long-term leases are similar to those of *istibdāl*; with respect to buildings, however, the *mutawallī* would seek a lessee (through *ḥikr*) only after failing to effect an *istibdāl*. Leased buildings must be in a state of total disrepair and so unproductive that no benefit could be derived from them without repair. Farmland could only be leased if: (1) its revenue had dropped below expenses; (2) attempts to let it for a limited period of a few years, which would have made it possible to develop it, had failed; and (3) no sharecropping (*muzāraʿa*) arrangements had proven possible.

When the *qāḍī* was asked to approve letting *waqf* property, he had to ascertain its physical condition and satisfy himself that all other alternatives – renovation with *waqf* money, taking out a renovation loan, long-term rent with advance payment, sharecropping (in the case of land) and *istibdāl* (in the case of a building) were impracticable.[16] It is not clear why *istibdāl* was permitted for buildings but not for farmland.

In the early nineteenth century, the most prevalent transaction in Jerusalem was *khulū* (a loan for renovating *waqf* property in which the creditor uses the property until repayment of the loan). This we know from Baer's research based on documents in the Jerusalem *sijill* dating 1800–15.[17] Other transactions permitted in Jerusalem during this period, but employed less frequently, were long-term leases (*ijāra ṭawīla*), other leases, and *istibdāl*.

Research findings present a fairly clear picture of the way these transactions were carried out and show that the *waqf* did not stagnate during the Ottoman period. *Istibdāl*, developed in the early period of Islam, was not the most prevalent method. In its stead, new devices for long-term leases spanning several generations were developed. A distinction was made between ownership and right of use. Jurists accepted these transactions easily, because they legally maintained the *waqf* status of the original properties. Leases had two objectives: (1) to enable the *waqf* to restore and conserve urban properties ravaged by time and nature and close to collapse, and (2) to make possible the use of uncultivated and neglected farmland or vacant urban land that could not be restored or developed from ordinary *waqf* revenue. These methods returned *waqf* properties to the market and attracted outside capital for their development. Although the rents were relatively low, the *waqf* gained more in this fashion than by leaving the properties idle. It should be emphasized that the main benefit of these leasing transactions was the preservation of *waqf* property. The party that gained the most was the lessee. The few available empirical studies do not attest to efforts by the *waqf* itself to invest in the development of its own assets.

Jerusalem *sijill* documents dating from 1900–17 point to a

change. Of the 24 transactions carried out in this period, not one was of the *khulū* type. There were 14 permanent leases of the *ḥikr* type, 5 cases of *istibdāl* relating to vacant land to be developed through new construction, 5 transactions in which the lessee was allowed to build privately against rent payments (a variation of *ḥikr*), and 1 transaction in which *waqf* money was used for development. (The *mutawallī*s of the Abū Midyan Waqf built shops on the roof of an existing property.)

During the Mandate period, a total of 84 transactions intended for development were carried out, compared with 108 permits for property transfer in the first 15 years of the nineteenth century (2.5 times as many by annual average). A comparison of the types of transactions carried out in Jerusalem over a period of more than 100 years elicits interesting results: most of the nineteenth-century transactions (91 out of 108) were of the *khulū* type (including 17 additions to existing *khulū* and 7 transactions using the *ijāra ṭawīla* method, which the Shāfiʿī school accepted), 7 leasing permits and 10 *istibdāl* permits. In the Mandate period, by contrast, most of the transactions (56 of 84: roughly two-thirds) were *istibdāl* sales, 12 were permanent leases (14 per cent) and 16 were investments for economic development (20 per cent).

ISTIBDĀL

The *istibdāl* transactions in Jerusalem fall into the categories shown in Table 7.1.

TABLE 7.1 CATEGORIES OF *ISTIBDĀL* TRANSACTIONS IN JERUSALEM

	Type of transaction	*No. of transactions*
a	*Istibdāl* according to explicit stipulation in the dedication deed	2
b	Ordinary exchange of property for property	4
c	Trespassing and compromise	2
d	Expropriation for public purposes	9
e	Sale of one property for the rehabilitation of another	7
f	Sale of property for economic development	32
Total transactions		56

Istibdāl *according to explicit stipulation in the endowment deed*

In the two cases in which founders allowed for *istibdāl* by themselves or the *mutawallī* who would succeed them, the transaction was indeed carried out. Amīna al-Khālidī, for example, dedicated properties which had been placed under lien for debt. She ordered the *mutawallī*s to sell some of them in order to repay the debt and lift the lien, for as long as it remained in effect, the properties could not be registered as *waqf*. To find a buyer, the *sharīʿa* court took the exceptional step of advertising in a newspaper, inviting the public to bid, with the intention of accepting the highest offer.[18]

Property for property

Under *sharīʿa* law, such an exchange must be of advantage to the *waqf*, and the new property must be in a better-renowned location than the former. An analysis of the three Mandate-era exchanges leads us to the conclusion that the *waqf* indeed received a property in better condition and with a higher revenue than the original one. The other party to the transaction received a property that had a better future revenue potential, provided an appropriate initial investment was made. In several ordinary *istibdāl* transactions, the factor of duress, theoretically a prerequisite under the *sharīʿa*, was not present at all; the *qāḍī*s approved the transactions on the basis of economic utility for the *waqf* alone.[19]

Trespassing and compromise

One permissible cause for *istibdāl* is trespass. In such cases, a usurper has made claim to *waqf* property and the *mutawallī* could not undisputably prove *waqf* ownership. Two permits for such *istibdāl* were issued as part of compromise (*mūṣālaḥa*) agreements between *mutawallī*s and the *ma'mūr al-awqāf* of the SMC. The first was given in a dispute between the ʿAnabūsī and the Hindiyya Waqfs and the *ma'mūr al-awqāf*, representing *al-Awqāf al-Mundarasa* in a dispute dating back to the Ottoman period. Suits had been brought previously in several instances. The reason for arriving at a compromise was that an appeal had recently been filed with the Privy Council in London, and there was concern that one or perhaps both of the *waqf*s would lose their property altogether, because neither had conclusive evidence. It was also argued that the compromise would save them onerous legal costs. The fact that this was a dispute between two *waqf*s made it easier for the court to agree that a compromise was of benefit to both.[20]

In the second case, a compromise was reached between the SMC and the *mutawallī* of the Zāwiyya al-Adhamiyya Waqf, which had earmarked its revenue for the al-Lāz family. In the late 1930s, the *mutawallī* wished to sell two plots in a prime east Jerusalem business location. The price asked was £P16,000–20,000 – an unusally large sum. In a thorough investigation, the SMC established that the founder, the former *shaykh* of the *zāwiyya*, had rented the two plots from the Zāwiyya Waqf in a *muqāṭaʿa*-type transaction and had then dedicated them as if he owned them. It instructed the *ma'mūr al-awqāf* to have himself appointed *mutawallī* by the *sharīʿa* court and then sue to rescind the endowment that had been made 50 years earlier. The *qāḍī* proposed a compromise, under which the SMC agreed to pay the *mutawallī* £P3,000 for the land and another £P200 to cover legal expenses. Although the SMC justified the transaction on the grounds of the religious sensitivity of the location (which was adjacent to a cemetery), there is no doubt that the considerations were purely economic. The compromise was approved by the *sharīʿa* court in 1947, and it took only a few years to construct commercial buildings at the location.[21]

Expropriation for public purposes

One of the innovations of our times that has affected the *waqf* is the modern legal concept of 'eminent domain', allowing the expropriation of land for public purposes.[22] The Jerusalem *sijill* of the late Ottoman period makes no mention of the expropriations of *waqf*s. The Ottomans did occasionally expropriate *khayrī* *waqf*s for public or development purposes, even before British law was applied, but these were ad hoc decisions by ruling authorities and did not include compensation for the original owners.[23]

Mutawallīs and *qāḍīs* came to regard expropriation by Mandatory municipal or central authorities as a type of *istibdāl* arising from duress. They therefore sought authorization from the *sharī'a* courts to accept compensation for expropriated properties and to invest the proceeds in alternative assets. Authorization was required in order to register the new property as a *waqf*. Expropriation by itself, based as it was on civil law, was not considered grounds for *istibdāl* under *sharī'a* law, and the *mutawallīs* had to offer other grounds. One was duress; another was utility (the compensation offered being greater than the real value of the property). The ostensible gravity with which these contrived grounds were discussed by the court casts doubt on all such arguments found in the *sijill*. Most requests for permits of this kind (seven out of nine) were presented to the *qāḍī* post factum – after the *mutawallī* had already accepted compensation and now sought to register a new property in the *waqf*'s name.[24]

In 1930, the government expropriated cultivated land in the Baq'a neighborhood from the Shaykh Muḥammad al-Khalīlī Waqf in order to build an Arab college and deposited an advance of £P5,612 against future compensation in the name of the *qāḍī* and the *mutawallīs*. The *mutawallīs* later used the full compensation payment to purchase two large houses in Muṣrāra costing £P7,000 and a 27-room house in Baq'a costing £P7,500.[25]

In the 1920s, the government expropriated a plot on Mount Scopus from the Shaykh Badr al-Dīn al-Jamā'ī al-Kinānnī Waqf for the Hebrew University to be built there. The *mutawallīs* were evidently satisfied with the expropriation, which promised handsome compensation for unused land that they could not afford to develop.[26] They accepted the compensation and purchased a four-story house in Muṣrāra and two houses in Baq'a expected to bring in a considerable income.

Sale of one property for the rehabilitation of another

The *sharī'a* makes no provision for selling a sound *waqf* property in order to use the proceeds for rehabilitating another. Nevertheless, the Jerusalem *sharī'a* court authorized seven transactions formally presented in this manner.[27] Such a transaction is termed '*istibdāl* sale for money' (*bay' 'an ṭarīq al-istibdāl bil-darāhim*, or *bay' 'alā wajh al-istibdāl*).[28] In one case, the *mutawallī* of the Abū-Jibna family *waqf* was allowed to sell 3 dunams of a large plot in eastern Jerusalem to the Jerusalem municipality for £P640. The money was intended to renovate a *waqf*-owned house at a cost of only £P225. The balance was to be invested in building a new house for the *waqf*. The circumstances make it clear that the real reason for seeking the permit was not renovation but rather the *mutawallī*'s wish to derive a greater revenue from unused *waqf* land.

Sale for economic development

Most of the transactions in Mandatory Jerusalem were made to ensure the economic development of *waqf* properties by adapting them to modern market conditions. They invoked the *istibdāl bil-darāhim* device in these transactions, mainly because of the economic benefit to the *waqf* from selling property and investing the proceeds in a manner calculated to earn much higher revenues.

From this point of view, the greatest possible achievement was the sale of land for building purposes in areas originally zoned for agriculture. The prospect of doing so was a function of the expansion of Jerusalem's built-up area at the time. This benefited the *waqf* in two ways: the purchaser invested in the property in order to develop it, and the *waqf* invested in new construction. By so doing, they acquired new buildings for the *waqf* at nominal costs and also developed another vacant plot of the endowment. The *mutawallī*s of the 'Alī Karīm al-Dīn al-Nammarī family *waqf* obtained no fewer than 18 permits of this type in the 1930s. This *waqf* had extensive holdings in the Baq'a and Qaṭamūn neighbourhoods of Jerusalem (properties that had formerly belonged to the village of Mālḥa). The *mutawallī*s used the permits to sell 25 dunams divided into 32 building plots[29] and another 20 dunams for use as sports grounds.[30] The *waqf* earned approximately £P15,000, sufficient for the construction of 30 new houses, with a potential revenue (at the price level of the late 1930s) of £P5,000 annually.

The SMC, too, sold land for economic development. In one

case, it sold 12 dunams owned by the al-Bīra Mosque Waqf, located on the Jerusalem–Ramallah road.[31] One of the SMC's most interesting *istibdāl* transactions relates to Ḥājj Amīn al-Ḥusaynī. As noted above, Ḥājj Amīn dedicated land and buildings in the Shaykh Jarrāḥ quarter of Jerusalem as a *waqf* through a contribution from a former Turkish Army officer, Zakariyya al-Dāghastānī (Zakī Bey). In January 1937, he contracted for the construction of two buildings on the *waqf* land. The contract referred to the plot as his own. Each building was to contain 11 shops and 4 apartments. Building costs were estimated at £P4,000–4,500.[32] The project was approved by the local *waqf* committee and the SMC. In Jaffa, 16 shops (including a café) were built for £P4,000 on *mundaras waqf* land, and the *waqf* reserved the right to add another five stories. The SMC records show that the *qāḍī* of Jaffa was in no hurry to approve the transaction and had to be prompted by the *mutawallī*, 'Izzat Darwaza, several times.[33] The attitude of the Jerusalem *qāḍī* was more pragmatic.

The SMC approved the sale to Ḥājj Amīn of two dunams in Shaykh Jarrāḥ belonging to the Dome of the Rock Waqf for £P500 (£P400 per dunam was then considered appropriate). The transaction was considered *istibdāl* in circumstances of duress (the land was unproductive and liable to heavy taxation).[34] Once approval was given in June 1937, four shops and seven apartments were built. Like all other SMC development projects, this required the approval of the local *waqf* committee, public bidding and SMC supervision of the construction work. In the *waqf* committee, the question arose whether the project was to be run by the SMC, or whether Amīn al-Tamīmī was to be appointed *mutawallī*. Evidently fearing British intervention, al-Tamīmī, as a senior SMC member, decided on the latter course; the SMC acted only as a trustee.[35] This did not deter him from accepting a loan of £P1,500 from the SMC for a 'private' *waqf* in November 1938, in order to complete the construction.[36]

In conclusion, *sijill* documents show clearly that most of the *istibdāl* transactions in Mandatory Jerusalem were of the *istibdāl bil-darāhim* type: the *waqf* sold unused urban land and invested the proceeds in construction on other vacant plots it possessed.

Alternatively, if the *waqf* owned no other land, the *mutawallī* bought an existing structure.

SMC documents show that the SMC, which had inherited administrative powers, preferred to describe them to outsiders as 'supreme *sharīʿa* authority'. Even when a *qāḍī* had already approved a sale by pointing to the relevant *sharīʿa* grounds as well as to the results of an investigation by experts, the SMC still took pains to spell out the legal reasons for approval.

In the few cases where the SMC rejected applications, its considerations were political. However, it always explained its refusals by reference to *sharīʿa* law. In 1938, for example, the SMC rejected an *istibdāl* application for the sale of 8.5 dunams belonging to the Shaykh Muḥammad Tamīm Waqf located in the undesirable Tulūl al-Maṣābin neighbourhood in exchange for 3.7 dunams with a residential building in the more attractive Mamilla neighbourhood (both parts of Jerusalem). It justified its rejection by reference to the economic recession which had lowered land prices. This was therefore not the right time to sell real estate: the *sharīʿa* rationale of benefit to the *waqf* did not exist. The SMC adopted this attitude even though an inquiry by experts, including an engineer from the Waqf Department, had confirmed that economic benefit would accrue to the *waqf*, and after the *qāḍī* had pronounced in favour of the project; so had a *sharīʿa* court inspector. The SMC also ignored the *mutawallī*'s argument (backed by documents) that because the land was liable to heavy taxes, this was a case of duress. If the *waqf* was unable to pay them, there was a real danger that the bailiff would sell it at the market price. The *mutawallī* appealed the rejection, but the file contains no information on the outcome of the appeal.[37]

The circumstances of the case raise doubts about the true reason for the rejection: a unique testimony in another file may help to elucidate the matter. In this file, a father presented a request to subdivide a 46-dunam orchard in Bayt Dajan village and sell three dunams of it, which were the portion of his son (then still a minor). The reason given was that the father had incurred heavy debts. The SMC rejected the application, stating that it was not convinced that subdividing the land was to the minor's advantage, even though the *qāḍī*, the experts and the *sharīʿa* court inspector had found for the applicant. The real motive for the SMC's attitude is disclosed in a letter by the assistant inspector of the *sharīʿa* court, whom the SMC sent to see the *qāḍī* shortly before the application came up for discussion (6 October 1935):

> The Council is interested in finding out the true reasons for the application . . . and [to discover] whether the aforementioned intends to furtively sell part of . . . [the orchard] to a speculator or to Jews.[38]

In reply, the *qāḍī* apologized and admitted that after further investigation, it had turned out that the applicant had indeed drawn up a fictitious document intended to show that he and his son owed a speculator a large sum of money. The father's real objective was to evade the SMC's close supervision and sell the orchard.[39] In short, we find that the SMC rejected requests by *mutawallī*s only when it feared that ownership would ultimately pass into Jewish hands.

Basically, the SMC's attitude toward *istibdāl* and other such devices was liberal, and it tended to disregard *sharīʿa* constraints. The only considerations that caused it to come out against such transactions were political.

In granting *istibdāl* permits, the *qāḍī*s in Mandatory Jerusalem ignored the prevailing opinion of the Ḥanafī school, which allowed *istibdāl* only if both duress and utility were present. They ruled on the principle of utility only, making no serious effort to find precedents or cite Ḥanafī minority views, even though they were known to exist.

LONG-TERM LEASING

*Traditional leasing methods (*ijāratayn, muqāṭaʿa *and* ḥikr*)*

In only a few leasing transactions in Mandatory Jerusalem were traditional methods applied. Only one leasing permit of the *ijāratayn* type was given. It was to allow the Municipality to lay a sewer pipe under land belonging to the Abū Midyan Waqf.[40] The only permit of the *muqāṭaʿa* type was given to the son of the original lessee of property belonging to the Shaykh Ibrāhīm al-Ansārī Waqf, allowing him to build a house on his father's original *muqāṭa'a* plot in return for doubling the rent.[41] Only two transactions of the *ḥikr* type appear in the *sijill*. In one, the *mutawallī*s of the Shaykh Sulaymān al-Dajānī Waqf were authorized to let vacant *waqf* land near David's Tomb on Mt Zion to three beneficiaries of the Dajānī family, at a rent of £P21 per annum – then considered a fairly high sum. The lessees undertook to build their residence on the land and to endow it as their own family *waqf*. To ensure this, they endowed money in advance, in the sum of the estimated building costs. The permit was granted in view of the scanty revenues from the land and the *waqf*'s inability to bear the cost of developing it. 'Outsiders', it was stated, were 'coveting' the land (*wa-hiya matma' anẓār al-ajānib*); leasing was the best way of keeping it a *waqf*. One of the *waqf* beneficiaries opposed the transaction, arguing in a letter to the SMC that the two *mutawallī*s' real interest was to transfer the land to their children. He also claimed that the land had been let for years, so that the claim that nobody was interested in renting it (as witnesses had testified before the *sharī'a* court) was false. He cited examples of homeowners in the Nabī Dā'ūd neighbourhood who had ultimately sold properties to outsiders. The SMC and the *qāḍī* disregarded his claims. Each of the three lessees deposited £E100 with the *mutawallī* and endowed the sum as a family *waqf* against the possibility of future sale.[42] Thus the traditional *ḥikr* method was used to ensure that *waqf* ownership was maintained and to prevent sale to non-Muslims.

In conclusion, transactions of this type (*ijāratayn*, *ḥikr* and *muqāṭa'a*) were carried out only in rare and exceptional circumstances. Clearly, they were falling into disuse in the Mandate period. They were replaced either by *istibdāl* or by a new leasing method, described below. These findings correspond with the overall trend in Muslim countries in the modern era to totally abolish *ḥikr* – that is, to invalidate the distinction between the land and the real property on it. In Iraq, legislative action had been taken since 1960 to abolish leasing. In Egypt, *ḥikr* was abolished in 1952, the relevant legislation being expanded in 1953 and 1960; under these Acts, which were part of Nasser's land reforms, lessees acquired full rights to the land against a payment of three-fifths of its value. In Turkey, *ḥikr* was abrogated in 1935 against an advance payment of 20 years' rent.[43] An Egyptian expert, al-Māḥī, suggested that Iraq proclaim an *istibdāl* for all tithes from farmland against advance remittance of 20 years' revenue.[44]

Permanent leases by the SMC for development

From 1933 on, the *sijill* contains *sharī'a* court permits for letting apartments belonging to SMC-administered *waqf*s under a new, untraditional method. In September 1933, the court authorized the SMC to let all lands of al-Ghawr (Khirbat Abū Samra)[45] in the Jordan Valley, the property of the Dome of the Rock Waqf, for 29 years, under a civil contract. (Among the six lessees was Jamāl al-Ḥusaynī, the secretary of the SMC.) At the end of this period, the lease would be renewed automatically (whether for the lessees or their heirs), provided they observed the terms of the contract. Its main provisions were:

1. The lessees would construct an irrigation system for the entire area within nine years.
2. They would remit one-fifth of the produce to the *waqf*.
3. Should they violate the terms, anything built on the land would revert to the *waqf*, and the lease would be null and void.[46]

At about the same time, a large plot in Jericho belonging to the Nabī Mūsā Waqf was leased to two lessees who undertook to develop the rocky land. They undertook to plant, within three years, orange groves and banana orchards, using modern methods (*'alā al-fann al-ḥadīth*!). They were to pay £P0.5 per dunam per year for the first nine years and £P1.25 per dunam after that.[47] In January 1936, one of the two asked to forfeit a sizeable part of his share because he could not afford to develop it. At the request of the SMC, the *sharī'a* court let it to 'Abbās Ḥilmī Pāshā, the former *khedive* of Egypt. Ḥilmī, however, rented the land on terms similar to *ḥikr*: he made no commitment to develop and work it but agreed to pay higher fees – £P6 per dunam for the first nine years and £P15 subsequently – as well as the land taxes.

Cultivation of the land and construction on it were at his discretion. The agreement would expire only when no trace of the lessor's buildings and orchards were left.[48]

Similar agreements were signed for the lease of Nabī Rubīn and Sidnā 'Alī lands, both in the jurisdiction of the Jaffa *Sharī'a* Court. In the late 1930s, large tracts belonging to the Nabī Rubīn Waqf (in the Soreq River valley) and Birkat Ramadan (near Netanya) were leased under the same terms as appear in the Jerusalem *sijill* with regard to the SMC.[49] In 1940, the *waqf* inspector criticized these leasing agreements as contrary to *waqf* interests and conducive to the loss of the land.[50]

None the less, the SMC continued to draw up similar agreements. In October 1939, it let land belonging to the Jericho Mosque Waqf under the same terms as the Nabī Mūsā Waqf. The agreement detailed the types of fruit trees to be planted (oranges, lemons, pistachios and dates) and the area of each orchard.[51] (The idea to do so dated back to 1932, when an application of this kind had first been made.)[52]

In 1944, the SMC let 12.5 dunams in Shaykh Jarrāḥ, belonging to the Dome of the Rock Waqf, on similar conditions. The lessees were the *mutawallīs* of the Amīna al-Khālidī Waqf – established, as noted above, for building a hospital for the Muslim poor. An orchard was to be planted there and the lessees would pledge the income from its produce to building the hospital within ten years. If the *mutawallīs* failed to complete construction, the agreement would be null and void.[53]

In 1940, the SMC concluded one of its largest transactions of this type when it let the lands of Khirbat Dayr 'Amrū, an area of about 6,000 dunams northwest of Jerusalem, in order to set up a farm and an agricultural school for orphans. The Committee for Arab Orphans, headed by Aḥmad Bey Sāmiḥ al-Khālidī, then principal of the Arab College, undertook to build the school within ten years and to put the farmland to full use.[54] The rent was set at £P50 for the entire parcel. Shaykh As'ad al-Imām, one of the witnesses heard by the *sharī'a* court, explained that this fee was too low for the SMC Waqf Department to derive any benefit, but that it was justified in terms of public interest (*maṣlaḥa 'āmma*).[55] The SMC records confirm that public considerations outweighed economic ones. The SMC had acquired the land in 1929 and left it fallow for many years. In 1934, the *ma'mūr al-awqāf* of Jaffa recommended that the land be let under a long-term lease, because it was suited for orchards only and required an investment of £P2,000. Since the trees would take six years to yield fruit, he proposed that the land be let at £P50 for the first six years, and the rent gradually increased thereafter, up to a maximum of £P300 per year. When bids were invited by the SMC in that year, the highest bid was from Maḥmūd al-Najjār of Liftā, at £P18,000 over 29 years! The deal fell through and the press blamed the engineer of the Waqf Department and the secretary of the SMC. The director-general of the Waqf Department denied that they were responsible, stating that al-Najjār had changed his mind. Thus the land remained unused for several more years. The SMC was aware of the rent being no more than nominal. The Jerusalem *ma'mūr al-awqāf*, writing to the *qāḍī* at the instance of the SMC, wrote that the deal should not be seen from the economic point of view only, but also in light of the need to safeguard and improve the land (*fī iʿtiqādinā inna ta'jīr hādhihi al-arāḍī ilā al-lajna al-mushār ilayhā fī maṣlaḥat al-waqf laysa min al-wajha al-māliyya faqaṭ wa-lakin min wajhat ḥafẓ al-arāḍī lil-awqāf wa-taḥsinihā*).

It is worth noting that during the first four years of the lease, the Orphans' Committee invested just over £P18,000 worth of donations in planting orchards and in construction on the land. Only after two years did the lessees make a profit of £P250 per year, rising to £P776 per annum after four years. They had intended to construct a school at an additional cost of £P20,000 but hesitated to do so unless the SMC committed itself to renewing the lease on the same terms after its expiry. Eventually, the committee concluded a new agreement with the SMC on more favourable terms.[56]

In late 1945, the SMC let 14 dunams belonging to the *mundaras waqf* of Mālḥa to the al-Iṣlāḥ Association for 29 years, against an annual rent of £P5, for the purpose of building a school. At the end of that period, the school and its annexes would revert to full *waqf* ownership. This transaction, too, was not especially profitable in the business sense. It was approved by the local *waqf* committee and the SMC following a petition by residents of Mālḥa who needed a school. The *waqf* committee believed it advantageous because the lease would preserve the *waqf* status of the land and also serve the public interest by providing a school for Muslim children.[57]

These SMC transactions were a new type of lease, drawn up like modern civil leases. They differed from the traditional leasing methods in the following respects:

1. The *sharīʿa* reasoning for renting *waqf* property was not present. The property had not fallen into disrepair; rather, it was unused farmland, and the purpose of the lease was to develop it.[58] Only in one exceptional case was there an effort to justify the permit in terms of the *sharīʿa*.
2. No attempt was made to ascertain whether the lessee *waqf* had the financial capability of developing the property. In the period here reviewed, the SMC had reserve funds available to invest in the development of some of the land, but it declined to do so.
3. Although the leases were not unlimited, they were automatically renewed, provided the lessee observed their conditions.
4. Traditional leases specified that real property built, and orchards planted, by the lessee would become his personal possession. Under the SMC lease agreements, assets added by the lessee reverted to the Waqf Department if the lessee violated the terms of the contract. This clause proved its worth when the Waqf Department repossessed land it had leased to the Muslim Brotherhood, after the Brotherhood failed to build or plant on it.[59] This, however, was the only instance of repossession.
5. Rents were merely nominal, as with the *ijāratayn*, but unlike the *ijāratayn*, there was no down payment. Consequently, the element of benefit to the *waqf* which, together with duress, was a prerequisite under *sharīʿa* law, was nonexistent.
6. The only profit accruing to the Waqf Department (except for the lease of the al-Ghawr lands against a fifth of the

produce) was the exemption from land taxes. Economically speaking, the *waqf* lost out on these leases because it forfeited land permanently, in return for a nominal rent. We must therefore conclude that the leases were given in order to put the assets to economic use by attracting private investors.

7. In the lease agreements, the Waqf Department laid down the type of development, the manner of use and a precise development timetable to which the lessee must commit himself. Failure to meet these was liable to place the lessee in breach of contract.

The question is why the SMC did not employ *istibdāl* in order to sell uncultivated land, as it did for the al-Bīra Mosque Waqf. Waqfs surely earned more from *istibdāl* than from leasing property in perpetuity for rents from which it could not profit. To account for this, we must relate SMC actions to the political and economic circumstances of the time.

In the 1930s, the struggle for land was one of the focal points of the national conflict in Palestine. The Arab Executive Committee established a national fund (*ṣandūq al-umma*) to raise money for 'saving land from the Jews'.[60] In 1929, the Palestinian leadership went over from a passive to an activist stance on this issue.[61] The SMC took part in their struggle, and Ḥājj Amīn al-Ḥusaynī used to boast of its role (although he clearly overstated the case). The SMC was active at two levels: purchase of land from farmers who had fallen into debt, and keeping Arabs from selling land to Jews. Starting in 1934, funds resulting from tithe agreements between the SMC and the Mandatory government became available. It invested these funds in the purchase of land which it then turned into *mushāʿ* – into land owned by a village community, thus hoping to prevent its sale (which now required the unanimous consent of all members of the community). Examples were the purchases of 6,000 dunams in Tayba village, 1,600 dunams in ʿAtīl and two-thirds of the land of Zaytā (in the Ṭūlkarm subdistrict).[62] When the SMC realized that it lacked the resources to go on with this, it launched a public information campaign against land sales to Jews.[63] This climaxed with the issue of a *fatwā* signed by 100 Palestinian *ʿulamā'*, most of them employees of the SMC,[64] proclaiming the sale of Palestinian land to Jews a crime against the faith.[65]

SMC operations regarding the economy of the Arab population as a whole also had its nationalist angle. The rivalry between the Jewish and Arab economies over the development of crops, the introduction of modern farming methods and penetration into foreign markets were part and parcel of the overall national conflict. Two crops were of particular interest to the Arab economy: citrus fruit and bananas.[66] The Arabs took up the challenge of worldwide citrus exports with much vigour. This entailed employing new technologies and belied the claim that the Arab economy was unable to adjust to technological change. Between 1932 and 1936, vast areas (some 92,000 dunams) were newly planted with citrus; this was twice as much as all citrus orchards previously owned by Arabs. About 25,000 dunams were planted in 1934 alone.[67] In its publications, the SMC claims to have planted 40,000 fruit trees. In the 1940s, the SMC decided to punish lessees who planted fruit other than citrus by imposing a surcharge of £P0.2 per dunam on their rent for the first six years, to be reassessed every seven years. Recalcitrant lessees were to be obliged to accept arbitration.[68]

One of the problems of Arab agriculture was the near-total lack of irrigation. Little was done in this regard, except building an irrigation system for several thousand dunams of bananas in the Jericho region.[69] Bananas required a larger investment (of £P30–40 per dunam) than olives, figs or grapes, but citrus required even more: some £P50 per dunam.[70] The SMC was apparently unable to meet this expense from its own funds, but did succeed in attracting outside investors. The solution of *istibdāl* conflicted with the SMC's exhortations to the Muslim public to refrain from selling land, and to convert land into *waqf*s. The leasing of land for a nominal fee was sometimes the only option open to safeguard the land, develop it and, in particular, integrate it into the Arab national economy. In this policy, the SMC preferred the pursuit of political aims over considerations of the *waqf*'s economic interest. The above example of Khirbat Dayr 'Umrū proves that the SMC could have commanded realistic rents, had it so insisted.

The SMC also engaged in draining marshlands and in afforestation.[71] Kupferschmidt believes that it did so in order to compete with the Jewish National Fund.

An overall view of the circumstances, as well as the cases cited, points to the following motives of the SMC in its leasing transactions:

1. to reinforce Arab claims to uncultivated land; working such land would prevent its falling into alien hands;
2. to counteract private land sales to Jews; the SMC urged the Muslim public to endow its property as *waqf*s and thereby make it inalienable;
3. to overcome the difficulty of finding Arab capitalists willing to invest first in purchasing land and then in its development, until it became economically viable;
4. to make sure that properties were developed according to the SMC's priorities; as we have seen, the SMC was interested in developing citrus cultivation in order to compete with the Jews for foreign markets.

These were primarily considerations of political advantage and public interest. The SMC thought of itself as a governing institution protecting the interests of the Muslim population, especially with regard to land and its economic development.

CHANGING THE *WAQF*'S ORIGINAL NATURE

Sharīʿa law proscribed modification of the original character (*taghyīr al-maʿālim*) of *waqf* properties. It did so in order to honour the founder's wishes and perpetuate the original property as a living memorial to him. Even when renovating a structure owned by a public *waqf*, the *mutawallī* may not render it in a better condition than it was when first donated. For example, interior walls must not be moved, new windows or doors may not be put in nor existing ones blocked; paint or plaster may only be applied where it had been found originally. An exception could only be made if the founder had specifically provided so in the *waqfiyya*. Family *waqf*s, by contrast, could be improved and given a new purpose if the beneficiaries gave their consent.[72] The *waqf* laws do not state whether consent must be unanimous or by majority. Apparently, general consent is required. On several occasions, beneficiaries sought the dismissal of *mutawallī*s for renovations that had altered the original nature of the property.[73] This constraint, however, seems to have been too hard for the public to abide by under the economic circumstances of the Mandate period. *Mutawallī*s who wished to improve or modify a property in order to increase its income would apply to the court, which usually approved the request on the basis of the principle of benefit to the interest of the *waqf*. For family *waqf*s, the court did not always take care to ascertain the beneficiaries' opinion; sometimes it approved modifications *post factum*. Several examples are given below.

The *mutawallī*s of the 'Anabūsī and Hindiyya *waqf*s carried out extensive development work, with the full backing of the *sharī'a* court. First they obtained a permit to attach a *waqf*-owned shop to another, adjacent property. The latter had been let to a bank, and the lease allowed the bank to expand. The *mutawallī*s declared that they would invest £P212 to make the change; the bank would raise its yearly rent from £P500 to £P800.[74] Ten years later, a new *mutawallī* received a permit from the *qāḍī* to add a storey to the building. The bank paid £P2,500 as its share in the building costs, against the right to use the new storey for eight years without further payment. The court gave its consent to a civil-law agreement between the *waqf* and the bank, allowing for a third rental period on terms to be agreed by the sides.[75] Earlier, the *mutawallī*s had obtained a permit to replace a row of old shops near Jaffa Gate and replace them with shops of more modern design. They had attached approved building plans and taken care to meet the Health Department requirements for such premises. They were allowed to invest £P5,000 (a substantial sum) in the project, mostly from *waqf* moneys. The *qāḍī* consented that if the *waqf*'s own funds did not suffice, they could take out a loan to make up the difference, or else rent some of the *waqf* property for three years against advance payment.[76] In 1947, the *mutawallī*s of the same *waqf* were authorized to use £P3,500 of *waqf* money to participate in the paving of a road and sidewalk by the municipality alongside the 14 shops it owned on Mamilla Street. They had stated that the work would make the *waqf* properties more attractive and increase rent revenues. To finance the work, the shops would be let for five years at £P50 per year each, the rent to be paid in advance.[77]

None of the permits granted to the *mutawallī*s of family *waqf*s stated that the beneficiaries had given their consent. In the case of the 'Anabūsī Waqf, there is reason to assume that such consent was virtually impossible to obtain, in view of the large number of beneficiaries and disputes then current among them over its management.

The above examples show that the *sharī'a* court in Jerusalem did not obstruct development of *waqf*s even if this entailed their modification – they proved ready to deviate substantially from the letter of the *sharī'a* law. *Mutawallī*s with entrepreneurial inclinations were able to develop *waqf* properties by moving with the forces of the market. Even post factum permission could be obtained without difficulty.

In only one case did the SMC seek permission of the *sharī'a* court to change and develop the properties of a *waqf* under its direct administration. In 1924, the *ma'mūr al-awqāf* asked the court to authorize, *post factum*, development work already carried out by the Waqf Department at a sanctuary (Turbat Ghabayin) in the Old City. It had built a shop in the tomb courtyard as an additional source of revenue. Department officials explained that the property needed renovation, but that the *waqf*, as it was, could not afford the expense. The *qāḍī* ignored the fact that the property was administered by the SMC under a central administration, not as a separate *waqf*. In fact, the SMC could not claim that it had no money for renovation at a time when it was purchasing property, erecting many new buildings and renovating dozens of buildings each year. In any case, the work had already been completed by the time the case was heard, and the *qāḍī* allowed the SMC to register the shop in the name of the *waqf*.[78]

It should be noted that the SMC built 224 new buildings and renovated 300 old ones during the years 1932–36 alone.[79] For most of these works, the SMC did not seek approval from the *sharī'a* court. In the case of the Ghabayin tomb, the *ma'mūr al-awqāf* evidently sought the court's permission because he required legal documents permitting him to register the new shop as a *waqf*.

The SMC's largest building project conducted for economic reasons only was the construction of the Palace Hotel. For its development, the hotel was to make use of land belonging to a Jerusalem cemetery. At the outset, in 1925, Ḥājj Amīn estimated the investment at £P40,000–50,000. A British company was chosen as building contractor, and it was Ḥājj Amīn's intention that the government should pay the contractor directly, from the tithes the authorities collected for the *waqf*s. This was tantamount to an indirect government guarantee. Before meeting with the finance secretary, Ḥājj Amīn drafted a letter setting the investment in the project (then not yet defined as a hotel) at £P20,000, to be repaid over ten years. In another letter, Ḥājj Amīn put the amount needed at £P20,000–30,000. The British company, for its part, estimated the construction costs at £P40,000. In June 1926, the inspector of *waqf*s turned to the president of the SMC and, pointing out that the Waqf Department did not have revenues or enterprises comparable to those of other communities, suggested that work be started at once by allocating £P10,000 from the Temple Mount renovation fund. In July, the SMC approved a loan of £P5,000 from the fund for the project, which was expected to bring in £P1,500 in rents per year. At the time, the project was to have a ground floor of shops and three floors of hotel rooms above them. The municipality predicated its approval on the SMC's consent for the road to be to widened, using cemetery ground to do so. At first, the Temple Mount Renovation Committee refused to forward the loan to the Waqf Department.[80] After the 1927 earthquake, however, Ḥājj Amīn ordered the transfer of £P10,000 from the fund, half for the Mamilla building project and the rest for repair of buildings damaged in the quake. £P1,200 was transferred to a building project at the Bāb al-Sāhira cemetery, just north of the Old City. This was done to exploit the paving of Salāḥ al-Dīn Street (which soon turned into a major business street) by the municipality and to prepare part of the plot for building shops. This required the demolition of a part of the cemetery's stone wall, and the *ma'mūr al-awqāf* recommended doing so.[81]

The contract for the construction of the Palace Hotel, finally signed by the SMC on December 29, 1927, set the building costs at £P56,000. It entitled the contractor to quarry on *waqf* land in the Mamilla neighbourhood without payment.[82] When the building was completed in 1929, the SMC claimed that rent income from the hotel would cover expenses within ten years. By then, however, the building costs had risen to £P73,500, and the SMC had to take out a bank loan, guaranteed by the government. None the less, the SMC continued to assert that the hotel (having been rented for 15 years at £P7,300 per annum) would generate enough income to repay the investment within ten years.[83] But the SMC's published data were unreliable: apparently, the rent was only £P3,000 per year, paid in advance.[84]

Permits to change the purpose of *waqf* properties of a secular nature did not, as a rule, elicit negative public reaction. This only happened when they involved religious sensitivity. In 1927, for example, Shaykh ʿAbd al-Razzāq al-ʿAlamī, Shaykh Saʿīd Kassāb and Ḥasan al-Budayrī complained to the SMC and the *ma'mūr al-awqāf* because of building work at the above-mentioned cemeteries, which entailed the disinterment of bones and their reburial elsewhere. A suit was brought, and counsel for the SMC claimed that traditional jurists had been divided on the issue. He quoted Ḥanafī authorities who had sanctioned this type of transaction. The court chose to avoid the issue of religious law and rejected the suit on procedural grounds. The claimants, it ruled, had no standing in the case; only the *mutawallī* did. The claimants asserted, correctly, that *sharīʿa* law accorded any Muslim a standing in claims involving *khayriyya waqf*s (everyone being a potential beneficiary).[85] Just the same, the Court of Appeals upheld the ruling.[86] In its public response, appearing in the newspaper *al-Jāmiʿa al-ʿArabiyya*, the SMC prided itself on its construction works throughout the country, which had increased its revenues by £P2,225 per year. The shops it had built at the Mamilla cemetery brought in £P750 per annum, new shops at the Bāb al-Sāhira cemetery £P170, and new shops in the Wād neighbourhood of the Old City £P20.[87]

The SMC, having supervisory rights over the *sharīʿa* courts, may have been interested in seeing the claim turned down on a technicality rather than on substance. The latter approach would have discouraged others from filing similar suits. It is worth noting that, according to the *sijill*, the SMC had never sought a permit for its development work at the cemeteries or, later, for the construction of the Palace Hotel. There may have been additional cases of *waqf* development under SMC administration never recorded in the *sijill*.

INVESTMENT IN NEW PROPERTY

The *sharīʿa* allows a *mutawallī* of a public *waqf* to use its revenues for the purchase of new assets, assuming that this is done only after the charitable objectives of the *waqf* have been provided for. In the case of a family *waqf*, the consent of the beneficiaries is required. In one case, the *qāḍī* dismissed the *mutawallī* of a family *waqf* merely for having invested *waqf* money for three years in the purchase of a house and liening the rent income of another year, instead of distributing it among the beneficiaries.[88] Six requests for permission were made to the Jerusalem *sharīʿa* court: one for a family *waqf* and five for public *waqf*s. All were granted. In the case of the family *waqf*, the *mutawallī*s were allowed to take loans to purchase three mansions in the Baqʿa and Muṣrāra neighbourhoods. The loans brought funds previously acquired by *istibdāl* up to the sum needed. The *qāḍī* himself visited the mansions.[89]

The SMC did not seek permission from the *sharīʿa* court unless the properties it wished to buy belonged to a *waqf* and the court's consent was needed by its *mutawallī*s. In January 1929, a building near the *sharīʿa* court building (*Maḥkama*) on the Temple Mount was purchased from the Khalīl Bey al-Ṣāliḥ Waqf for £P1,150, on the grounds that it had been partly destroyed and the rest structurally damaged in the 1927 earthquake.[90] The SMC subsequently purchased from the al-Khalīlī Waqf a complex of 24 shops and a house, also adjacent to the *Maḥkama*, for £P2,000. The permit obtained by the *waqf* stated explicitly that the *istibdāl* had been made in order to comply with instructions from Ḥājj Amīn (*tanfidhan li-awāmir ṣāḥib al-samāḥa al-Ḥājj Amīn al-*

Ḥusaynī), who was anxious that the property should not be transferred (*tatasarrab*) to the Jews.[91] The proceeds were deposited in a bank in the joint name of the *qāḍī* and *mutawallī*, in order to ensure that an alternative property was indeed purchased.[92]

Another SMC purchase was a house under the *Maḥkama* building, adjacent to the Western Wall, from the Shaykh ʿUthmān al-ʿAlamī family *waqf*. At the time, the *waqf* was being provisionally administered by the SMC's Waqf Department, and the SMC exploited this to buy the house before a new *mutawallī* could be appointed. Experts testified that the house was in disrepair and in need of renovation, and was no longer fit for habitation because the SMC offices opened onto its court. Consequently, its future revenue potential was nil. The permit stated that the transaction would be of advantage to both *waqf*s, and from the SMC's standpoint, it was 'obligatory and important' (*ḍarūrī wa-muhimm*) to annex the property to the Temple Mount Waqf as a matter of public interest (*maṣlaḥa ʿāmma*).[93] In 1947, the SMC purchased 8.6 dunams south of the Temple Mount from the Ṣalāḥ al-Dīn al-ʿAlam Waqf for £P800. The permit stated that expenses for the land were exceeding revenues, and that it was important to safeguard its *waqf* status because of its proximity to the Temple Mount. Its transfer to the SMC's Waqf Department would ensure that.[94]

The SMC also purchased farmland to keep it out of Jewish hands – for political rather than economic reasons. Such purchases were not recorded in the *sijill*. In 1934 alone, after the tithe agreement had been implemented, the SMC invested £P39,282 in buying land with this aim in mind.[95] In 1946, the sum had fallen to only £P201.[96] It is interesting to study the purchase of Khirbat Dayr ʿAmrū, which was let in 1946. The sum paid for it in 1929 (£P5,855) was raised from donations for the victims of the 1929 disturbances.[97] In a suit against the SMC, the heirs of the original owner of the land produced a letter from the *ma'mūr al-awqāf*, Jamīl al-Shihābī, to the effect that following the purchase, the SMC should dispose of part of the land by means of *istibdāl* in order to reimburse itself for the purchase. The rest of the land should then be returned to the heirs of the original landowner except for a four-dunam plot and a house that would serve the mosque. If no purchaser were found, the land should revert to the original owner.[98]

In conclusion, purchases of new property for privately administered *waqf*s, made as investments, were rare in the Mandatory period, either because the *waqf*s did not have sufficient income or because the *mutawallī*s preferred to use existing reserves for other purposes. Purchases by the SMC, in contrast, were made with political rather than economic aims in mind. The SMC purchased family *waqf* property in the vicinity of the Temple Mount and the Western Wall because of the great sensitivity surrounding that area and from fear that the Jews intended to use their possession of the Western Wall as a lever to gain control of the Mount. Other purchases were made to acquire land from Arabs so as to prevent them selling it to non-Arabs. These transactions were incompatible with *sharī'a* law, because they were not justified in terms of economic benefit. The SMC did not register most of its acquisitions in the *sijill*. It seems to have preferred registering the property in its name or in that of its representative, the *ma'mūr al-awqāf*, because this exempted the property from the constraints of *waqf* status. Family *waqf* properties purchased by the SMC were, however, recorded in the *sijill* because their *mutawallī*s needed a permit. Once that was obtained, the SMC became their legal owner, and their *waqf* status expired.

THE *QĀḌĪS*' ATTITUDE TO *WAQF* TRANSACTIONS

In most sales, as well as in the *istibdāl* transactions made by Ḥājj Amīn, the applications were worded to fit the *sharī'a* grounds of duress, despite the patently economic objectives. First, it was argued that the land could no longer be worked, because it had become part of a built-up area. Second, it was described as unproductive, and its taxes were therefore an unnecessary expense. Indeed, the Mandatory land taxes in urban areas encouraged the owners of vacant lots to sell them to developers.[99] In 1935, when villages near Jerusalem were included in the municipal planning area, the villagers as well as the SMC protested. Ḥājj Amīn asserted that this was being done to force the owners to sell their land to Jews in order to avoid the heavy taxes. Meeting with 150 village notables, he recommended that the government be petitioned and the mosque preachers mobilized to counteract the commercial tactics of real-estate middlemen.[100]

Another point sometimes made to present the sale of *waqf* properties as conforming with the *sharī'a*, was that the land had become a pedestrian walkway and that squatters might therefore make it their target. Most permits stated, as required by the *sharī'a*, that the *waqf* could not afford to develop and utilize the property. Some permits declared that no one was interested in renting it or exchanging it through *istibdāl*. Many of the files have nothing to say about efforts by the *sharī'a* court to verify these details, and the impression one gets is that no such efforts were made.[101] The remarkably large number of permits given to the al-Nammarī Waqf to sell land shows that no investigation was undertaken. This *waqf* undoubtedly had vast capital reserves, both from its assets and from the many sales already made. In some of the permits, including some granted to the *ma'mūr al-awqāf*, the only reason given was economic benefit to the *waqf*; duress was not cited, not even ostensibly.[102] In one case, the permit states laconically: 'The benefit confirms the duress.'[103] The *qāḍī*s in Mandatory Jerusalem seem to have rejected the views of the minority Ḥanafī school, which permits *istibdāl* even if it is made for economic benefit alone.[104] They recognized the crucial need to approve such transactions, but usually tended to cite contrived grounds of duress. The testimony of experts, who were merely people of progressive socio-economic views, and of witnesses for the *mutawallī*, gave the court a pretext to issue permits without investigating details. The attitude of the Jerusalem *qāḍī*s differed from their contemporaries in Iraq. The latter subjected claims of duress to painstaking examination; they rejected *istibdāl* requests when they found that the property in question had not become absolutely unproductive, as *sharī'a* law requires, or turned them down because some of the land had already been sold previously by *istibdāl*, earning income that could be used to develop the remaining land.[105]

The attitude of Jerusalem *qāḍī*s towards other transactions was similar: they made every effort to facilitate them for reasons of economic benefit to the *waqf*. In most instances, however, they held on to the *sharīʿa* pretext of duress, even if it was clear to them that its use was fictitious. When permission for *istibdāl bil-darāhim* was sought, for example, the need to renovate a *waqf* house was proffered as proof of duress, even though – in one case – the renovations cost £P40, whereas the property itself was sold for over £P400. If renovation was the sole reason for the sale, a smaller portion of the land could have been sold. The *sharīʿa* court thus supported the *mutawallī* in clearly flouting *sharīʿa* law. The *qāḍī* obscured this by invoking an entirely different point of law (permitting *istibdāl bil-darāhim* when a *waqf* property is in disrepair and cannot be exchanged for another).[106] In another permit, granted to the *mutawallī* of the Muḥammad al-Khalīlī Waqf to sell a plot to the Municipality of Jerusalem for use as a garbage dump, the *qāḍī* based his decision on the same law.[107] The permit stressed that the property in need of renovation included the founder's tomb and a library in his name. The evident purpose in doing so was to tone down emotional reactions and make it easier to ignore the violation of the *sharīʿa*. What the *mutawallī* and the *sharīʿa* court were actually signalling was that the sale of property of no special importance for perpetuating the founder's name is preferable to the destruction of some other property directly linked with the founder.

To sum up, the prevalent way of transferring *waqf* property in Jerusalem, and in Palestine as a whole, during the Ottoman period was a permanent lease (mostly by *khulū* in the early nineteenth century and by *ḥikr* in the early twentieth century). Although *istibdāl* was used, it was not the most common method. Both leasing and exchange (or sale) were developed to solve the same problem: how to raise outside capital to restore *waqf* properties and render them profitable. There is no doubt that the *istibdāl*, especially the *istibdāl bil-darāhim*, served this function more efficiently than leasing. Moreover, the *waqf* benefited much more extensively from *istibdāl* than from leasing, usually done at comparatively low rents.[108]

The probable reason for the general avoidance of *istibdāl*, especially of *istibdāl bil-darāhim*, during the Ottoman period was the conservative attitude of some of the *'ulamā'*. Their caution stemmed from the belief that the transactions could neither be efficiently supervised nor protected from corruption or liquidation. Al-Māḥī, the Egyptian expert who studied Iraqi *waqf*s, criticized the conservatism of the Iraqi *qāḍī*s in granting permits for *istibdāl*. In Egypt, he noted by contrast, the *sharī'a* courts collaborated with the Waqf Ministry in approving *istibdāl* on the grounds of benefit only.[109] Abū Zahra asserts similarly that in Egypt, benefit to the *waqf* (*maṣlaḥa*) was the sole consideration. An Egyptian law of 1931 empowered the *sharī'a* court to carry out *istibdāl* unless the Waqf Ministry objected within 15 days. According to Abū Zahra, the Egyptians developed an effective technique for the supervision of *istibdāl*, using experts who inquired about the parties to the transaction and especially about beneficiaries who stood to gain. Only then were bids solicited.[110] In Mandatory Syria, too, the *'ulamā'* opposed the widespread use of *istibdāl*, but the French authorities introduced reforms in civil legislation that allowed it to be widely practised.[111]

In the 1950s, Abū Zahra wrote, *istibdāl* was accepted in most Arab countries except Saudi Arabia. He personally favoured *istibdāl* for economic development purposes and wondered 'why the *waqf* should remain stagnant and not change with circumstances and the times'. As an example, he mentioned the inclusion of farmland in areas intended for building. Unless its original purpose was changed, its income would become negligible in comparison to the benefit from its sale and the purchase of an alternative plot.[112] Al-Māḥī also proposed that, in view of the poor state of agriculture in Iraq, *waqf* farmland should be exchanged for urban property and that urban *waqf*s should be utilized for building and development. He proposed that funds be raised from the following sources:

1. by letting the land to building contractors for 20–30 years;
2. by taking government loans or seeking government guarantees for other loans;
3. by *istibdāl* and investment of the proceeds in construction.[113]

Unlike Baer's finding with regard to the early nineteenth century, transactions in the Mandatory period did not contribute to the loss of *waqf* properties. On the contrary, they enriched and developed them and made it possible for the tradition of endowments to survive and for *waqf*s to prosper in the modern era. One may well say that the *mutawallī*s, the *qāḍī*s and the SMC successfully met the challenge of modern economic transformation.

NOTES

1. Sh. D. Goitein and A. Ben Shamesh, *Muslim Law in the State of Israel* (Hebrew, Jerusalem, 1957) pp. 169–70; A. Granovski, *The Land Regime in Palestine* (Hebrew, Tel-Aviv, 1949) pp. 127–30, M. Kurd *'Alī, Kitāb Khiṭṭaṭ al-Shām* (Damascus, 1927), vol. 5, 123ff.
2. M. Qadrī Pāshā, *Kitāb Qānūn al-'Adl wa'l-Inṣāf li'l-Qaḍā' 'alā Mushkilāt al-Awqāf* (Cairo, 1902) art. 1: *al-waqf hua ḥabs al-'ayn 'an tamlīkihā li-aḥadin min al-'ibād . . .*
3. G. Baer, *A History of Land Ownership in Modern Egypt: 1800–1950* (London: Oxford University Press, 1962) p. 169.
4. G. Gilbar, 'The *Waqf* and Economic Growth' in G. Baer and G. Gilbar (eds), *Studies on the Muslim Waqf* (Oxford: Oxford University Press) (forthcoming); idem, 'Muslim *Waqf* and Distribution of Capital and Income, Towards a Quantitative Analysis', ibid.
5. al-Khaṣṣāf, *Kitāb Aḥkām al-Awqāf* (Cairo: Diwan 'Umūm al-Awqāf al-Miṣriyya, 1902) p. 22.
6. Ibid.
7. M. Qadrī Pāshā, *Kitāb Qānūn al-'Adl wa'l-Inṣāf li'l-Qaḍā' 'alā Mushkilāt al-Awqāf* (Cairo, 1902) arts. 133; 332. See the discussion in M. Hoexter, 'Le contrat de quasi-alienation des *awqāf* à Alger à la fin de la domination turque: études de deux documents d''*nā*', *Bulletin of the School of Oriental and African Studies*, 47 (1984) p. 248ff.
8. M. Qadrī Pāshā, *Kitāb Qānūn al-'Adl wa'l-Inṣāf li'l-Qaḍā' 'alā Mushkilāt al-Awqāf* (Cairo, 1902) art. 133.
9. M. Qadrī Pāshā, *Kitāb Qānūn al-'Adl wa'l-Inṣāf li'l-Qaḍā' 'alā Mushkilāt al-Awqāf* (Cairo, 1902) art. 135.
10. Ibid.
11. al-Maqrizī, *al-Mawā'iz wal-i'tibār bi-dhikr al-khiṭṭaṭ wāl-āthār* (Cairo: Bulāq, 1853), 2, p. 296. See M. Abū Zahra, *Muḥāḍarāt fī al-Waqf* (2nd ed., Cairo: Dār al Fikr al-'Arabī, 1971) p. 14.
12. M. Abū Zahra, *Muḥāḍarāt fī al-Waqf* (2nd ed., Cairo: Dār al Fikr al-'Arabī, 1971) p. 167.
13. Ibn al-Nujaym. *al-Baḥr al-rā'iq fī sharḥ kanz al-daqā'iq* (al-Maṭba'a al-'Ilmiyya), 241.
14. Ibid.
15. H. Gerber, *Economy and Society in an Ottoman City: Bursa 1600–1700*

(Jerusalem: Magnes Press, 1988) pp. 172, relating to *ijāratayn*.
16. M. Qadrī Pāshā, *Kitāb Qānūn al-ʿAdl wa'l-Inṣāf li'l-Qaḍā' ʿalā Mushkilāt al-Awqāf* (Cairo, 1902) art. 332.
17. G. Baer, 'The Dismemberment of *Awqāf* in Early 19th Century Jerusalem', *Asian and African Studies*, 13, no.3 (1979) p. 221.
18. *Sijill*, 486/56/416, 486/118/20, 485/46/168.
19. *Sijill* 437/21/24, 477/16/163, 443/112/67.
20. *Sijill* 443/126/87.
21. *Sijill* 377/182, 510/86/487, 513/21/256, *CIH*, 13/38/1,13/2/45.
22. Expropriation Ordinance: *Official Gazette*, 1926, 157.
23. Examples: *ISA, ʿAwnī ʿAbd al-Hādī files*, 34/153; U.M. Kupferschmidt, *The Supreme Muslim Council: Islam under the British Mandate for Palestine* (Leiden: E.J. Brill, 1987) p. 115ff.
24. F.M. Goadby and M.J. Doukhan, *The Land Law of Palestine* (Hebrew, Tel Aviv, 1935) pp. 321–32; *Sijill* 482/25/74, 508/123/80, 508/123/80.
25. *Sijill* 443/141/104, 475/56/93, 475/65/3.
26. Interview with Shaykh Asʿad al-Imām on 23 June 1990; *Sijill* 479/3/119, 481/53/332, 485/31/133, 507/39/175; *CIH*, 13/47/5,24/55.
27. *Sijill* 419/372/97, 445/22/130, 451/130/202, 474/102/159, 500/139/175, 424/2/9, 432/310/63.
28. *Sijill* 451/130/202, 445/310/130.
29. Examples: *Sijill* 453/64/315, 453/89/210.
30. *Sijill* 455/147/150.
31. *Sijill* 500/101/114. On revenues from *istibdāl* see Al-Majlis al-Islāmī al-Sharʿī al-Aʿlā, *Bayān al-Majlis al-Islāmī al-Sharʿī al-Aʿlā* 1929, p. 3 (1,400 £P); Al-Majlis al-Islāmī al-Sharʿī al-Aʿlā, *Bayān al-Majlis al-Islāmī al-Sharʿī al-Aʿlā* 1931, p. 8 (2,000 £P).
32. *CIH*, 13/37/10,8/2.
33. *CIH*, 378, 13/24/1,5/20.
34. *Sijill* 474/112/179.
35. *CIH*, 378, 13/37/10,9/20.
36. *ISA, SMC*, P/989, 43.
37. *ISA, SMC*, P/989, 45.
38. *ISA, SMC*, P/989, 78.
39. Ibid.
40. *ISA, Land Court*, B/739, 56/25.
41. *Sijill* 427/495/175, 440/36/30.
42. *CIH*, 1/50, 13/19/2,1/10.
43. Gabriel Baer, 'Ḥikr', *Encyclopaedia of Islam* (2nd ed.) suppl., pp. 368–70.
44. M.M. al-Māḥī, *al-Ḥukūma al ʿIrāqiyya, Taqrīr ʿan ʿAwqāf al-ʿIrāq wa-Wasā'il Iṣlāḥiha* (Baghdad, 1937) p. 42.
45. From 8 km north of Jericho to the Nuʿayma valley north of Jericho.
46. *Sijill* 461/141/192.
47. *Sijill* 461/138/191.
48. *Sijill* 471/63/24.
49. U.M. Kupferschmidt, *The Supreme Muslim Council: Islam under the British Mandate for Palestine* (Leiden: E.J. Brill, 1987) pp. 130–8; *CIH*, 13/32/5,15/60; *ISA, SMC*, P/989, 77.
50. Al-Majlis al-Islāmī al-Sharʿī al-Aʿlā, *Majmuʿat taqārīr al-taftīsh*, p. 11.

51. *Sijill* 479/79/223.
52. *CIH*, 13/32/5,12/60.
53. *Sijill* 498/78/517.
54. *Sijill* 480/97/185.
55. Interview dated 2 January 1989.
56. *CIH*, 3/52(12), 45, 13/40/2,59/10.
57. *CIH*, 378, 13/43/10,10/20.
58. *Sijill* 498/97/185.
59. Interview with Shaykh As'ad al-Imām who was secretary of the Muslim Brethrens Associasion.
60. Y. Porath, *The Palestinian Arab National Movement 1929–1939; From Riots to Rebellion* (London: Frank Cass, 1977) p. 94.
61. J. Qano, *The Affairs of the Land Dispute between Jews and Arabs in Palestine* (Hebrew, Givat Haviva, 1980) p. 27.
62. Y. Porath, *The Palestinian Arab National Movement 1929–1939: From Riots to Rebellion* (London: Frank Cass, 1977) p. 94; U.M. Kupferschmidt, *The Supreme Muslim Council: Islam under the British Mandate for Palestine* (Leiden: E.J. Brill, 1987) p. 139.
63. B. Kimmerling, *The Land Struggle, a Chapter in the Sociology of the Jewish–Arab Conflict* (Hebrew, Jerusalem, The Hebrew University, 1973) p. 73.
64. *al-Fatwā al-Khaṭīra allatī Aṣdarathā al-Muftūn wa'l-Quḍā wa'l-Mudarrisūn wa'l-Khuṭabā' wa'l-A'ima wa'l-Wu'āẓ wa-Sā'ir 'Ulamā' al-Muslimīn wa-Rijāl al-Dīn bi-Filasṭīn bi-Sha'n Bay' al-Arḍ li'l-Ṣahyūniyyīn.* (Jerusalem, (1935)).
65. Y. Porath, *The Palestinian Arab National Movement 1929–1939: From Riots to Rebellion* (London: Frank Cass, 1977) pp. 98–9.
66. Z. Abramovitz and Y. Gleft, *The Arab Economy in Palestine and the Middle Eastern Countries* (Hebrew, Tel-Aviv, ha-Kibutz ha-Me'uhad, 1944) p. 51ff.
67. A. Cohen, *The Economy of the Arab Sector in Palestine under the Mandate* (Hebrew, Givat Haviva, 1978), pp. 24–6.
68. *CIH*, 13/43/1,40/40.
69. A. Cohen, *The Economy of the Arab Sector in Palestine under the Mandate* (Hebrew, Givat Haviva, 1978) p. 11.
70. Z. Abramovitz and Y. Gleft, *The Arab Economy in Palestine and the Middle Eastern Countries* (Hebrew, Tel-Aviv, ha-Kibutz ha-Me'uhad, 1944) p. 53.
71. Al-Majlis al-Islāmī al-Shar'ī al-A'lā, *Bayān al-Majlis al-Islāmī al-Shar'i al-A'lā 1923–4*, p. 20; *Bayān* 1928, p. 12.
72. M. Qadrī Pāshā, *Kitāb Qānūn al-'Adl wa'l-Inṣāf li'l-Qaḍā' 'alā Mushkilāt al-Awqāf* (Cairo, 1902) arts. 236, 412.
73. *CIH*, SMC, P/989, 70.
74. *Sijill* 437/97/113.
75. *Sijill* 467/127/83.
76. *Sijill* 453/26/256.
77. *Sijill* 512/49/86, 507/24/151.
78. *Sijill* 427/438/118.
79. Al-Majlis al-Islāmī al-Shar'ī al-A'lā, *Bayān al-Majlis al-Islāmī al-Shar'ī al-*

Aʿlā 1923–4, p. 18; *Bayān* 1924–5, p. 5; *Bayān* 1928, p. 5: *Bayān* 1931, p. 3.

80. *CIH*, 378, 13/24/1,2/20.
81. Ibid., 13/26/10,3/20.
82. Ibid., 13/26/10,3/20.
83. Al-Majlis al-Islāmī al-Sharʿī al-Aʿlā, *Bayān al-Majlis al-Islāmī al-Sharʿī al-Aʿlā* 1929, p. 8.
84. *Al-Jāmiʿa al-ʿArabiyya*, 17 October 1927.
85. *Sijill* 444/19/95.
86. *Sijill* 420/25/105.
87. *Al-Jāmiʿa al-ʿArabiyya*, 17 October 1927.
88. *Sijill* 478/291/267.
89. *Sijill* 446/79/16.
90. *Sijill* 443/79/16.
91. *Sijill* 445/2/111.
92. *CIH*, 13/40/1,31/40, document 389 dated 19 November 1940.
93. *Sijill* 458/138/119.
94. *Sijill* 505/71/745.
95. *ISA, SMC*, P/988, 37.
96. Ibid., 38.
97. *ISA, Land Court*, B/794, 149/45.
98. Ibid.
99. M. Doukhan, *Land Laws in the State of Israel* (Hebrew, 2nd ed., Jerusalem, 1953) p. 430.
100. *CIH*, 13/35/5,20/60.
101. Examples: *Sijill* 505/21/663, 445/58/175.
102. Examples: *Sijill* 469/76/95, 469/82/103.
103. *Sijill* 479/24/144.
104. M.Z. al-Abyani Bey, *Kitāb Mābaḥith al-Waqf* (Cairo, 1924) p. 61. For the practice in Morocco see O. Pesle, *La théorie et la pratique des habous dans le rite malekite* (Casablanca, n.d.) p. 134ff.
105. For the practice in Iraq see M.S. al-ʿĀnī, *Aḥkām al-Awqāf* (3rd ed., Baghdad, 1965) p. 190.
106. *Sijill* 419/372/97.
107. *Sijill* 424/2/9.
108. See for example M. Kurd ʿAlī, *Kitāb Khiṭṭaṭ al-Shām* (Damascus, 1927) 5, p. 105.
109. M.M. al-Māḥī, *al-Ḥukuma al ʿIrāqiyya, Taqrīr ʿan Awqāf al-ʿIrāq wa-Wasa'il Iṣlāḥiha* (Baghdad, 1937) p. 188.
110. M. Abū Zahra, *Muḥāḍarāt fī al-Waqf* (2nd ed., Cairo: Dār al Fikr al-ʿArabi, 1971) pp. 173–4.
111. R.C. Deguilhem Schoem, 'History of *Waqf* and Case Studies from Syria in the Late Ottoman Period and French Mandate' (Ann Arbor, MI, University Microfilms, 1986) pp. 131, 141.
112. M. Abū Zahra, *Muḥāḍarāt fī al-Waqf* (2nd ed., Cairo: Dār al Fikr al-ʿArabī, 1971) p. 165.
113. M.M. al-Māḥī, *al-Ḥukūma al ʿIrāqiyya, Taqrīr ʿan 'Awqāf al-ʿIrāq wa-Wasā'il Iṣlaḥiha* (Baghdad, 1937) p. 188.

Part 4

8

Supervision of *waqfs*

One of the weaknesses of the *waqf* system is the absence of efficient supervision over its administration. The *sharī'a* rules entrust the *qāḍīs* with supervisory powers, but neither the Ottoman nor the Mandatory government gave them the means to discharge this duty. Neither did they devise auditing rules to ensure sound management. Accordingly, *qāḍīs* had to rely on complaints from beneficiaries. This weakness was easily exploited by the *mutawallīs* for personal gain from *waqf* resources; it also caused *waqfs* to fall into neglect. Cases of corruption or neglect have given the *waqf* the image of a declining and mismanaged institution.[1] Modern Muslim governments sometimes mention this when arguing that the *waqf* should be abolished. However, this negative image has not yet been empirically studied by drawing on primary *waqf* sources.

Like the preceding chapters, the discussion below is based on a methodical study of the *sijill* of the Jerusalem *sharī'a* court over the past century. We have examined the degree of corruption within *waqfs* on the basis of complaints by beneficiaries against *mutawallīs*. In this type of complaint, the beneficiary spelled out his allegations against the *mutawallī*, and the *qāḍī* was required to establish the facts and rule accordingly. Of course, not all such claims were brought before the *qāḍī*; he only dealt with the tip of the iceberg. However, the very fact that such grievances were filed and that *mutawallīs* were dismissed and made to account for their activities is important in itself and permits one to draw certain conclusions.

Other types of documents in the *sijill* describe measures taken by *qāḍīs* to control the management of *waqfs*. These documents may answer questions about the efficiency of supervision and the extent to which *qāḍī*s participated in attempts to overcome the defects of the *waqf* as an institution.

The *sijill* – especially the documents in which *qāḍī*s authorized *mutawallī*s to modify or trade in *waqf* properties – are the major source for study of their management. The documents can help us answer the question of whether the *waqf*s were administered under traditional or modern economic principles, whether they were neglected, or whether they were developed and allowed to flourish.

EMBEZZLEMENT, NEGLECT OR MISMANAGEMENT

Sharī'a rules permit the dismissal of a *mutawallī* in three cases:

1. wilful embezzlement or corruption – such an act is considered breach of trust and is called '*khiyāna*' ('perfidy');[2] acts regarded as 'perfidious' include violations of the terms set forth by the founder, unless done in good faith; mortgaging or sale of *waqf*s without permission from the *qāḍī*s; *mutawallī*s acting as if the *waqf* were their own; use of *waqf* properties and moneys for personal needs; letting *waqf*s without benefit to the endowed property;[3] arbitrary failure to maintain property; failure to collect *waqf* revenue, and failure to grant beneficiaries their full entitlement;[4]
2. malfeasance (*fisq* – an offense less serious than *khiyāna*);
3. incapacity or incompetence.

Demands by beneficiaries for the investigation of *mutawallī*s or suing for their dismissal were the most effective means of control available to beneficiaries and the *sharī'a* court. It must be noted, however, that the initiative in such cases came from the beneficiaries, not from the court. Dismissal of the *mutawallī* was the strongest sanction available.

In the last years of Ottoman rule in Palestine, 13 complaints urging the dismissal of *mutawallī*s were presented in Jerusalem. The *qāḍī* turned down two of them as unjustified. In one case, he suggested that the beneficiaries petition the *sharī'a* court following standard procedures. In ten cases, the *qāḍī* did dismiss the *mutawallī*: four for embezzlement, two for infringement of *sharī'a* rules, two for failure to give the beneficiaries their full entitlement, and two because the beneficiaries no longer wished the *mutawallī*s to continue in office.

An interesting legal inquiry recorded in the *sijill* during this period is that of the *shaykh* of the Afghanī Sufi Lodge in Jerusalem, Shaykh 'Alī 'Abd al-Qādir al-Bāsh. He was accused of giving loans to peasants and charging interest, using funds provided for the lodge by the Ottoman government. In his trial, he admitted that he had appropriated *waqf* resources in order to campaign in Istanbul for his appointment as *mutawallī*. He had been given the appointment even though he was illiterate!

The number of lawsuits actually adjudicated during the late Ottoman years was small compared with the Mandatory period. From 1918 to 1948, beneficiaries sought the dismissal of *mutawallī*s in 74 cases (see Table 8.1), including 57 for embezzlement and corruption. Thirty-five cases led to dismissal or other sanctions.

In 35 cases, embezzlement was the main charge, and 22 of them resulted in dismissal. In only six of these cases, however, was embezzlement recorded as the reason for dismissal. In the other cases, the *qāḍī* cited other reasons which also appeared in the beneficiaries' petitions.

Embezzlement charges were phrased in various ways. Sometimes the *mutawallī* was accused of having appropriated *waqf* funds for his own uses (*maṣāliḥuhu al-khāṣṣa*), of owing money to the *waqf* (*dhimatuhu mashghūla*) or of failing to keep his personal accounts separate from *waqf* accounts. Thus, for example, a beneficiary sued the *mutawallī* of the al-Ḥarīrī Waqf for embezzlement. Each side appointed a *sharī'a* lawyer and a panel of experts (*lajnat muḥāsaba*) to audit the *mutawallī*s' accounts together with representatives of the *qāḍī*. It transpired that the *mutawallī* had concealed some of the *waqf* revenues for the three years preceding the lawsuit and had withdrawn funds from *waqf* funds to finance personal legal expenses. Most of the expenses listed in the *mutawallī*'s financial statement were not substantiated, and many of the beneficiaries had not received any payment, let alone their full entitlement. On the basis of these

TABLE 8.1 BENEFICIARIES' PETITIONS FOR THE DISMISSAL OF *MUTAWALLĪ*S DURING THE MANDATE PERIOD

Charge	*No. of cases (out of 74) in which the charge was made**
Embezzlement and corruption:	
Embezzlement	43
Takeover of *waqf*s	18
Unauthorized residence on *waqf* property	8
Letting properties at inadequate rates	19
Unnecessary expenditure	6
Charging fees without the *qāḍī*'s consent	2
Borrowing from *waqf* funds	3
Transferring one year's funds to the next year's budget	6
Inaccurate bookkeeping	9
Neglect:	
Failure to renovate property	28
Failure to collect revenue	9
Failure to utilize property	2
Failure to pay taxes	1
Failure to prosecute trespassers	14
Letting property to *waqf* debtors	1
Inefficient rental property	2
Breach of founder's stipulations:	
Failure to remit full entitlements	51
Failure to comply with founder's stipulations concerning charities	3
Violation of *sharī'a* rules:	
Unauthorized modification of *waqf* properties	4
Unauthorized transactions with *waqf* properties	8
Unnecessary renovations and improvement in *waqf* properties	7
Unauthorized long-term rental of *waqf* properties	10
Transfer of revenues from one *waqf* to another	3
Failure to share management with colleagues	6
Mismanagement	2
Mutawallī's unsuitability as *waqf* administrator	15
Failure to present financial statements or negligent presentation	30
Failure to present receipts of rental contracts	6
Unauthorized destruction of *waqf* properties	1

Note: * In most cases, more than one charge was made.

findings, the *qāḍī* fired the *mutawallī*.[5] About a year later, a former *mutawallī* of this *waqf* who had earlier been dismissed for having charged an unauthorized fee was appointed again. Three years later, his predecessor, the *mutawallī* who had been dismissed in the original suit, sued him in turn for embezzlement. The incumbent admitted his guilt and also confessed to having paid some of the beneficiaries more than their due in order to keep them quiet (*ḥattā iskātihim*).[6]

In mismanagement complaints, one of the allegations was that the administrator had not granted the beneficiaries their full entitlements as set forth in the endowment deed. This was the main charge in 25 of these cases, and although it was not emphasized in the others, one may assume that the beneficiaries might never have sued at all had they received their due. In some cases, the nature of the allegations suggests that negligence and mismanagement had long been rife, but that the beneficiaries sued only when they no longer received their entitlements.[7] (Neglect, mismanagement and embezzlement have been stressed here because they are the subject of this chapter, but it must be remembered that at the other end of the spectrum, there were many instances of proper maintenance and development, described in the preceding chapters.)

METHODS OF CONTROL

What sanctions was the *qāḍī* able to apply in order to discharge the duty of supervision? The *sharīʿa* court was vested with the following powers:

1. to appoint one of the beneficiaries as an overseer of the *mutawallī*;[8] if the beneficiaries complained about the *mutawallī*, the *qāḍī* was entitled to enlist one of the plaintiffs in whom he had trust (*thiqa*) as an additional *mutawallī*;[9] in either case, the *mutawallī* was not allowed to conclude a contract or carry out any transaction without the consent of the overseer or of the second *mutawallī*;
2. to order an annual audit (*muḥāsaba*);[10]
3. to order an inspection of properties by experts (*kashf*);[11]
4. to dismiss a *mutawallī*.

The last of these sanctions has been discussed above. Below we describe the other methods, as well as several additional ones adapted to modern times.

Appointing an additional mutawallī *or overseer (*nāẓir *or* mushrif*)*

During the Mandatory period, approximately 30 family and public endowments (from among roughly 200 active *waqf*s supervised by the *sharīʿa* court) were managed by more than one *mutawallī*. The reason usually given in the *sijill* for appointing a 'co-*mutawallī*' was 'the importance of the *waqf*'. This, however, was a euphemism used by the beneficiaries from different branches of the founder's family for wanting to safeguard their own interests and to ensure close control of a *mutawallī* from another branch of the family. Thus, for example, the Maḥbūba al-Khālidī Waqf was administered for 30 years by two brothers (Muṣṭafā Bey and ʿAbd al-Ghanī al-Khālidī). In 1927, the *qāḍī* appointed their nephew, Fu'ād ʿAṭāllāh, as a third *mutawallī*. The formal pretext was that 'the *waqf* needed another *mutawallī* in view of its importance and its many activities.'[12] The real reason, however, was that ʿAṭāllāh's offspring were dissatisfied with the way their two elderly uncles ran the *waqf*; it was they who had brought about Fu'ād's appointment. Several months after the appointment, Fu'ād sued in the *sharīʿa* court for the dismissal of his two uncles. In the course of the litigation, the brothers resigned one after the other; the *qāḍī* found Fu'ād's allegations justified.[13]

The *qāḍī*s evidently had good reason to exercise their prerogative to appoint beneficiaries as additional *mutawallī*s or overseers. Such internal control ensured close and constant supervision of the *mutawallī*, and it gave the beneficiaries some assurance that their affairs were not subject to the decisions of a single person. In 23 of the 30 *waqf*s in Mandatory Jerusalem that were managed by more than one *mutawallī* or had a *nāẓir*, 36 petitions for the dismissal of *mutawallī*s were filed during the Mandate years. The *mutawallī* was dismissed in half of these cases. Thus the *qāḍī* used his right to appoint additional *mutawallī*s as a stage in the enforcement of full control.

The *waqf*s for which the *qāḍī* appointed an overseer over the *mutawallī* were in no better condition than those run by multiple *mutawallī*s.[14] Various *mutawallī*s managed to evade their overseer's vigilance for long periods of time, until they were finally sued in the *sharīʿa* court. In one case, the *qāḍī* ordered a *mutawallī* to deposit trust revenues in a bank account from which he could not withdraw funds without the co-signature of one of two supervisors.[15] Thus the *qāḍī* ensured the efficacy of the *nāẓir*'s supervisory powers by actively involving him in all administrative matters. He employed an effective sanction, well suited to modern times. However, as stated, it was invoked only once in Mandatory Jerusalem.[16]

Beneficiaries preferred internal control rather than entrusting their endowments to the Waqf Department of the SMC, about which they felt apprehensive. Evidently, *qāḍī*s also preferred this option since, as long as management of the *waqf* had not yet been assigned to the *ma'mūr al-awqāf*, the *qāḍī* wielded the supervisory powers himself. By the end of the Ottoman period, the appointment of overseers and additional *mutawallī*s had become the norm in public *waqf*s. The appointment of multiple *mutawallī*s was meant to satisfy various groups of beneficiaries. Thus, for example, Maghribīs from various countries of origin were represented on the boards of *mutawallī*s of two Maghribī *waqf*s (the Abū Midyan and the Takrūrī Waqfs).[17]

Audits (muḥāsaba)

The *qāḍī* was supposed to inspect the financial statements of the *waqf* once a year. If the *mutawallī* was known to be honest, it sufficed for him to submit a general statement. However, if the *mutawallī* was suspect in the eyes of the *qāḍī* or the beneficiaries, he had to present the *sharīʿa* court with a detailed financial statement, including all income and expenditure. The *qāḍī* would then order the *mutawallī*s to report for an investigation (lasting two or three days, if necessary) of every detail therein.[18] A *mutawallī* who failed to file a financial statement was deemed guilty of malpractice (*su' istiʿmāl fi al-waẓīfa*).[19] The *waqf* account books, known as *daftar al-muḥāsaba*, were kept according to the Islamic calendar. They itemized *waqf* properties and the revenues generated by each, the names and entitlements of each beneficiary, and every *waqf* expenditure. The *mutawallī*s had to verify every item by attaching receipts, rental contracts, and other relevant documents.

Table 8.2 gives an example of a financial statement (for 1930) presented to the *sharīʿa* court: it comes from the *mutawallī* of the Muḥammad al-Khalīlī Waqf, a trust with substantial income from properties in Jerusalem, Jaffa and Hebron.[20]

It is worth noting at this juncture that these audits were not very effective. The *mutawallī* presented the *daftar* and the above documents. The examining committee made sure that there were no discrepancies. If none were found, the committee declared the books 'compatible with reality' (*lā yakdhibahu al-ẓāhir*; literally: 'do not belie appearances'). If there were any, the *mutawallī* had to provide an explanation. One member of the Jerusalem Muslim establishment who used to audit *waqf* books said in an interview that even though he habitually approved account books that were 'compatible with reality', he did not consider most of them truthful. He stated that there were *mutawallī*s who refused to show the court their books, adding that no one could force them to do so unless the beneficiaries filed a complaint.[21]

In 30 suits for the dismissal of *mutawallī*s filed with the Jerusalem *sharīʿa* court during the Mandatory period, we find, among others, the allegation that the *mutawallī*s had failed to show the books of account to the beneficiaries or to others entitled to see them. In 11 suits, *mutawallī*s were dismissed for this reason.[22] *Qāḍī*s did not regard the mere failure to submit a *daftar al-muḥāsaba* for the routine annual audit as sufficient reason for dismissal. Rather, they ordered him to do so, even if belatedly.[23] But non-compliance with such an order was considered a grave matter. For example: a *qāḍī* ordered the dismissal of a *mutawallī* of the Ṣāliḥ al-Takrūrī Waqf, describing the man as a recalcitrant whose behaviour had made his reliability suspect (*sulūkihi hādhā mujīb lil-rayba fī amānatihi*).[24]

Once a suit was filed, it was usually found that the *mutawallī*s had not presented annual statements for many years, in some cases not even once since their appointment. Thus, for example, a

TABLE 8.2 FINANCIAL STATEMENT (*MUḤĀSABA*) OF THE MUḤAMMAD AL-KHALĪLĪ WAQF FOR 1930 (IN £P)

Income

1,800	Rent from Hebron public bath
2,700	Rent from Jaffa public bath
4,200	Rent paid by Ibrāhīm al-Ḥabasha
2,500	Rent paid by al-Khalīlī
3,000	Rent paid by Maḥmūd Fayḍī
1,800	Rent paid by ʿAmrān al-Bashītī
1,500	Rent paid by ʿAbd al-Salām al-Khalīlī
8,000	Rent paid by Tawfīq Fayḍī al-Nābulsī
2,700	Rent paid by Abu ʿAlī al-Ḥawāsh
5,000	Rent paid by Ḥusayn Naṣra al-Maʿṣara
2,000	Rent paid by al-Tutanjī
1,300	Rent paid by al-Arna'ūt
4,700	Rent of Dār al-Shihābī
4,700	Rent of Dār Taḥsīn al-Ḥabalī
5,500	Rent of Dār al-Almānī
6,000	Rent paid by ʿAbd Buṭrus
1,500	Rent paid by al-Maṣlaḥ, let to the municipality
2,500	Rent from land in Baqʿa let to the Water Commission
10,000	Rent from land in Baqʿa let to the army (for two years)
12,600	Deposit made at Barclay's Bank, June 1930
13,600	Second deposit at Barclay's Bank
97,600	

Expenditure

1,325	*Werko* (property) taxes for Jerusalem properties for 1928
1,225	Ditto for 1929
445	*Werko* taxes for land in Baqʿa and Bāb al-Sāhira
1,200	*Werko* taxes for Dār Ẓāhir
1,325	*Werko* taxes for properties in Jaffa for previous years
7,800	Renovation of Tomb of Khalīl by al-Balbīsī
300	Renovation of a room
300	Whitewash
400	Expenses for Shaykh Amīn al-Danaf
1,900	Furniture, etc.
750	Sewing of shroud for tomb, including tailor's fee
1,500	Haulage of water to Dār Taḥsīn and Dār al-Shihābī
900	Cesspool at the large house, together with Muḥyi al-Dīn al-ʿAmarī
800	Cesspool at the large house at the north end of Dār al-Ghubayya, to the east
1,000	Installation of metal door at Dār al-Walad
100	Velvet tablecloth
250	Aluminum chimney for olive press
150	Wood and aluminium windows and panes at al-Ḥafra
500	Plumbing, etc.
400	Debt to Ḥasan ʿAlam al-Khalīlī
22,730	

Note: The surplus, £P74,870, went to six beneficiaries, among them the *mutawallī*, who received twice the share of the others.

beneficiary of the al-Shihābī Waqf alleged in a petition against the *mutawallī* that the latter had not presented accounts since he had been appointed 14 years previously. When a financial statement was eventually prepared by order of the *qāḍī*, the *mutawallī* was shown to have embezzled *waqf* funds.[25] In another suit filed by a beneficiary of the Yaḥyā al-Khalīlī Qulaybū Waqf, the plaintiff accused the *mutawallī* of not having presented accounts since assuming office 38 years earlier![26]

Inspection by experts (kashf)

Another sanction to which *qāḍī*s could resort was the appointment of a committee of experts to inspect the *waqf* properties.[27] Such committees were appointed by the *qāḍī* whenever a request was made for permission to renovate, let or perform some other transaction with *waqf* properties. Committees of identical composition were also set up to investigate charges by beneficiaries against *mutawallī*s for neglect or unauthorized renovation or construction work. This action was called *kashf*. After completing its visit, the committee would report back to the *qāḍī*, who would then rule whether the *mutawallī* had discharged his duties faithfully or negligently, or had acted illegally. The committee was composed of three experts, one representing each side and a third representing the *qāḍī*. If they failed to reach a consensus, it was in the *qāḍī*'s sole discretion to appoint a new committee. The *sijill* of Jerusalem shows that scores of committees of these types were appointed.

Neglect tended to go hand-in-hand with mismanagement, since the *mutawallī*s and, at times, the beneficiaries expected to make an immediate profit (a large end-of-year balance for distribution among the beneficiaries) at the expense of the future. In 29 lawsuits from the Mandatory period, plaintiffs alleged that *mutawallī*s were negligent in the upkeep and renovation of *waqf*s. In ten of these suits, *mutawallī*s were dismissed, eight of them because of the findings of a *kashf* committee. The efficacy of these control devices cannot be doubted. However, they were invoked only when beneficiaries petitioned the *qāḍī* with allegations relating to the physical condition of *waqf* properties.

CONCLUSIONS

The *sijill* of twentieth-century Jerusalem attests to instances of corruption among the *mutawallī*s of non-*maḍbūṭ waqf*s. Differences between the types and the number of beneficiaries of *waqf*s and the way they were managed were clearly discernible. Embezzlement was far more common in public *waqf*s than in family endowments. Among the family endowments, corruption was more prevalent in *waqf*s where beneficiaries belonged to several families or to different branches of one family than in endowments whose beneficiaries all belonged to one branch of a single family. It is nevertheless a fact that *mutawallī*s suspected of malpractice were brought to trial, that their activities were monitored and their accounts audited, and that those found guilty were fired and forced to return embezzled funds. This shows that the corruption was not as entrenched in the period discussed here as in earlier eras, when it was suspected that *qāḍī*s and powerful, high-ranking officials were partners in corruption. There is no evidence that *qāḍī*s, *ma'mūrī al-awqāf* or members of the SMC collaborated with *mutawallī*s. One must, however, take into account that some cases of corruption and mismanagement were perhaps hushed up and resolved quietly within the religious establishment, unbeknown to the public and with no written documentation.

Examination of the Jerusalem *sijill* shows that action for the dismissal of *mutawallī*s was brought more frequently under the Mandate than in the late Ottoman period.

Although there is no study comparing the level of moral rectitude in the *waqf*s to that of other administrative and public systems, there is no doubt that the inefficiency of control over the *waqf* bears much of the blame for the erosion of *waqf* ethics.

In sum, inability to supervise the *mutawallī*s was the major defect of the *waqf* in all periods. In the twentieth century, however, corruption was not intrinsic.

NOTES

1. See for example Sh.D. Goitein and A. Ben Shemmesh, *Muslim Law in the State of Israel* (Hebrew, Jerusalem, 1957) pp. 169–70; A. Granovski, *The Land Regime in Palestine* (Hebrew, Tel-Aviv, 1949) pp. 127, 130; M. Kurd 'Alī, *Kitāb Khiṭṭaṭ al-Shām* (Damascus, 1927) 5, p. 123ff; G. Baer, 'The Dismemberment of *Awqāf* in Early 19th Century Jerusalem', *Asian and African Studies*, 13, 3 (1979) pp. 220–41; B. Yediyildiz, 'La porte économique des Vakfs Turcs au XVIIIe siècle', in G. Baer and G. Gilbar

(eds), *Studies on the Muslim Waqf* (Oxford: Oxford University Press) (forthcoming).
2. M. Qadrī Pāshā, *Kitāb Qānūn al-ʿAdl wa'l-Inṣāf li'l-Qaḍā' ʿalā Mushkilāt al-Awqāf* (Cairo, 1902) arts. 248, 335.
3. M. Qadrī Pāshā, *Kitāb Qānūn al-ʿAdl wa'l-Inṣāf li'l-Qaḍā' ʿalā Mushkilāt al-Awqāf* (Cairo, 1902) art. 252.
4. M. Qadrī Pāshā, *Kitāb Qānūn al-ʿAdl wa'l-Inṣāf li'l-Qaḍā' ʿalā Mushkilāt al-Awqāf* (Cairo, 1902) art. 253.
5. *Sijill* 473/196/174.
6. *Sijill* 478/373/115.
7. See, for example, *Sijill* 438/55/177, 478/291/267.
8. M. Qadrī Pāshā, *Kitāb Qānūn al-ʿAdl wa'l-Inṣāf li'l-Qaḍā' ʿalā Mushkilāt al-Awqāf* (Cairo, 1902) art. 158.
9. Ibid., art. 251.
10. Ibid., art. 217.
11. Ibid., art. 221.
12. *Sijill* 439/96/69.
13. *Sijill* 438/362/222, 441/49/68, 449/98/187.
14. *Sijill* 483/375/5.
15. *Sijill* 486/48/407.
16. *Sijill* 489/314/65, 483/182/136, 478/373/115, 478/116/16.
17. *Sijill* 475/63/100, 475/22/36, 475/22/34, 474/128/83.
18. M. Qadrī Pāshā, *Kitāb Qānūn al-ʿAdl wa'l-Inṣāf li'l-Qaḍā' ʿalā Mushkilāt al-Awqāf* (Cairo, 1902) art. 218.
19. *Sijill* 438/34/27.
20. *ISA*, *Land Court*, 752b, file 40/31.
21. Interview with Zayn al-ʿĀbidīn al-ʿAlamī.
22. *Sijill* 452/381/246, 496/382/191, 466/9/179, 456/247/231, 509/229/87, 483/233/233, 483/378/6, 449/98/187, 450/62/16, 478/116/160.
23. *Sijill* 498/382/191.
24. *Sijill* 509/229/87.
25. *Sijill* 496/29/219.
26. *Sijill* 452/375/214.
27. M. Qadrī Pāshā, *Kitāb Qānūn al-ʿAdl wa'l-Inṣāf li'l-Qaḍā' ʿalā Mushkilāt al-Awqāf* (Cairo, 1902) art. 221.

9

Summary and conclusions

At a time when the *waqf* institution tended towards extinction in most Muslim countries, it continued to occupy an important place among the Muslims of Mandatory Palestine. A creation of the old social order in Islam, it had a vital function as a voluntary institution in medieval Muslim society. It filled a void left by the concept of the role of the state by providing the population with public services and with a lever for economic development. It also met various needs in the lives of individuals and families. It reached its peak in the Ottoman empire, when three-quarters of all cultivated land had *waqf* status and most municipal institutions were funded by *waqf* resources. Since the nineteenth century, however, the *waqf* has receded to the point of being abolished in several Muslim countries. Its central importance first began to decline with the introduction of Ottoman reforms in the nineteenth century. Inasmuch as reform measures related to the *waqf*, they were meant to adapt it to the evolving socio-economic conditions of modern times. Public criticism of the *waqf* in the modern era spoke of it as an embodiment of the constraints of the old social order, and therefore subject to reforms. It was identified with an elite – the *'ulamā'* – that modern regimes attempted to weaken by redistributing *waqf* resources among diverse population groups (as happened in Egypt, for example). Waqfs were regarded (unjustifiably so, as this study shows) as neglectful of their properties and as holding back economic development and agrarian reform, thereby harming the economy as a whole. They were also perceived as an institution riddled with corruption. This included the *qāḍīs* who were supposed to exercise the power of supervision. Finally, the family *waqf* was perceived as a ruse to circumvent Islamic inheritance laws – the commands *Allāh* and his prophet had handed down in the *Qur'ān* and the *Sunna*.

The patterns of *waqf* management in Mandatory Palestine were different from those chosen by other non-Muslim regimes, whether merely mandatory or full-fledged colonial administrations. There is a marked difference between the two in their attitude toward the *waqf*. Mandatory regimes were subject to the provisions of the mandate, which required them to administer *waqf*s under religious law. Yet there was a considerable difference between the *waqf* administration under the French mandates in Syria and Lebanon and the British mandate in Palestine. In Syria and Lebanon, public *waqf*s were supervised and, to a great extent, controlled by the French, who intervened with a heavy hand and imposed various reforms – for example, in the matter of *istibdāl*. In Palestine, by contrast, the British at first refrained from intervening in *waqf* administration. But after 1937, when they finally imposed close supervision on *waqf* management, they refrained from reforming the institution itself and actually repealed several Ottoman reforms. British legislation on points affecting the *waqf* did so indirectly, and did not leave its mark on daily realities.

Colonial regimes, in contrast, attempted to impose Western legal norms on their Muslim populations. In India, the British created a legal hybrid that became known as 'Anglo-Mohammedan law', in which British judges applied the *sharīʿa* according to English legal principles. One of the results of this method was a British ruling (of 1913) abolishing family *waqf*s because they were incompatible with the concepts of English law. The French adopted a similar policy in Algeria, instituting what was termed 'Algerian Muslim law'. Unlike the British in India, the French left the *sharīʿa* courts intact but integrated them into the French legal system under French principles of law. They imposed a reformist style on the *sharīʿa* by placing the burden of reform on the *qāḍī*s and the *ʿulamāʾ* themselves, in their capacity as employees of the state. Policy on the *waqf* was a function of French land policy, tailored to facilitate French colonization in Algeria. Consequently, the French made the *waqf* (especially the public *waqf*) fully subordinate to the state. The difference between British and French attitudes was brought out by the fact that, in 1932, the French authorities had to meet a Saudi demand for Algerian *waqf* revenues pledged to Mecca and Medina (*awqāf al-*

ḥaramayn). In Palestine, by contrast, it was the Supreme Muslim Council, rather than the authorities, which forwarded revenues pledged to the *ḥaramayn*. These were arbitrary sums and bore no relation to actual revenue. Thus the model of *waqf* administration in Mandatory Palestine was unique among non-Muslim regimes, whether mandatory or colonial.

Conditions in Mandatory Palestine allowed the *waqf* to maintain its status and centrality in Muslim society, and, to a certain extent, even to strengthen its hold. To go beyond the time-frame of this book for a moment, let us note that there was a down-turn in this trend under Jordanian rule in eastern Jerusalem (after 1948). But it regained its strength when Israel moved into the eastern section of the city in June 1967. From that time onward, the reconstituted Supreme Muslim Council again used the *maḍbūṭ waqf* as the mainstay of its activities. Approximately 90 new public and family *waqf*s were established in Jerusalem between 1967 and 1990. The pivotal importance of the *waqf* for Muslim society in Palestinian is a consequence of the political circumstances that brought it under non-Muslim rule. In Mandatory Palestine, as well as under Israeli rule, Islam was on the defensive (as Kupferschmidt puts it). The Supreme Muslim Council, which the British had endowed with autonomous powers in religious matters, including the management of *waqf*s, came into being because of the Muslims' need, under non-Muslim rule, to conduct their (religious and other) affairs by themselves. In eastern Jerusalem, this became true again after 1967.

The status of the *waqf* in society should not be assessed under the institutional aspect, which is all too often shaped by political aims and considerations. Rather, the development of the *waqf* is to be measured principally at the levels of individuals and the community, as indicated, most of all, by the number of new *waqf*s formed. In the Mandate period, 61 new endowments were made in Jerusalem, about one-third fewer than in the preceding period (an average of two endowments per year, compared with three between 1900 and 1917). Ḥājj Amīn al-Ḥusaynī's exhortations for the Muslim public to declare its real property *waqf*s were not heeded in any practical sense. But the decline in establishing new *waqf*s was not sharp, at a time when the social and economic changes that accompanied the entry into the modern age were dramatic indeed. The most pronounced change in the Mandate era, continuing a trend that dated back to the late Ottoman period, was the decline in the formation of public *waqf*s. As the modern state came to regard personal welfare and community services as falling within its domain, the predisposition to form *khayrī waqf*s diminished. In Mandatory Jerusalem, only nine public *waqf*s were established. The traditional purpose of the public *waqf*, support of houses of worship (mosques and Sufi *zāwiyya*s), remained the major motivation in the formation of such endowments. The Maghribī (Takrūrī) Waqf, for people who traced their descent to certain geographical areas in Africa, was a direct continuation of the tradition of some 100 other Maghribī *waqf*s already existing in Jerusalem, chief among them the Abū Midyan Waqf.

At the level of the individual and his or her immediate setting (family, community of origin, town), the paradigm of the family *waqf* underwent no substantial change. Evidently, people's motives for establishing family *waqf*s remained unchanged. An analysis of the patterns of *waqf* entitlements and of the personal and family background of *waqf* founders in Jerusalem leads us to conclude that the establishment of a family *waqf* was thought of as an act of charity bound to earn the believer a reward in the afterworld.

For many, the *waqf* was a device to circumvent the law of inheritance. The major objective of many founders was to protect family property from being taken over by outsiders following the marriages of daughters. Many founders in Jerusalem deprived cognate offspring of their entitlements for this reason. Several founders added stipulations barring women who had married out of the family from receiving entitlements as long as they remained married. Founders who addressed themselves to this problem did so in order to ease the circumstances of their children and children's children. They regarded this as a way to strengthen the family's future status. Perpetuating the founder's name and establishing a living memorial to himself and his works were part and parcel of that status. As an alternative to a freely drawn will under civil law (following the Western model), the *waqf* offered an excellent solution for founders who had no children or other close relatives. Such founders were concerned that, according to Islamic law, their property would end up with distant relatives or in the state's treasury. However, one should not belittle the individual founders' religious, spiritual and psychological motives in making their endowments. The greater the number of disadvantaged persons whom the founder served, the greater the reward. In their deeds, many founders set aside a sum of money for clerics to recite chapters of the *Qur'ān* for the benefit of their souls. Other worldly belief combined with a sense of social responsibility that regarded it an injustice to exclude orphaned grandchildren from their grandfathers' estate, as the *sharī'a* law did. Both motives together caused founders to go out of their way to include orphaned grandchildren – of the living or of future generations – in the entitlements, allowing them to step into the place of their deceased father. The conclusion of the present study is that the family *waqf* is the product of social and religious motives combined.

In the Mandate period, the characteristics of founders underwent a perceptible change. Members of the former ruling classes and of families of notables, from whom many of the founders in the Ottoman period sprang, were replaced by members of small-to-average families from the middle and lower middle classes. This is also reflected in the types of endowments: large endowments – such as those of cultivated land outside Jerusalem, along the lines of the Ottoman governmental endowments – were few in number in the Mandate period.

The new era introduced new methods of charity and social welfare. The Charities Ordinance, enacted by the British in 1925, made it possible to make a charitable endowment under civil law, exempting the founder from the constraints of the *waqf*. Such endowments could be administered by modern methods. British inheritance legislation also made it possible for Muslims to draw up civil wills. But the Muslims of Palestine were not drawn to these options, which – one might have supposed – were likely to diminish the vitality of the *waqf*. The traditional cultural constraints were strong enough to deter Muslims from availing themselves of civil alternatives to procedures offered by the *sharī'a*.

Muslims who wished to circumvent the inheritance law preferred to do this by means of devices sanctioned by the *sharīʿa*. The establishment of new *waqf*s in Palestine in the twentieth century amounted, so to speak, to a vote of confidence by Muslims in the *waqf* as an institution. The founders failed to see in the *waqf* those defects which modern scholarship attributes to it.

The traditional image of neglect, inefficient management and economic conservatism is not corroborated by the Jerusalem *sijill*. Neglect and inefficiency were indeed present, and some *mutawallī*s were dismissed on these grounds. However, there were also many instances of renovation and maintenance, of new construction on, and development of, *waqf* land; some *waqf*s acquired new and more profitable properties by raising external capital by various methods (loans, long-term leases and exchange and sale of property). Because data on privately owned property are not available, we cannot arrive at a meaningful comparison between the physical and economic condition of *waqf* property and that of private assets.

Regarding ongoing maintenance, *waqf*s administered by the SMC seem to have fared better than privately managed endowments, especially after 1937, when the SMC ceased to engage in ostentatious projects (see below). In the collection of *waqf* revenue, however, the *mutawallī*s were more efficient than the SMC's clerks. In protecting the rights of *waqf*s to their property, both the SMC and the *mutawallī*s usually performed well, although the SMC was able to invest greater resources in doing so. Both the SMC and the *mutawallī*s disregarded founders' wishes for financing charities and social welfare.

The principal methods used in the Ottoman period to renovate run-down *waqf* properties and develop unused property were of the traditional kind: long-term leasing, such as *ijāratayn*, *ḥikr*, *muqāṭa'a* and *khulū*. *Istibdāl* was not prevalent in this period, chiefly because of the conservative attitude of the *ʿulamā'*. Under the Mandate, by contrast, *istibdāl bil-darāhim* (the sale of a property and the investment of the proceeds in another one) was the most prevalent type of transaction. It allowed capital to be raised to render vacant urban land profitable by selling part of it and investing the proceeds in new building on the remainder. The extensive development of *waqf* properties in Jerusalem, particularly in the new business district in the vicinity of Ṣalāḥ al-Dīn Street, helped preserve the status of the *waqf* in the city. Even though the number of new endowments decreased slightly, the *waqf* as such gained in economic strength. Credit for this should go to the *qāḍī*s, who found ways to permit modern economic management of *waqf*s, overcoming traditional *sharīʿa* constraints. The SMC, too, as an administrative and supervisory body, made a substantial contribution to the evolution of the modern market attitude. For political reasons, the SMC leased out large tracts of land at nominal rents, adopting an attitude of dirigisme to Arab economic development. While the Ottoman attitude had remained traditional and had aimed at keeping *waqf* properties in their original state, during the Mandate period, *waqf* management changed significantly in order to adjust to modern conditions. A modern perspective towards economic development was adopted, sweeping aside the principle of preservation alone.

The prevailing image of 'institutionalized' corruption in the *waqf* system, embracing beneficiaries, *mutawallī*s, *qāḍī*s and members of the social elite, is not altogether confirmed by the Jerusalem *sijill*. In the Mandate period, the *sharīʿa* court received 82 applications for the dismissal of *mutawallī*s. About 35 were indeed dismissed during these 30 years for embezzlement or corruption. This fact supports the standard image of *waqf* corruption, particularly if one assumes that not all cases of corruption reached the courts, and that the *sijill* merely shows the tip of the iceberg. However, the very fact that beneficiaries sued *mutawallī*s and that some suits ended with the dismissal of the latter indicates that there was no institutionalized corruption. Rather, it points in the opposite direction: the dismissal of *mutawallī*s was a deterrent. This was particularly true of family *waqf*s in which the *mutawallī* was, as a rule, the recipient of the largest entitlement. In the absence of comparative data, it is hard to assess whether the *waqf* was more corrupt under the Mandate than in the preceding period, or more corrupt than other contemporary Muslim institutions. To do so would require additional research, the findings of which should then be compared with this study.

The major weakness of the *waqf* was the lax supervision to which *mutawallī*s were subject. The *qāḍī*s did not carry out their supervisory duty successfully. The traditional remedy was the appointment of a trustworthy *mutawallī* who would be subordinate to the beneficiaries. The *qāḍī* intervened only if official application was made to the court. During the Mandate period, the *mutawallī*s' annual financial statements were not audited regularly. A new supervisory method was to force *mutawallī*s to deposit *waqf* revenues in a bank account from which withdrawals could be made only if countersigned by the *qāḍī* or the *nāẓir*. But this was done on rare occasions only. The *qāḍī*s attached considerable importance to renovation and construction, but precisely such activities made it easier for the *mutawallī* to line his own pocket. The *qāḍī*s ordered experts to inspect the site before the work began to satisfy themselves that it was necessary (*kashf*). Sometimes they did so again after it was completed, to verify the costs.

The *qāḍī*s were central actors in determining the way in which the *waqf* developed. Although in Mandatory Jerusalem they were dependent on the SMC, they succeeded in maintaining considerable autonomy with respect to the internal administration of *ghayr al-maḍbūṭ waqf*s. As early as 1923, the *Sharī'a* Court of Appeals ruled that supervision of *waqf*s, including the appointment and dismissal of *mutawallī*s, was the prerogative of the *qāḍī*, rather than of the SMC or of the two committees that represented it – the local *waqf* committee and the appointments board. (The ruling, it is worth noting, flew in the face of the views of Ḥājj Amīn al-Ḥusaynī.) When adjudicating entitlement disputes and interpreting the wishes of the founders, the *qāḍī*s followed the fundamental principles that Muslim religious lawyers had set forth in the Middle Ages: their assumption was always that the founder had wanted to provide for as many of his offspring as possible (*ghard al-wāqif dā'iman yumīl ilā iṭ'ām dhuriyatahu*). Accordingly, they upheld the entitlements of women and cognate offspring and the right of orphaned grandchildren to inherit their fathers' share. The *qāḍī*s may have done so because their attitude was often apologetic – they tended to speak of the *waqf* above all as a charitable institution, and thereby implicitly to defend it against the charge that it was designed to circumvent the Islamic inheritance law. This should not exclude the possibility that the *qāḍī*s, or some of them, were motivated by social conscience and wished to improve the lot of those deprived under the inheritance rules. As a rule, the *qāḍī*s respected the founders' wishes for the *waqf* to be administered by one of his offspring rather than an outsider. To uphold this principle, they sometimes had to compromise over a candidate's suitability and administrative competence. Most appointments went to persons who were acceptable to the various branches of the family and had the largest shares in the overall entitlements (members of the generation closest to the founder).

The unique contribution of the Mandate-era *qāḍī*s to reconciling the *waqf* with modern economic and social conditions is evident in their attitude towards transactions involving *waqf* properties. *Mutawallī*s met with no difficulties when they sought permission, even *post factum*, for the renovation, development or sale of *waqf* properties, provided this was to the *waqf*'s benefit. The main contribution of the Jerusalem *qāḍī*s was their use of *istibdāl bil-darāhim*: 'exchange' of *waqf* property for monetary compensation or, in plain words, the sale of one property and the investment of the proceeds in another. In this fashion, the *qāḍī*s resurrected a method that dated from early Islam and which had been suspended for many generations because of the prevailing conservatism. In approving such transactions, the Jerusalem *qāḍī*s waived an important *sharī'a* principle: the requirement of duress (*ḍarūra*). This liberalism contrasts sharply with rulings given by *qāḍī*s in Iraq during this period. In Mandatory Syria, when *istibdāl* was applied, it was in the context of French Mandatory legislation and under external pressure. In Jerusalem, by contrast, it was the result of a development within the Muslim religious establishment, triggered by modern economic constraints (including high taxes for vacant urban land). This development cannot be construed as innovative Islamic legal thinking (*ijtihād*) on the part of the *qāḍī*s. Indeed, they took pains to mask their disregard of the duress principle by referring to it quite artificially in their permits. They would, for instance, argue that the property needed urgent renovation or failed to generate revenue; that it was liable to heavy taxation, and so on. Thus the *qāḍī*s in Jerusalem resorted to a method traditionally practised by their predecessors in Palestine and elsewhere in the Muslim world; what made their contribution unique was that they went to great lengths to relax existing legal constraints for the sake of economic development.

The SMC, too, approached its task in a modern, fairly liberal spirit, and the combination of the SMC's attitude with the flexible stance of the *qāḍī*s led to the developments described above. The SMC, acting as it did as administrator and supervisor of the *waqf*s, was motivated by economic considerations as well as by its political aims and public interest. When, in a few cases, it obstructed the *mutawallī*s' transactions, it acted on the fear that the property would be sold to Jews. The SMC made great efforts to renovate and develop *waqf* property, put up new buildings and purchase others. Its president successfully enlisted Muslims abroad to help finance various works, most particularly the great renovation project on the Temple Mount. Its development schemes reached their peak with the construction of the Palace Hotel at the site of an ancient Muslim cemetery next to Mamilla Street. But this ostentatious project failed and had, for many years to come, an adverse effect on the SMC budget – precisely at the time of the world-wide economic depression. Under easier circumstances, it might have turned out a great success. Waqf-owned lands outside Jerusalem were leased for nominal sums to individual Muslims or to organizations that undertook to install irrigation systems and produce crops that the Arab national economy needed, for example, citrus fruit.

One of the most interesting findings of the present study is that the *ghayr maḍbūṭ waqf*s had not been subject to central governmental supervision during the Ottoman period. Because of a certain confusion between the terms *mulḥaq* and *maḍbūṭ waqf*, the British gave the SMC supervisory powers over *waqf*s that were not of the *maḍbūṭ* kind (Paragraph 5 in the ordinance setting it up). This was understood to mean that the SMC had the authority to order *mutawallī*s of family (and other *ghayr maḍbūṭ*) *waqf*s to submit annual reports for auditing. Ḥājj Amīn also attempted to have local *waqf* committees empowered to dismiss *mutawallī*s. But on the whole, the SMC took little interest in family *waqf*s and did not consistently follow through on its duty to supervise them. Such supervision as there was came to be applied selectively, when the SMC discovered that a *mutawallī* intended to sell property to non-Muslims or that there was a risk of property being transferred to private ownership and losing its *waqf* status. After the changes made in 1937 (see immediately below), the SMC exploited its standing and supervisory powers in order to take over the administration of several public *waqf*s. It claimed the provision of religious services as its exclusive prerogative, thus merging the concepts of *khayrī* and *maḍbūṭ*. When similar attempts had been made earlier, during the period of the Young Turks, the *qāḍī*s in Palestine had foiled them. But in the Mandate era, the SMC had the *qāḍī*s' full co-operation.

Over the years, the SMC adopted principles of sound administration and remedied various defects. Until 1937, however, neither its president nor its members were accountable to, or supervised by, the Muslim community (through the SMC appointments committee). Neither did the Mandatory government hold them accountable. After 1937, the three-member *waqf* committee (appointed under the Defence Regulations) intervened in, and closely supervised, *waqf* affairs. Its approval was now needed for any SMC decision that had budgetary implications. This did not eradicate corruption altogether, but it did prevent most possibilities of *waqf* resources being used for political purposes and so being of help in frustrating the policy and practice of the government.

A comparison of the Mandatory with the late Ottoman *sijill* reveals a great deal of institutional continuity. After all, the British fully adopted Ottoman legislation on *waqf* matters and revoked several reforms. The only difference was that the British government did not itself take over the powers of the Ottoman government over *waqf* affairs; instead, it transferred them to a Muslim body, the SMC. Muslims continued to make endowments in Jerusalem even under a non-Muslim government and regardless of the overall political, social and economic changes, but the nineteenth-century decline in the rate of *waqf* formation continued in the Mandate period. The purpose of the *waqf*, however, remained what it had been, as attested to by the entitlement patterns of family *waqf*s. The way *mutawallī*s were appointed also remained virtually unchanged. The *mutawallī*s of family *waqf*s were usually the founders' immediate offspring. The ongoing administration of *waqf* properties continued much as it had under the Ottomans. The *sharīʿa* court methods of supervising *waqf*s were also direct extensions of traditional methods: appointing beneficiaries as *mutawallī*s; employing beneficiaries as supervisors; auditing accounts (never practised fully), and physically inspecting properties before permitting development or modification. The major supervisory lever in non-*maḍbūṭ* *waqf*s, in the Mandate period as before, were the complaints by beneficiaries.

Overall continuity notwithstanding, the *waqf* underwent several changes under the Mandate reflecting modern circumstances. As we have seen, the establishment of new *waqf*s – and in particular, *waqf*s for public purposes – declined. Among *waqf* founders, urban notables were increasingly replaced by people of average and small families who had made money by their own efforts. As a consequence, the properties endowed were smaller, and the share of small urban properties increased. New administrative norms took hold among the Muslim population, through contacts with the British administration and the Yishuv (the Jewish community) and led to attempts – not always successful – to tighten *waqf* supervision and eradicate corruption. During the Mandatory period, the *qāḍī*s doubled the number of beneficiaries who were appointed as additional *mutawallī*s or *nāẓir*s. In some cases, they ordered periodic physical inspections of properties, used commercial banks to check on *waqf* income and expenditure and occasionally instructed *mutawallī*s to provide financial collateral as a deterrent against embezzlement. They were very harsh with *mutawallī*s who abused their office, often dismissing them for unsound or corrupt administration. Stricter methods were applied to public endowments under the supervision of the *sharīʿa* court than to private *waqf*s.

However, the most salient change – a change that allowed the *waqf* to continue and to develop in the modern era – was the emergence of a new approach in managing property. The *waqf* succeeded in adjusting to modern conditions by bringing its property administration into line with modern economic practice, eliminating some of the traditional constraints that had earlier prevented a modern response to the forces of the market. Small and insignificant family *waqf*s, such as those of the Nammari and Shitayya families, were now able to sell their original holdings and invest the proceeds in new construction, thereby quickly turning themselves into prosperous economic ventures. The maintenance of the status quo was no longer the dominant concern, as it had been in the Ottoman period; instead, development and improvement took pride of place.

Bibliography

ARCHIVES

CIH – Archives of The Center for Islamic Heritage (*Qism al-turāth al-Islāmī*).
ISA, Land Court – Israel State Archives, Land Court.
ISA, SMC – Israel State Archives, Supreme Muslim Council.
ISA, CSO – Israel State Archives, Chief Secretariat Office.
ISA, ʿAwnī ʿAbd al-Hādī's files – Israel State Archives, ʿAwnī ʿAbd al-Hādī's files.
Sijill – The Records of the *Sharīʿa* Court of Jerusalem.

OFFICIAL PUBLICATIONS

In Arabic

Dustūr (Arabic translation by Nawfal Nawfal, Beirut 1301 h.).
Al-Majlis al-Islāmī al-Sharʿī al-Aʿlā, *Bayān al-Majlis al-Islāmī al-Sharʿī al-Aʿlā*. *Bayāns* from the years 1923–4, 1924–5, 1928, 1929, 1931.
Al-Majlis al-Islāmī al-Sharʿī al-Aʿlā, *Majmūʿat al-Balāghāt li-Sanat* 1345, 1346h.
Al-Majlis al-Islāmī al-Sharʿī al-Aʿlā, *Majmūʿat Taqārīr al-Taftīsh*.
Al-Fatwā al-Khaṭīra allatī Aṣdarathā al-Muftūn wa'l-Quḍā' wa'l-Mudarrisūn wa'l-Khuṭabā' wa'l-A'ima wa'l-Wuʿāẓ wa-Sā'ir ʿUlamā' al-Muslimīn wa-Rijāl al-Dīn bi-Filasṭīn bi-Sha'n Bayʿ al-Arḍ li'l-Ṣahyūniyyin. Jerusalem (1935).

In English

Great Britain, *Report on the Economic Conditions of Agriculturists in Palestine and the Fiscal Measures of Government in Relation thereto*. Jerusalem, 1930 (W.J. Johnson and R.E. Crosbie).
Great Britain, Colonial Office, *Report by His Majesty's Government to the Council of the League of Nations on the Administration of*

Palestine and Trans-Jordan for the Year 1935 (London, 1936).
Palestine, Government of, *Official Gazette.*
Palestine, Government of, *Palestine Laws.*

BOOKS AND ARTICLES

Abramovitz, Zvi and Y. Gleft. *The Arab Economy in Palestine and the Middle Eastern Countries* (Hebrew). Tel-Aviv: ha-Kibutz ha-Me'uhad, 1944.

Abū Zahra, Muḥammad. *Muḥāḍarāt fī al-Waqf.* 2nd ed., Cairo: Dār al-Fikr al-ʿArabī, 1971.

al-Abyānī Bey, Muḥammad Zayn. *Kitāb Mabāḥith al-Waqf.* Cairo, 1924.

Aḥad Fuḍalā' al-Muslimīn. *Bayān wa-Radd ʿAla Bayān al-Majlis al-Islāmī al-Aʿlā Muwajjah li-Kull Muslim fī al-ʿAlam al-Islāmī ʿĀmmatan wa-fī Filasṭīn Khāṣṣatan.* Jerusalem, 1924.

ʿAly Pasha, M. 'Le *Waqf* est-it une Institution Religieuse', *L'Egypte Contemporain*, 18 (1927) pp. 385–402.

Anderson, J.N.D. 'Recent Developments in *Sharīʿa* Law: The *Waqf* System'. *The Muslim World*, 42 (1952) pp. 257–73.

al-ʿĀnī, Muḥammad Shafīq. *Aḥkām al-Awqāf.* 3rd ed. Baghdad, 1965.

Arbitrat, J. 'Essai sur les contrats de quasi-elienation et de location perpetuelle auxquels l'institution du hobous à donne naissance'. *Revue Algérienne et Tunisienne de Législation et de Jurisprudence*, 17 (1901) 121–51.

Arnon-Ohana, Yuval. *The Internal Struggle within the Palestinian Movement 1929–1939* (Hebrew). Tel Aviv, 1981.

ʿAshūb, ʿAbd al-Jalīl A. *Kitāb al-Waqf.* n.p.,1935.

Baer, Gabriel. 'The Dismemberment of *Awqāf* in Early 19th Century Jerusalem'. *Asian and African Studies*, 13, 3 (1979) pp. 220–41.

Baer, Gabriel. 'Ḥikr.' *The Encyclopaedia of Islam.* (2nd ed.), suppl., pp. 368–70.

Baer, Gabriel. *The History of Land Ownership in Modern Egypt 1800–1950.* London: Oxford University Press, 1960.

Baer, Gabriel. 'Jerusalem's Families of Notables and the *Waqf* in the Early 19th Century' in *Palestine in The Late Ottoman Period*, ed. D. Kushner. Jerusalem and Leiden: Yad Itzhak Ben Zvi and E.J. Brill, 1986, pp. 109–22.

Baer, Gabriel. *Population and Society in the Arab East.* London: Routledge & Kegan Paul, 1964.

Baer, Gabriel. 'The *Waqf* as a Prop for the Social System (16th–20th Centuries)' in *Studies in the Muslim Waqf*, eds Gabriel Baer and Gad Gilbar. Oxford: Oxford University Press, forthcoming.

Baer, Gabriel. '*Waqf* Reform in Egypt', in *Middle Eastern Affairs* (St Antony Papers no. 4), 1 (1958) pp. 61–76.

Baer, Gabriel. 'Women and the *Waqf*: An Analysis of the Istanbul *Taḥrīr* of 1546'. *Asian and African Studies*, 17 (1983) pp. 9–27.

Barkan, Omer L. and Ekrem H. Ayverdi. *Istanbul Vakiflari Tahrir Defteri 953 (1546)* Tarihli. Istanbul, 1970.

Barnes, R.J. *An Introduction to Religious Foundations in the Ottoman Empire*. Leiden: E.J. Brill, 1987.

Barron, John B. *Mohammedan Wakfs in Palestine*. Jerusalem, 1922.

Ben Shemesh, Avraham. *The Land Laws of Palestine* (Hebrew). Tel Aviv, 1953.

Busson de Janssens, Gérard. 'Contribution à l'étude de habous public algériens'. Ph.D. dissertation, 1950.

Clavel, Eugene. *Droit Musulman, Le wakf ou habous*. 2 vols, Cairo: Impr. Diemer, 1896.

Cohen, Abraham. *The Economy of the Arab Sector in Palestine under the Mandate* (Hebrew). Givat Haviva, 1978.

Coulson, Noel J. *Succession in the Muslim Family*. Cambridge: Cambridge University Press, 1971.

Coulson, Norman J. *A History of Islamic Law*. Edinburgh: Edinburgh University Press, 1964.

Crecelius, Daniel. 'Incidences of *Waqf* Cases in Three Cairo Courts'. *Journal of the Economic and Social History of the Orient*, 29 (1986) pp. 175–89.

Dequilhem-Schoem, Randy C. *History of Waqf and Case Studies from Syria in the late Ottoman Period and French Mandate*. Ann Arbor, MI: University Microfilms, 1986.

Doukhan, Moshe. *Land Laws in the State of Israel* (Hebrew). 2nd ed., Jerusalem, 1953.

Eisenman, R.H. *Islamic Law in Palestine and Israel*. Leiden: E.J. Brill, 1978.

Fayzee, Asaf A.A. *Outline of Muḥammadan Law*. 3rd ed. London: Oxford University Press, 1964.

Gerber, Haim. *Economy and Society in an Ottoman City: Bursa 1600–1700*. Jerusalem, 1988.

Gerber, Haim. *Ottoman Rule in Jerusalem 1890–1914*. Berlin: Klaus Schwarz verlag, 1985.

Gerber, Haim. 'The *Waqf* institution in Early Ottoman Edirne'. *Asian and African Studies*, 17 (1983) pp. 29–45.

al-Ghāzī, Kāmil. *Nahr al-Dhahab fī Ta'rīkh Ḥalab*. Aleppo, 1342h.

Gilbar, Gad. 'The *Waqf* and Economic Growth', in *Studies in the Muslim Waqf*, eds Gabriel Baer and Gad Gilbar. Oxford: Oxford University Press, forthcoming.

Goadby, Frederic M. and Moses J. Doukhan. *The Land Law of Palestine*. Tel Aviv, 1935.

Granovski, Avraham. *The Land Regime in Palestine* (Hebrew). Tel-Aviv, 1949.

Goitein, Shlomo D. and Avraham Ben Shemesh. *Muslim Law in the State of Israel* (Hebrew). Jerusalem, 1957.

Heffening, W. 'Wakf'. *Encyclopaedia of Islam*, 1st ed., 4, 1096–103.

Hilmi, Omer Efendi, *A Treatise on the Laws of Evkaf*, trans. C.R. Tyser and D.G. Demetriades. Nicosia, 1899.

Hoexter, Miriam. 'Le contrat de quasi-aliénation des *awqāf* à Alger à la fin de la domination turque: études de deux documents d'anā'. *Bulletin of the School of Oriental and African Studies*, 47 (1984) pp. 243–59.

Hoexter, Miriam. '*Waqf* al-Ḥaramayn and the Turkish Government in Algiers', in *Studies in the Muslim Waqf*, eds Gabriel Baer and Gad Gilbar. Oxford: Oxford University Press, forthcoming.

Hoexter, Miriam. 'The *Waqf* and the State', in *Studies in the Muslim Waqf*, eds Gabriel Baer and Gad Gilbar. Oxford: Oxford University Press, forthcoming.

Ḥukm al-Sharī'a fī al-Waqf al-Khayrī wa'l-Ahlī, Bayān min al-'Ulamā'. Cairo, 1346 h.

al-Ḥuṣarī, Aḥmad. *al-Tarikāt wal-Wiṣāya fī al-Fiqh al-Islāmī*. Amman, 1972.

Ibn 'Ābidīn. Muḥammad A. *Khashiyyat al-Durr al-Mukhtār*. 2nd ed., Cairo, 1386/1966.

Ibn al-Nujaym. *al-Baḥr al-Rā'iq fī Sharḥ Kanz al-Daqā'iq*. al-Maṭba'a al-'Ilmiyya.

al-Imām al-Ḥusaynī, Muḥammad As'ad. *al-Manhal al-Ṣāfī fī al-Waqf wa-Aḥkāmihi*. Jerusalem, n.d. (1982).

Ipširli, Muḥammad. 'The *Waqfs* of Palestine in the Sixteenth Century According to the *Taḥrir* Registers', in *The Third International Conference on Bilād al-Shām: Palestine 19–24 April 1980*. 2 (1984) pp. 96–107.

Ipširli, Muḥammad. and M. al-Tamimi. *Awqāf wa-Amlāk al-Muslimīn fī Filastīn*. Istanbul: Munaẓamat al-Mu'tamar al-Islāmī, 1982.

Jamāl al-Dīn, Aḥmad. *al-Waqf Muṣṭalahātihi wa-Qawā'idihi*. Baghdad:

Maṭba'at al-Rābiṭa, 1955.

Jennings, R.C. 'The Development of Evkaf in a new Ottoman province: Cyprus, 1571–1640', in *Studies in the Muslim Waqf*, eds Gabriel Baer and Gad Gilbar. Oxford: Oxford University Press, forthcoming.

Jennings, R.C. 'Women in Early 17th Century Ottoman Judicial Records the *Sharī'a* Court of Anatolian Kayseri'. *Journal of the Economic and Social History of the Orient*, 18 (1975) pp. 176–89.

Khadr, M. 'Deux actes de *Waqf* d'un Qarahanide d'Asie central'. *Journal Asiatique*, 145 (1967) pp. 305–35.

al-Khaṣṣāf, Aḥmad. *Kitāb Aḥkām al-Awqāf*. Cairo: Diwān 'Umūm al-Awqāf al-Miṣriyya, 1902.

Khayat, Habib A. *Waqfs in Palestine and Israel – from the Ottoman Reforms to the Present*. Ann Arbor, MI: University Microfilms, 1962.

Kimmerling, Barukh. *The Land Struggle, a Chapter in the Sociology of the Jewish–Arab Conflict* (Hebrew). Jerusalem: The Hebrew University, 1973.

Kupferschmidt, Uri M. *The Supreme Muslim Council, Islam Under the British Mandate for Palestine*. Leiden: E.J. Brill, 1987.

Koprulu, Fuad. 'L'Institution de Vakf et l'importance historique de documents de Vakf'. *Vakiflar Dergisi*, I (1938) (section française) pp. 3–9.

Kozlowski, Gregory C. *Muslim Endowments and Society in British India*. Cambridge: Cambridge University Press, 1985.

Kurd 'Alī, Muḥammad. *Kitāb Khiṭṭaṭ al-Shām*. Damascus, 1927.

Layish, Aharon. 'The Family *Waqf* and the *Shar'ī* Law of Succession', in *Studies in the Muslim Waqf*, eds Gabriel Baer and Gad Gilbar. Oxford: Oxford University Press, forthcoming.

Layish, Aharon. 'The Mālikī Family *Waqf* according to Wills and Waqfiyyāt'. *Bulletin of the School of Oriental and African Studies*, 46 (1983) pp. 1–32.

Layish, Aharon. 'The Muslim *Waqf* in Israel'. *Asian and African Studies*, 2 (1966) pp. 41–76.

Layish, Aharon. 'The Muslim *Waqf* in Jerusalem after 1967: Beneficiaries and Management', Le *Waqf* dans le monde musulman contemporain (XIXe–XXe siècles), ed. Faruk Bilici, *Varia Turcica*, Istanbul, Institut Français d'études Annatoliennes, 26 (1994) pp. 145–68.

Layish, Aharon. 'The *Sijill* of the Jaffa and Nazareth *Sharī'a* Courts as a Source for the Political and Social History of Ottoman Palestine'. In *Studies on Palestine during the Ottoman Period*, ed. Moshe Ma'oz, Jerusalem: Magnes Press, 1975, pp. 525–32.

Layish, Aharon. *Women and Islamic Law in a Non-Muslim State.* Jerusalem and New York: Israel Universities Press and John Wiley, 1975.

Lewis, Bernard. 'al-Ḥaramayn'. *The Encyclopaedia of Islam.* 2nd ed., 3, 175–6.

Lewis, Bernard. *The Emergence of Modern Turkey.* London: Oxford University Press, 1961.

al-Māḥī, Muḥammad Muṣṭafā. *al-Ḥukūma al-ʿIrāqiyya, Taqrīr ʿan Awqāf al-ʿIrāq wa-Wasā'il Iṣlaḥihā.* Baghdad, 1937.

Mandaville, J. 'The Jerusalem *Sharīʿa* Court Records: a Supplement and Complement to the Central Archives', in *Studies on Palestine during the Ottoman Period*, ed. Moshe Maʿoz, Jerusalem: Magnes Press 1975, pp. 517–24.

Mandaville, J. 'The Ottoman Court Records of Syria and Jordan'. *Journal of the American Oriental Society*, 86 (1966) pp. 311–19.

Mannāʿ, ʿĀdel. 'The *Sanjaq* of Jerusalem between Two Invasions (1798–1831), Administration and Society'. Ph.D. dissertation in Hebrew, Jerusalem, The Hebrew University, 1986.

Mannāʿ, ʿĀdel. 'The *Sijill* as a Source for Study of Palestine during the Ottoman Period, with Special Reference to the French Invasion', in *Palestine in The Late Ottoman Period*, ed. David Kushner, Jerusalem: Yad Izhak Ben-Zvi and Leiden: E.J. Brill, pp. 351–62.

al-Maqrīzī, *al-Mawāʿiẓ wal-Iʿtibār bi-Dhikr al-Khiṭṭat wal-Āthār.* Cairo: Bulāq, 1853.

Marcus, Abraham. 'Piety and Profit: The *Waqf* in the Society and Economy of 18th Century Aleppo', in *Studies in the Muslim Waqf*, eds Gabriel Baer and Gad Gilbar. Oxford: Oxford University Press, forthcoming.

Marcus, Abraham. 'Men, Women and Property: Dealers in Real Estate in the 18th Century Aleppo'. *Journal of the Economic and Social History of the Orient*, 26, 1–2 (1983) pp. 137–63.

ʿA. al-Sayyid Marsot, 'The Political and Economic Function of the *ʿUlamā'* in the 18th Century', *Journal of the Economic and Social History of the Orient,* 16, 2–3 (1973) pp.130–54.

Massignon, Louis. 'Documents sur Certains *Waqfs* de lieux saints del Islam.' *Revue des études Islamiques*, 19 (1951), pp. 43–76.

Mercier, Ernest. *Le code du habous ou ouakf selon la législation musulman.* Constantine, 1899.

Milliot, L. *Démembrements du habous: gza, guelsa, zina', istighraq.* Paris: E. Leroux, 1918.

Ochsenwald, W.L. 'A Modern *Waqf*: The Hijaz Railway 1900–1948'.

Arabian Studies, 3 (1976) pp. 1–12.
Pearl, David. *A Textbook on Muslim Law*. London, 1979.
Pesle, O. *La théorie et la pratique des habous dans le rite malekite*. Casablanca, n.d.
Porath, Yehoshu'a. *The Emergence of the Palestinian Arab National Movement 1918–1929*. London: Frank Cass, 1974.
Porath, Yehoshu'a. *The Palestinian-Arab National Movement 1929–1939: From Riots to Rebellion*. London: Frank Cass, 1977.
Powers, David S. 'The Islamic Inheritance System: A Socio-Historical Approach', in *Islamic Family Law*, eds Chibli Mallat and Jane Connors, London/Dordrecht/Boston, 1990, pp. 11–29.
Powers, David, S. 'The Mālikī Family Endowment: Legal Norms and Social Practices'. *International Journal of Middle Eastern Studies*, 25 (1993) pp. 379–406.
Powers, David S. 'Revenues of Public *Waqfs* in Sixteenth Century Jerusalem'. *Archivum Ottomanicum*, 9 (1984) pp. 163–202.
Powers, David S. '*Fatwās* as a Source of Legal and Social History: A Dispute over Endowment Revenues from Fourteenth-Century Fez'. *Al-Qanṭara*, 11,2 (1990) pp. 320–40.
Qadrī Pāshā, Muḥammad. *Kitāb Qānūn al-'Adl wa'l-Inṣāf li'l-Qaḍā' 'alā Mushkilāt al-Awqāf*. Cairo, 1902.
Qano, Jaque. *The Affair of the Land Dispute between Jews and Arabs in Palestine* (Hebrew). Givat Haviva, 1980.
Rāfeq, 'Alī. 'The Law Court of Damascus, with Special Reference to the Craft-corporations during the First Half of the Eighteenth Century', in *Les Arabes par leurs archives*, Paris, 1976, pp. 141–59.
Reiter, Yitzhak. 'Family *Waqf* Entitlements in British Palestine (1917–1948)', *Islamic Law and Society*, 2, 2 (1995) pp. 174–93.
Reiter, Yitzhak. 'The *Waqf* Institution in Acre' (unpublished M.A. thesis). Jerusalem: The Hebrew University, 1986.
Roded, Ruth. 'The *Waqf* and the Social Elite of Aleppo in the Eighteenth and Nineteenth Centuries'. *Turcica*, 20 (1988) pp. 71–91.
Roded, Ruth. 'The *Waqf* in Ottoman Aleppo', in *Studies in the Muslim Waqf*, eds Gabriel Baer and Gad Gilbar. Oxford: Oxford University Press, forthcoming.
Salname Vilayet Beyrut, 1311–1312. Istanbul, n.d.
al-Sayyid Marsot, A.L. 'The Political and Economic Function of the '*Ulamā*' in the 18th Century'. *Journal of the Economic and Social History of the Orient*, 16, 2–3 (1973) pp. 130–54.
Sekaly, Achile. 'Le Problem des *Waqfs* en Egypt'. *Revue du monde Musulmanne*, 3, 1-4 (1929) pp. 75–126; 277–337; 395–454; 601–59.

Shaham, Ron. 'Christian and Jewish *Waqfs* in Palestine during the Ottoman Period'. *Bulletin of the School of Oriental and African Studies*, 54 (1991) pp. 460–72

Shim'oni, Ya'aqov. *The Arabs of Palestine* (Hebrew). Tel-Aviv: 'Am 'Oved, 1947.

Shitrit, Bekhor Shalom. *The Supreme Muslim Sharī'a Council* (Hebrew). n.p., 1949.

Shpitzen, Arieh. 'Legal Personality and Jewish Endowments in late Nineteenth Century Jerusalem' (Hebrew), *Qatedra*, 19 (April 1981), pp. 72–82.

Tute, R.C. *The Ottoman Land Code*. Jerusalem, 1927.

al-'Umar, Muḥammad A. *al-Dalīl li-Iṣlāḥ al-Awqāf*. Baghdad, 1948.

Yediyildiz, Bahaeddin. 'La porte économique des vakfs Turcs au XVIII siècle', in *Studies in the Muslim Waqf*, eds Gabriel Baer and Gad Gilbar. Oxford: Oxford University Press, forthcoming.

Zilberman, Ifrah. 'Change and Continuity amongst Muslim Migrants in a Suburb of Jerusalem', unpublished Ph.D. dissertation. Cambridge, University, 1988.

NEWSPAPERS

The Palestine Weekly.

Al-Jāmi'a al-'Arabiyya.

Index

For Product Safety Concerns and Information please contact our EU
representative GPSR@taylorandfrancis.com
Taylor & Francis Verlag GmbH, Kaufingerstraße 24, 80331 München, Germany

www.ingramcontent.com/pod-product-compliance
Ingram Content Group UK Ltd.
Pitfield, Milton Keynes, MK11 3LW, UK
UKHW042201240425
457818UK00011B/328

* 9 7 8 0 7 1 4 6 4 3 4 2 7 *